Milton the Puritan

Books by A. L. Rowse

Literature

Shakespeare:

Shakespeare the Man
William Shakespeare: A
    Biography
Shakespeare the Elizabethan
Shakespeare's Sonnets
    A Modern Edition,
    Introduction and Notes
Shakespeare's Southampton:
    Patron of Virginia
Christopher Marlowe: A
    Biography
Simon Forman: Sex and
    Society in Shakespeare's
    Age

Milton the Puritan
Jonathan Swift: Major
    Prophet
Matthew Arnold: Poet and
    Prophet
Discoveries and Reviews:
    from Renaissance to
    Restoration
The English Spirit: Essays in
    History and Literature
Times, Persons, Places

A Cornish Childhood
A Cornishman at Oxford
A Cornishman Abroad
Cornish Stories
A Cornish Anthology
Peter, the White Cat of
    Trenarren
Brown Buck: A Californian
    Fantasy

Poems of a Decade
Poems Chiefly Cornish
Poems of Deliverance
Poems Partly American

Poems of Cornwall and
    America
Strange Encounter: Poems

History

The Elizabethan Age:

The England of Elizabeth
The Expansion of Elizabethan
    England
The Elizabethan Renaissance:
1. The Life of the Society
2. The Cultural Achievement

Tudor Cornwall: Portrait of a
    Society
Sir Richard Grenville of the
    Revenge
Ralegh and the
    Throckmortons
The Elizabethans and
    America
The Cornish in America

The Heritage of Britain
The Spirit of English History
Bosworth Field
The Tower of London in the
    History of the Nation
Windsor Castle in the History
    of the Nation
Oxford in the History of the
    Nation

The Early Churchills
The Later Churchills

All Souls and Appeasement
The End of an Epoch
Homosexuals in History:
    Ambivalence in Society,
    Literature and the Arts

A. L. ROWSE

Milton the Puritan

Portrait of a Mind

© *A. L. Rowse 1977*

ISBN: 0 333 21850 7

First published 1977 by
MACMILLAN LONDON LIMITED
*4 Little Essex Street London WC2R 3LF
and Basingstoke
Associated companies in New York   Dublin
Melbourne   Johannesburg and Delhi*

Printed in Great Britain by
LOWE & BRYDONE LIMITED
Thetford, Norfolk

To
J. M. Steadman
prime authority on Milton
to recall walks and talks at
the Huntington

Contents

Preface

THIS is not a biography of Milton, as *Shakespeare the Man* was of Shakespeare. Milton was above all an intellectual, and this is a study of his mind, of his intellectual outfit, ideas and prejudices, the line he took about the issues that led to the Civil War, with its consequences.

There is an overweighty Milton industry as there is about Shakespeare, burying the man and his work beneath a mountain of dead academicism. The intelligent reader will hardly need to burden himself with this and can safely ignore most of it, in both cases. Though this is not a biography of Milton, I hope I have rendered him more alive than many academic treatises on the subject.

Milton was essentially a controversial figure in his own time, and remains so – this helps to keep him alive. But over the controversial issues of the Civil War, in which he engaged himself so bitterly, it may help the reader if I explain briefly my own values, by which I judge these issues.

My ultimate values are aesthetic; for me, works of art and imagination, and of men's hands – the poetry of Shakespeare and Milton, music, drama, painting, architecture, sculpture – lift men out of the slime. These things endure when most of what they supposed themselves to think has evaporated. Most of what most people think, especially in the realms of politics and religion – with which Milton so much concerned himself – is, strictly speaking, non-sense, i.e., does not make sense, or mean much in its own terms. The greatest intellects of Milton's own time – Bacon, Hobbes, Selden – realised this very well.

So my standpoint is one of scepticism, if of an aggressive scepticism. Imperceptive critics will identify it with a simple

Royalist outlook. They will be wrong, as usual. My point of view has much more in common with Hobbes, who saw through the fooleries on both sides, and was contemptuous of people's delusions, especially liberal-minded illusions about human nature – untrue to the facts. So too that man of genius among men of science, Sir William Harvey, discoverer of the circulation of the blood (though ordinary minds would not believe his discovery till a generation later): while the fighting fools fought themselves to a standstill at Edgehill, he sheltered under a hedge and read a book.

My opinion of humans is in keeping with Swift's – appropriately for the appalling age we live in. As for the appeals to their conscience with which Puritans undermined the social order and brought on the war, the last word was spoken by another sceptical intelligence, Sainte-Beuve, who saw that they were only 'the sophistries of the spirit of faction'.

The perceptive reader will see that there is something in common between our own society, falling apart, and the confusion and anarchy of the Civil War – as there is between this book and my *Jonathan Swift: Major Prophet*.

1976   A. L. ROWSE

CHAPTER ONE

Milton's Early Years

WILLIAM SHAKESPEARE and John Milton – each a man of
transcendent genius – stand at the opposite poles in English
literature. Milton was the complete intellectual, a man of
astonishing intellectual range and command of learning, than
whom one could not be more highly educated; essentially
didactic and doctrinaire, always convinced that he was in
possession of the truth and that hardly anybody else was, with a
disagreeable element of fanaticism in him. Shakespeare, hailed
as 'a child of nature', received quite a sufficient education for
his own purposes – those of drama and poetry – was a very
quick and clever reading man who instinctively absorbed and
made his own whatever he needed, food for his exploring and
searching mind; the least doctrinaire and fanatical of men.
Milton was a Cambridge man. Life and its manifold experiences formed Shakespeare's university – a much better training
for the essential dramatist. Where Shakespeare followed the
flow of life in all its diversity, Milton sought to impose order, his
own order, upon it and wrote one of the greatest epics, on the
most significant of human themes, in the world. Milton was a
great egoist, with every reason to be proud of himself and his
gifts; Shakespeare was the most unegoistic of men, much less
learned, but wise in human wisdom.

Milton, virtuous and chaste, was largely and formidably
concerned with religion – not in an illumined and mystical
sense like Dante or Eliot, or George Fox in Milton's own time,
but in a positive and rather secular way. He was deeply concerned about its place in society, the power it could command
and impose – like a Puritan; in its consequences for and influence upon society and still more the individual. His concern

11

with religion was intellectual and moral – and he was highly moralistic. Shakespeare was a conformist in religion, an accepter of the order of the universe, not disturbed by the intellectual problems it posed as such – as Marlowe was (Milton's precursor). This is not to say that Shakespeare had not a moral view of life: he had a deeply moral view, regarding both individual and society, enforcing the lesson of responsibility throughout society, from the top downwards, from ruler to ruled, and from them towards authority – more responsibly than any of the contemporary, university-trained intellectuals, such as Robert Greene or Marlowe.[1]

Shakespeare's frame of mind was sceptical, as is often the case with conformists – his contemporary Montaigne offers a parallel. He was prepared to *accept* the mystery of things, the mystery of the universe, as the sum of human wisdom, knowing instinctively how useless to probe further. John Milton would never accept anything on trust. He had to prove everything by the light of his own reason. Reason was to him the *summum bonum* – i.e., what appealed to his own reason; he was too much of an egoist to doubt himself. He was always convinced that he, almost alone, was in possession of the Truth. Intellectual pride was the marrow of his being.

This was a great strength to a genius such as his, for he derived inspiration from his abnormally developed ego. His self-esteem was inexpugnable; in a few lines of *Paradise Lost* he has a deliberate and conscious defence of it. (See later, page 233.) Here, too, his instinct was quite right. It is usual to disapprove of egoism, self-esteem, a good conceit of oneself. But this is a conventional cliché-reaction, for whether it is to be disapproved or approved depends upon whether the consequences are bad or good. Ordinary folk who display conceit, with nothing to show for it, are simply laughable. Milton's overweening conceit was thoroughly justified by his achievement – indeed, it was psychologically necessary to equip him for the pre-eminent task he meant to undertake from his early years. He always intended to achieve something exceptional with his life, and this needed all the boost his egoism and self-esteem could give it.

William Shakespeare had a translucent honesty of mind – Ben Jonson paid tribute to that. We love him for his candour: he had no illusions about himself or about other people, recognised his own frailty for what it was and saw that it was merely human, reflected equally in others:

> For why should others' false adulterate eyes
> Give salutation to my sportive blood?
> Or on my frailties why are frailer spies,
> Which in their wills count bad what I think good?
> No – I am that I am. . . .

We are not to approve or disapprove of one any more than the other; we simply find William Shakespeare's admission of human weakness more attractive.

He knew all about women – irresistible as he found them. He loved women, appreciated them, was chivalrous and compassionate about them, was their victim, sympathised when they were the victims of life and men, and therefore understood them through and through – no man more so. Thus the other half of human nature was an open book to him, largely closed to Milton; and, as opposed to the usual masculine imperceptiveness, the lack of intuition all too common with men, Shakespeare knew to his finger-tips what was to be learned from women. Not to know this knowledge, not to make use of this source of information, the other half of human experience, was very silly in his amused tolerant view:

> But love, first learnèd in a lady's eyes,
> Lives not alone immurèd in the brain,
> But, with the motion of all elements,
> Courses as swift as thought in every power,
> And gives to every power a double power,
> Above their functions and their offices. . . .
>
> From women's eyes this doctrine I derive:
> They sparkle still the right Promethean fire;
> They are the books, the arts, the academes,
> That show, contain, and nourish all the world.

What a contrast with John Milton's view of women! But, then, William Shakespeare was so deeply versed in the

ways of humans, in the experience of men and women's frail-
ties, in which he fully shared, that this gave him not only understanding but also sympathy and compassion. A sensitive man,
he hated cruelty and suffering. Hence his exceptional insistence
upon order, due obedience to authority, the mutual responsibility of ruler and ruled, each performing his duty. Otherwise,
society breaks apart in disruption and civil war, revolution with
its promise of better things but in the course of it bringing about
more suffering, letting loose more cruelty than before. For
hypothetical gains, all too definite losses – in lives, civilisation,
culture. He well understood how thin is the crust of civilisation
upon which we stand, and how easy it is to break through into
what dark waters beneath.

It happened to his daughter Susanna to have to entertain
Charles I's embattled Queen, passing through Stratford in the
full horror of the Civil War – the breakdown of society in three
kingdoms – in Shakespeare's own home, New Place, in 1643.
Shakespeare's intelligent daughter, who took after him, was
Royalist in her sympathies; the townsfolk, indoctrinated by a
succession of Puritan preachers, Parliamentarian in theirs.

There was little sympathy or compassion in John Milton's
composition, and not much sense of humour – a subversive element to the 'unco guid'. He was prepared to sacrifice anything
and everybody – first and foremost himself, we must admit – to
the cause of Truth, as he saw it, at the mercy of Reason, as he
conceived it. His type of rationalism, as we see again with the
philosophes who prepared the way for the French Revolution
(with all the destruction and suffering it brought about), was an
influence disruptive of society. It was a superficial rationalism
which did not see into the deeper rationale of things – the
anthropological necessity of habit, routine, custom, folk-ways;
or perceive, as Burke did, that societies cohere by instinctual
prejudice, social imitation, a thousand ties of affection, kinship,
mutual help, likes and even dislikes, interests, sympathies.
Burke's was an altogether profounder rationalism, in keeping
with the findings of modern psychology about the importance
of the unconscious and the subconscious. There was something
Shakespearian about Burke.

Like all the Elizabethan theatre-folk, Shakespeare disliked Puritans – Ben Jonson put admirable caricatures of them into *The Alchemist*, Tribulation and Ananias, and Zeal-of-the-land Busy in *Bartholomew Fair*. (The Puritans had it in for the theatre when their time came.) John Milton was a Puritan – we do not need to waste time on academic disputes as to what kind of Puritan – and a consummate prig.

Both Shakespeare and Milton were deeply interested in history – Shakespeare more sympathetically – and again contrastingly. Shakespeare's delight in history was imaginative and dramatic. Like all Elizabethans he was concerned with the moral aspects of history, the lessons to be learned from it – as to the inadequacies or crimes of kings, for example, and what happened to examples like Richard II or Richard III. Again there was compassion in his representations, of Richard II or Henry VI, Cardinal Wolsey or Catherine of Aragon.

Milton wrote history – notably his *History of Britain* – dogmatically, didactically. That was his main interest in it: to expose the foolery of monks, the inadequacies and crimes of monarchs, the superstitions of the people, the silliness of average humanity. He was very far from being an average man himself, and never ceased for a moment to be aware of his difference. He was reserved for a high calling; he prepared himself conscientiously, industriously, inhumanly for it from the years of his youth. He was to be God's prophet speaking through him to his chosen people, the English.

John Milton was born a citizen of London in 1608, eight years before Shakespeare's death in Stratford. Milton's father, John Milton senior, had come to London from the country just outside Oxford, Forest Hill, where the grandfather, Richard Milton, was a keeper in the royal forest of Shotover, which then spread more widely over those delightful hills. Richard Milton was, to boot, an obstinate recusant Catholic, fined for refusing to come to church. His son, brought up a chorister at Christ Church, conforming to the Anglican Church, refused to give way to the old man and was disinherited. Milton's younger brother, Christopher, became in turn a Catholic and – though he had no legal ability to speak of – was promoted to the bench by the *dévot* James II. There was a vein of stiff-necked obstinacy in the Milton family – anything to be out of step.[2]

The charming member of it was Milton's father, who not only made a fortune for himself (and his son, who thus was a *rentier*) but was also a talented composer. Theirs was a cultivated musical household. Both father and son played the organ; the father contributed madrigals to the famous *Triumphs of Oriana* in honour of Queen Elizabeth, besides motets and settings of the Psalms for the liturgy of the English Church. Its music was at its noblest, with the splendid and moving works composed for it by such men as Tallis and Byrd, Weelkes, Orlando Gibbons, Tompkins, William and Henry Lawes.

This last, Henry Lawes, was a friend of the family, to whom young John Milton owed the opportunity of providing the words for his masques *Arcades* and *Comus*. William Lawes was the original spirit, whose instrumental compositions, unpublished in his life-time, held the greatest promise for the future of English music. But, alas, he was killed in the odious Civil War. He had written, also, anthems for the beautiful liturgy of the Church. The brothers came out of its nursery, their father a vicar-choral in the cathedral at Salisbury.

The first paradox that confronts us in the character of John Milton is that he – an exquisite musical spirit, with an intense response to the beauty of the world of sound – should have set such little store by the moving liturgy and music of the Church. Often enough he inveighs against the liturgy; in at least one place he even deplores the music. He never expresses regret for the destruction of the cathedral and collegiate services, the smashing of the organs, the dispersal of the choirs, the tearing-up of service and music books, the breach of the long, creative tradition. It seems inexplicable that such an aesthete, so refined an ear, can have preferred the nasal cant of the Puritans. We can only put it down to his education.

The child *is* father of the man. John Milton was a brilliant, precocious – and pretty – boy. His father was very proud of him, and had him (*par exception* for a middle-class family) painted as a child. He also called in a tutor for the boy of ten, already avid for book-learning. The middle classes of the City were increasingly under the baneful influence of Puritanism – actually all too subversive and inflammatory. The age exhibited a mania for sermons, a Biblical craze which, as we shall see, had the worst possible consequences in civil war. People would have done far better to read Shakespeare – as Charles I did, a most appreciative reader, as Milton commented disdainfully.

Unfortunately the man chosen to tutor the boy was a Cambridge Puritan, a Scotch Presbyterian, Thomas Young. He was a good scholar, and the youth admired him, corresponded with him afterwards, exchanged Latin elegiacs with him, and defended him later when involved in controversy. (These clerics quarrelled about their nonsense like cats and dogs, as Thomas Hobbes pointed out – their vocational disease.) Young was widely known for his work on that favourite topic with Puritans, the observance of the Sabbath: *Dies Dominica*. It should be gloomy, as in Scotland, where he came from – and where he had already opposed King James's attempt to introduce the infectious presence of bishops among the godly. Young also attacked the King's very reasonable *Book of Sports*, allowing most of the recreations country people were accustomed to after their week of toil. Young was for a time chaplain to the English merchants in Hamburg; in his preface he confessed to a love for Germany. That was the place for him; it was a pity he didn't stay there.

Talented youths are apt to get fixed in the ways of thought and behaviour they pick up when young – that is why their time at the university is apt to be crucial in their development. A Labour cabinet minister of my acquaintance, who picked up his socialist ideas at Oxford, confessed sadly to me that one develops a fixation when young, gets caught in the toils, sets out on a career and then, disillusioned, finds it is too late to change it. Sometimes people manage to slough off the prejudices and fixations of their immaturity. John Milton never did – too obstinate and conceited; he would never take telling from anybody, not even from life itself. It is a curious thing psychologically that genius on one side often goes along with naïveté, a lack of development, on the other – sometimes sexually. In neither term does this apply to William Shakespeare, but young Milton became fixed, and this was confirmed by the next stages in his education.

At St Paul's School he came under the influence of the two Alexander Gills, father and son, successively high-masters. They came from the bleak eastern counties. The Elizabethan schoolmaster, charming Mulcaster, would have been a more genial influence; a believer in dramatics and the future of the English language, he trained his boys to perform plays and speak out before the great Queen. The elder Gill had a special devotion to Spenser, which Milton took over from him; and that was a good thing. But his intimacy with the younger Gill can only be regarded as deleterious.

They became close friends, writing in Latin to each other, sending each other verses – and Milton admired the younger Gill's excessively. This young man was of an all too familiar disposition, up against authority. At Oxford he challengingly drank a toast to Buckingham's assassin, coupling it with disrespectful words about virtuous King Charles. William Chillingworth, Laud's godson, reported this to Laud, who instituted a search, when further incriminating verses, abusing Buckingham and the King, were found.

This was no joke, after an assassination, and Gill received a severe sentence. Actually Laud remitted most of it and even helped Gill on his submission. Gill collected his more printable Latin verse with a fulsome dedication to the King, and a sycophantic poem to Laud – to whom he had further reason to be grateful. On his father's death he was appointed high-master. But he became notorious for his sadistic beatings – Aubrey has a number of unsuitable ballad verses said to have been sung under Gill's windows. Shortly, in 1639, after a shocking beating of a boy named Bennet, Gill was dismissed from his job. Laud tried to help him, but in vain. The Mercers' Company held to their decision, and Gill ended his days teaching a few boys privately in his house.

Such was Milton's early friend.

*

These influences were only confirmed by Cambridge, the chief
nursery of Puritanism from Cartwright's time onwards. This
acrid controversialist had set the pattern and laid down the
model of Presbyterian discipline which dominated Puritanism
up to the Civil War, and was indeed a potent factor in bringing
it on. Cartwright had advocated the execution of Roman priests
simply for the fact of their priesthood. We see what a barbarous, uncivilised type he was, mentor of the Puritans, with
their fixation on the harsh Old Testament. It is true that the
Catholics in Spain or Italy would have consigned a Cartwright
to the fire, such was the charity of these extremes: no model for
civilised men – and indeed the *via media* of the Anglican Church
was altogether more tolerant.

At Cambridge, Emmanuel College – the foundation of which
by the Puritanical Mildmay had aroused no enthusiasm in
Queen Elizabeth – proved a seminary of sedition, out of which
Harvard largely came. Christ's came second to Emmanuel,
and here Milton was entered in 1625. It is ironical to think what
difference it might have made if he had gone to his ancestral
Oxford. Later, he expressed a supercilious scorn – a characteristic note with him – for his father's kindlier nursery.

The first thing we learn about Milton at Cambridge is a piece
of insubordination. He quarrelled with his tutor, and was rusti-
cated for a period. There is nothing exceptional in this adoles-
cent behaviour – it follows a tedious pattern with ordinary
youths; what is out of the ordinary is that this should have happened to an exceptionally brilliant young scholar who already
set store by his refined superiority to others. An American
authority concludes, with some meiosis, 'it is evident that Milton's college life was not untroubled, and it is a safe conjecture
that he was ill-equipped to meet the attitude of persons less
willing than his earlier well-wishers to accept him at his own
valuation'.[3]

It was they, however, who were mistaken and Milton's own
valuation of himself that was correct. He returned to Christ's,
having won his point and acquired a new and more congenial
tutor (actually the previous one had been a Puritan: one Chap-
pell, whom Laud was tolerant enough later to promote, if to an

Irish bishopric). Milton continued at the University to win acclaim as an outstanding student, much to the fore in academic exercises, Latin declamations and disputations, Latin versification on set themes. In addition to the classics his proud father had put out money for him to acquire French and Italian, and this too paid interest.

Many of these early exercises have, quite exceptionally, been preserved, and in them we can observe the development of the young man's mind. The anniversary of Gunpowder Plot – the idiocy of which had done such damage to Catholicism in England – was a regular theme. Milton's verses express the acrid smell of his hatred of Rome; his glittering description of Satan, with glazing eyes, adamantine teeth grinding like the clash of arms, points forward to his later fascination with that figure, the rebel-hero of *Paradise Lost*.

The dominant academic exercise was that of the disputation. This was disapproved of by Bacon – and rightly, for in sharpening logical acuteness it led to the excruciating disputatiousness of the intellectual life of the time, in politics and the law, above all in the Church and among the sects, in religion and theology. As if one *learnt* anything that way! – as Bacon pointed out. Far better the patient exploration of the external universe, the secrets of nature, the facts of history and of life. And, for the rest – poetry and the arts, music, drama, painting, sculpture, architecture – what the cultivated Court of Charles I stood for, not the crackling dry bones of theological controversy.

Once more, we are up against the paradox why Milton did not appreciate this. For he was a refined, aesthetic type, not at all the ordinary insensitive clod. He himself characteristically insists upon this. A defensive note is discernible in these early works; he would never express any sense of inferiority, whatever he felt, but was always conscious of his difference from *l'homme moyen sensuel*, the average human fool. 'As many heads as I behold in this large audience, almost as many do I see of faces bearing malice against me.' Thus one Latin disputation. In another, 'why do I seem to them insufficiently masculine? . . . Doubtless it was because I was never able to quaff down large bumpers; or because my hand has not become calloused holding the plough; or because I never lay on my back in the sun like a cattle-drover; perhaps, in short, because I never proved myself a man in the same manner as these beasts. But – would they could lay aside their asininity as easily I can my femininity.'

This is supposed to be funny, after the manner of Latin declamations – and Milton never did have much humour. But it is intensely revealing. The young Milton was a pretty boy, after a feminine fashion: the 'Lady of Christ's'. We cannot expect his Victorian and Victorian-minded commentators, pre-Freudians, to have any glimmering of the significance of this. Milton belonged to a recognisable feminine type who would not accept it; one has known such examples. The effect often is to over-emphasise their masculinity; it leads to a discernible psychological strain, repression, the sharpening of the senses and faculties that goes with that, the finer edge, the acridity and liability to bitterness. It is all there in Milton – a world away from William Shakespeare, the completely released, normal, masculine heterosexual.

Milton was always conscious of difference, and repression was reinforced not only by his Puritanism but by his very refinement. He attached an exaggerated importance to chastity – the more unnecessary when women offered no temptation to him – and it reads rather absurdly when he commends himself on refraining from the pleasures of the bordello in Italy. He must have been rather provoking to sophisticated Italians – so good-looking in a feminine way, so innocent and chaste, and outspoken against their religion. Milton belonged to the rather feminine type whose inclinations, under pressure and repressed by religion, are forced into the heterosexual channel. With this make-up there was always effort and strain in his life.

We note, too, the recognisable sense of superiority that goes with it. 'Many complain that the majority of academics are hard to please, boorish, uncouth in manners, with no grace of speech or gift for winning men's minds.' Fancy telling them as much, even in Latin! 'I confess that one who is really a recluse and withdrawn from them into his own studies is more ready to address the gods than men'! Later, looking back on these years at the University, the fixed Puritan disapproved of the harmless dramatic entertainments of the students, especially of those intended for the Church, 'writhing their clerical limbs to the immoral gestures of Trinculos, buffoons, and bawds; prostituting the name of the ministry to the eyes of courtiers and court-ladies, with their attendants and mademoiselles'.

What a way to speak of these charming interludes! He goes on to describe himself at the time: 'while these acted and over-acted, among other young scholars I watched. They thought themselves gallants, and I thought them fools. They made sport, and I laughed. They mispronounced, and I was contemptuous. To complete the Atticism, they were out, and I hissed.' There we have the young Johnny Milton, the characteristic smell of superciliousness. It would be intolerable but for his genius – for which one forgives him everything.

Here is the other side to him. In these exercises he is already the controversialist with the sharp edge to his tongue (perhaps this very sharpness of tongue was rather feminine?). Professor Hanford concludes that he was compensating himself psychologically by exhibiting his brilliant talents, 'winning admiration certainly, but not perhaps good will. . . . He has begun what was to be with him a lifelong process of resistance and retreat. Henceforth the world is divided between friends and enemies.'[4] Retreating within the citadel of his inexpugnable sense of superiority, he already implies that what he has to say 'will fall on deaf or hostile ears'. His audience will be 'fit, though few', his rôle that of 'the one against the many, the chosen servant of God speaking to the unregenerate'. He was already assuming the part of 'a consistent intellectual and individual non-conformity'.[5]

Milton was intended for the Church – in a way, there was always something of the *prêtre manqué* about him – but, like Marlowe, though for very different reasons, he could not make up his mind to it. Marlowe went on to a notorious career as writer for the stage with lewd associates, a scandalous life and an early grave. For Milton, *per contra*, the Church was not good enough. While at Cambridge he accepted its institutions and wrote appropriate Latin elegies on two of its prelates who were

Cambridge figures.

The first is on Nicholas Felton, Bishop of Ely, of whom nothing ill is known, though he was one of the translators of the Authorised Version of the Bible. Fuller tells us that he had 'a sound head and a sanctified heart, was beloved of all good men, very hospitable to all, and charitable to the poor'. He devoted a considerable portion of his income regularly to poor relief; he was no less painstaking a preacher, a strong recommendation at that time. The second, Lancelot Andrewes, Bishop of Winchester, was a towering figure in the Church. Another of the celebrated Translators, he had vast patristic learning, and was much admired as a preacher. A High Churchman who believed in Catholic order, he was a celibate, so that no family claims disputed his widespread charity. An adherent of ritual, he was notably tolerant of those who disagreed with him. He was the patron of a younger generation of distinguished clerics who were to suffer grievously for their devotion to the Church – John Cosin, Matthew Wren and William Laud.

The young Milton's elegy on this eminent prelate was a formal affair, and had not the personal feeling of the High Church poet Richard Crashaw's tribute. In his time Andrewes had won over many Catholics to the Anglican Church by his learning and the sanctity of his life. This did not prevent Milton some years later from making a thoroughgoing attack on him and his 'shallow reasonings in defence of episcopacy'.

This is already foreshadowed in one of the most beautiful of Milton's early poems, 'Lycidas'. Suddenly, in the middle of an elegy on a young Cambridge man, we hear surprisingly, and inappropriately, an attack on clerics who

> Creep, and intrude, and climb into the fold

simply 'for their bellies' sake'. Well, ordinary men with ordinary talents must live; no doubt many of them went into the Church for a living – what was wrong with that? – and performed their laborious duties well enough. But this young perfectionist, making no allowance for average human nature, goes on to make a scathing attack on the clergy:

> Blind mouths! that scarce themselves know how to hold

> A sheep-hook, or have learnt aught else the least
> That to the faithful herdman's art belongs!

Supercilious again: but worse follows:

> The hungry sheep look up, and are not fed,
> But, swoln with wind and the rank mist they draw,
> Rot inwardly, and foul contagion spread. . . .

A shocking aspersion upon the Caroline clergy, struggling to repair some of the losses and depredations which had accompanied the Reformation.

The passage concludes with the usual hysteria against Rome:

> the grim Wolf with privy paw
> Daily devours apace, and nothing said.

A great deal too much, in fact, was said by everybody. Even the poetry of Anglican writers receives angry dismissal from this young prophet:

> And, when they list, their lean and flashy songs
> Grate on their scrannel pipes of wretched straw. . . .

Is this the way to describe the passionate divine poems of the later Donne, Dean of St Paul's; or the intensity of devotion of the saintly George Herbert, of Richard Crashaw, or Thomas Traherne – apart from the devotional poetry of devout laymen like Sidney Godolphin or Henry Vaughan? And, though Herrick's delightful verse is dominantly secular, there is nothing to show that he was not a dutiful parish priest.

Later, Milton was to refer to these years, contemptuously, as when 'our corrupted clergy were at their height'. We have seen what characters such prelates as Lancelot Andrewes and Nicholas Felton bore. In fact, the Caroline age was one of distinguished divines. Charles I, whose private life was unblemished, was not the man to prefer unworthy clerics. We do not have to ascend the heights of saintliness with George Herbert or of mystical devotion with Crashaw and Traherne; we may take lower levels with a cheerful and charitable prelate – such as Puritans were not – with Bishop Corbet, who wrote the delightful 'Farewell, rewards and fairies':

> Lament, lament, old abbeys,
>   The fairies lost command:
> They did but change priests' babies,
>   But some have changed your land;
> And all your children stoln from thence
>   Are now grown Puritans,
> Who live as changelings ever since
>   For love of your demesnes.

Or we may take a normal bishop such as Henry King, son of a bishop of London (of whom Puritans put it about that he died a Catholic: liars as they often were, he did not). Bishop King, a good poet too, was badly treated in the Civil War; he survived to display generosity in his see, 'a person never to be forgotten by his tenants and by the poor'. The Puritans, with their usual charity, described him as 'a proud prelate' and 'a most pragmatical malignant'.

Into King's rectory of Petworth, Parliament intruded the odious Francis Cheynell, who persecuted Chillingworth, then prisoner, upon his deathbed. The philosophic Chillingworth was one of the ornaments of Lord Falkland's intellectual circle at Great Tew, of which other eminent divines were Dr Sheldon, Dr Morley and the scholarly John Hales. Hales was a Fellow of Eton, who gave everything away in charity as fast as it came to hand; ejected by the triumphant Puritans, he died in poverty, uncomplaining.

We need go no further than these men, to immensely learned prelates like Archbishop Ussher or Bishop Hall, to Archbishop Williams who, though worldly, was tolerant and a patron of music and culture; or to the martyred Laud – more tolerant than his enemies – who died for the Church. All over England there were humble men of heart who struggled along, doing what they could according to their capacity in their parishes. John Milton had no humility, traditionally the first of Christian virtues; he was full of pride – hence his inner feeling for Satan – which Catholic Christianity holds the deadliest of the Seven Deadly Sins. He showed no understanding towards the bishops in their difficult task, nor charity – a quality in which he was singularly wanting; nor had he any justice of mind, which William Shakespeare so eminently exemplified.

One of the pleasant things about the too virtuous young Milton is his appreciation of the not very virtuous Shakespeare. His tribute appeared prefaced to the Second Folio of 1632, and its phrases express personal feeling and warmth:

> Dear son of memory, great heir of fame . . .
> Thou in our wonder and astonishment
> Hast built a live-long monument.
> For whilst to the shame of slow-endeavouring art
> Thy easy numbers flow. . . .

Evidently, as in his 'Sonnet on His Twenty-Third Year', Milton reproached himself as not yet justifying his high expectations. He was in fact laying deep foundations in learning for the great monument he was preparing to construct.

Milton later gave as his reason for not becoming a cleric Laud's demand for conformity. Laud's personality and policy have received utterly unsympathetic and uncomprehending treatment from the dominant Parliamentary and Whig tradition in historical writing. We should do him justice. Laud aimed at external uniformity, decency and order; with regard to the inner content of men's beliefs he was far more tolerant than the Puritans. His position was that of the philosophic Hooker, indeed of Queen Elizabeth herself: 'I desire to open a window into no man's conscience.' Hobbes thought Laud was a fool of a don to bother about such things; but, then, Hobbes was not a churchman and had no religious belief at all. Laud wished to repair some of the damage that had been wrought by the Reformation, recover some of its property pillaged by the gentry, restore some of the devastation in the churches, lift up the level of ritual and order. This was precisely what uncultivated Puritans hated him for; they wanted to carry the Reformation further. They succeeded for a time, bringing about still further deliberate destruction.

Once more we see the paradox that so cultivated a man as Milton should have been on the uncivilised side. It was his intellectual convictions, his doctrinal certainty, that misled him, as usually with doctrinaires. This is how he described what happened: he was sad at having to draw back, when the Church was in such need of reform. But 'perceiving what tyranny had invaded the Church that he who would take orders must subscribe slave' – we see what an exaggeration this is – he preferred 'a blameless silence before the sacred office bought and begun with servitude and forswearing'. Blaming others, he immediately contradicts himself: 'Church-outed by the prelates', he considered he had 'a right to meddle in these matters' just as if he were a cleric – and indeed, so far from maintaining silence, never ceased to shoot his mouth off on these matters.

Though the most brilliant student at Christ's, he had not been elected to a Fellowship as his junior, Edward King, had been. Rather remarkably, no one seems to have proposed it. King was much beloved; Milton was never popular: he reacted to that with contempt not only for the populace, but also for people in general. He remarked yet again on their envy, their complaints and calumnies – himself so virtuous. Then what profession should he take? Commerce? Business in the City? He considered this beneath him – though he owed the independence he enjoyed to his father having made a fortune as scrivener and usurer, lending out money at high rates of interest on good security. The law? He described the law as 'senseless clamour', and complacently thanked his father in a Latin poem for saving him from it – when his younger brother, Christopher, was drafted into it.

There remained the profession of poet. Milton being Milton, he did not take this in his stride and content himself with his gift and what came to him, like Herbert or Herrick, let alone Court poets like Carew or Suckling or Lovelace. For him, to be a poet was a divine calling. He was to be poet and prophet alike, expressing the highest sentiments in the noblest form. To this end he was preparing himself. He recognised a certain 'belatedness' in his development, his hesitation before the calling he proposed to follow, but so in the end he would win fame: 'no longer shall I be lost in obscurity among the stupid mob'. As for preparing himself for his vocation: 'my genius is such that no delay, no rest, no care or thought of anything else keeps me from it until I achieve the end I have in view and complete the full period of my studies'. What is extraordinary is that this ambitious programme, with its fixed end in view, he did achieve. It involved abnormal exertion of the will, with yet further strain upon this sensitive, feminine temperament. What wonder if the beautiful youth ultimately grew into a rather harsh man?

He spent these next six years, 1632–8, mainly in studious retirement at his father's country place, Horton in Buckinghamshire, practically within sight of the towers of Windsor Castle and Eton. Lucky young man to be able to do so. Nothing distracted him, as he said, from his aim. Certainly not the mere glimpse of a dark-eyed Italian girl, of the rare name Emilia ——, about whom he wrote in his Italian sonnets. (Shakespeare's Dark Lady, another Emilia, *née* Bassano, Mrs Lanier, was still alive, in her sixties; her husband's cousin, Nicholas Lanier, was a distinguished musician and connoisseur, agent for the King in building up his unparalleled collection of pictures.)

Milton's closest friend, a strong emotional attachment, was another Anglo-Italian, Charles Diodati, to whom alone he confided his inmost thoughts. His letters to Diodati – the friends corresponded in Latin and Greek – inform us as to his inordinate programme of studies. He was already familiar with most of classical literature; in Italian he read Dante and Petrarch: in English his chief admiration was Spenser; though he knew the language, he was rather anti-French (Charles I's spirited but tactless Queen, Henrietta Maria, probably counted for something in that). To all this Milton was now adding a wide study of the Bible and the Early Fathers; he seems to have acquired Hebrew, with some Syriac and Chaldaic. His notebooks show him reading ethics, politics and economics. He was now adding history; he had covered the history of Greece to its transition to the Byzantine Empire, thence to the Holy Roman Empire of the Germans. Would Diodati be so kind as to send him Giustiniani's *History of the Venetians?*

How staggering it all is! The young Milton was virtually

proposing to compass the whole of human knowledge, and we see the sympathies of mind that linked him with his charming Italian friend.

Charles Diodati belonged to a distinguished international family of Italian Protestants, with roots and contacts in Venice, Geneva, the Netherlands, Paris and London.[6] Charles's father, Theodore, was an eminent doctor who had settled in the City and lived not far from the Miltons in the neighbourhood of St Paul's. Born in 1609, and thus a year junior to Milton, Charles went to St Paul's School but left a couple of years earlier than his friend to go to Oxford. Physically he matured earlier: it is Milton – intellectually precocious, physically behindhand – who looks up to Charles with admiration as leader, as if he were the senior, and Charles plays this rôle in the relationship. I suspect that he was the more masculine partner: he shows himself a cheerful extrovert, gay and companionable, intelligent and quick, fond of the open air. The two young men, highly sympathetic to one another, were complementary.

Diodati writes from Oxford reproaching Milton as for ever studying. 'Why inexcusably persist in hanging over books and studies all day and all night? Live, laugh, make the most of youth and the hours – and cease worrying about the passions and concerns of men of old, and wearing yourself out.' Diodati, like Milton, had been intended for the Church, and in 1630–1 went to Geneva, where his family was entrenched, to study theology. However, he could not stand the rigours of Calvinism, which had been reinforced by the victory of the rigid Calvinists at the Synod of Dort, 1618–19. The issue at this historic assembly was that of Predestination against Free Will, upheld by Arminius (hence Free Willers, like Laud, were named Arminians).[7] Predestination, having numbers with it, prevailed. The intelligent House of Orange had been all for moderation; but the political sense of Prince Maurice, perceiving that the majority were for Calvinism, threw in his lot with them. The Predestined Elect had the joy of condemning the wisest brain in Holland, Hugo Grotius, to imprisonment for life. Diodati came back to England and turned to the more useful study of medicine.

When we next hear of the friends, Diodati has failed to write to Milton, though writing frequently enough to their bookseller in London and to his own brother; nor has he kept his promise to stay with Milton on his way to the country, where he was now practising physic. It seems that Diodati's feeling for his friend had somewhat cooled, for Milton writes a long defence of ideal Platonic friendship, its nature and obligations, in a tone of reproach. Milton would not have it depend upon correspondence and formal salutations, but upon 'a loving recollection of virtues on both sides. . . . It is impossible for me not to love men like you. God has instilled into me, if into anyone, a passionate love of the beautiful. . . . When anyone scorns what ordinary people think in their low view of things, and dares to express what the highest wisdom of the ages has thought best, I forthwith attach myself to that man by a kind of necessity.' Here we are in touch with the inwardness of Milton's nature.

This was the blissful decade, described so poignantly by Clarendon, when Parliament was in abeyance with its angry disputes, and there was an illusion of inner security while the King maintained peace with foreign powers. In such an atmosphere the interests of culture prevailed: the magnificent masques of Ben Jonson and Carew at Court, the *décor* by Inigo Jones. This architect of genius built more permanent works, the Banqueting Hall at Whitehall, the Queen's House at Greenwich; and erected the grandest portico in Europe, save for St Peter's, at the west end of St Paul's to which he was giving a classic exterior. (The Puritans hated it.) The King gave his patronage to artists such as Rubens and Van Dyck, by which we remember his Court with romantic nostalgia. Laud built his beautiful Canterbury quadrangle at his Oxford college, St John's.

In peace and security Milton could write his exquisite earlier poems, which many prefer – for they are easier to appreciate – to the greater works of his last years. It is no part of my plan to indulge in literary criticism of what others have so often discussed – 'L'Allegro' and 'Il Penseroso'; or the masques *Arcades* and *Comus*. We must, however, consider *Comus*, the most important of these, for the light it throws on our subject, his intellectual outlook and frame of mind.

Of all Milton's early works *Comus* is that which most foreshadows the later – to a degree which may not be realised – and expresses, though more agreeably and with exquisite charm, not only the tone and temper of his mind but the principle upon which it was fixed. It is the most beautiful of all Caroline masques, the most perfect as a work of art. Aesthetic criticism is not my quest, though we should notice that even in this sphere *Comus* clearly foreshadows the later works.

In the use of language, for example, there are many phrases in the classic style – it reminds one of the encroaching classicism in Caroline architecture – which would grow upon him, until it became the Miltonic style recognised as such. We note such phrases as 'my unacquainted feet', 'my severed company', 'innumerous boughs', 'arbitrate the event' (for, simply, 'decide'); or, again, 'invert the covenants' for 'turn the conditions upside down', or such a phrase as 'this corporal rind thou hast immanacled' for 'you have bound this body'. With regard to rhyme, too, much of the work is in regular rhyme; but even in the blank verse we meet with a good deal of irregular rhyme and assonance – as in *Paradise Lost* and the later works.

It is the theme, however, that is important to our purpose, the portrait of Milton's mind, its intellectual constitution and make-up. The very first speech announces that it is Virtue under stress that is going to be the subject, though in the event it will not be soiled

> With the rank vapours of this *sin-worn* mould.

In the phrase 'sin-worn' there is already a Puritan touch: I doubt if any other of the Caroline masques sported such a phrase. Already the young Puritan announces himself in the disdain at the thought

> To roll with pleasure in a sensual sty.

(As a matter of fact, a little rolling in the hay would have done him good and advanced the knowledge of life, in which he was so sadly deficient – responsible in the end for the grief of his personal life.)

Chastity, an attempt on the chastity of the Lady, is the subject. Milton already identified with virtue and chastity, and proclaims the self-esteem which provides an *obbligato* in all his work, a guiding motive consistently adhered to and even specifically expounded and defended later. It has much to be said for it – though the insistence is what raises a psychological query. Thus early it appears, unobjectionably:

> He that has light within his own clear breast
> May sit i' the centre, and enjoy bright day

– Milton evidently:

> But he that hides a dark soul and foul thoughts
> Benighted walks under the midday sun;
> Himself in his own dungeon.

Paradoxically, it was the introvert Milton who became imprisoned in the dungeon of his own egoism; where extroverts like Shakespeare, by no means virtuous or chaste, enjoyed a free and happy life.

Here is Milton already formed:

> Till oft converse with heavenly habitants
> Begin to cast a beam on the outward shape,
> The unpolluted temple of the mind,
> And turns it by degrees to the soul's essence,
> Till all be made immortal.

As for the unchaste, Puritan disapprobation declares itself:

> But, when lust,
> By unchaste looks, loose gestures, and foul talk,
> But most by lewd and lavish acts of sin,
> Lets in defilement to the inward parts,
> The soul grows clotted by contagion,
> Imbodies, and imbrutes, till she quite lose
> The divine property of her first being.

Why did the theme of chastity occupy so important a place in Milton's mind? He was already twenty-five – quite an advanced age for a Caroline young man to have retained a virginity as spotless as the Lady with whom he identifies:

> I would not taste thy treasonous offer. None

> But such as are good men can give good things

– what immature nonsense! –

> And that which is not good is not delicious
> To a well-governed and wise appetite

– i.e., Milton.

It is, indeed, revealing psychologically that the 'Lady of Christ's' identified with the Lady in *Comus*. But, in fact, she is so walled up in virtue that the temptation offered is no temptation at all, so that there is no real drama in the masque: it is just a beautiful exposition of its theme.

> These thoughts may startle well, but not astound
> The virtuous mind, that ever walks attended
> By a strong siding champion, Conscience.
> O, welcome, pure-eyed Faith, white-handed Hope,
> And thou unblemished form of Chastity!

Nevertheless, that the theme itself was crucial to Milton is clear from the fact that it becomes central again in both *Paradise Lost* and *Paradise Regained*, while Samson had succumbed to temptation – hence his trials. Why was temptation so very important to Milton? Partly, one sees, from the too rigorous, the inhuman control he imposed upon himself – so unlike Shakespeare. But one would very much like to know what, in fact, would have tempted Milton most. Probably power, more than anything.

In the moral of the masque we recognise Milton complete already, as he remained all through: Nature

> Means her provision only to the good,
> That live according to her sober laws,
> And holy dictate of spare Temperance.
> If every just man that now pines with want
> Had but a moderate and beseeming share
> Of that which lewdly-pampered Luxury
> Now heaps upon some few with vast excess,
> Nature's full blessings would be well dispensed
> In unsuperfluous even proportion. . . .

It is the Nonconformist ideal – which has come to prevail,

under his spiritual descendants, in our time.

The masque was performed in 1634 at splendid Ludlow Castle – its ruined towers now looking down upon the Teme, which runs below its walls – before the Earl of Bridgewater, then President of the Council of Wales. The invitation to write it had come from the composer of the music, Henry Lawes, a family friend. In 1637 he published it: 'although not openly acknowledged by the author, yet it is a legitimate offspring, so lovely and so much desired that the often copying of it hath tired my pen to give my several friends satisfaction, and brought me to a necessity of producing it to the public view'.

Why should Milton have not acknowledged it and withheld it from publication? It is not the first, nor the last, sign of perverseness in his disposition.

Next year, 1638, while his brother – seven years younger – was normally engaged in getting married, the elder, getting on for thirty, was making his preparations to go abroad, thus belatedly, to complete the imposing edifice of his education by the Grand Tour. In gathering introductions he was helped by the Diodatis and the advice of his neighbour at Eton, Sir Henry Wotton, who appreciated Milton's verse and suggested a plan of travel. At Eton, Milton also knew John Hales, whom Wotton used to call (in Latin) a walking library, and from whom Milton could have taken some lessons in Christian charity.

In Paris, Wotton's letters introduced the traveller to the ambassador, Viscount Scudamore. We have reason to remember this benefactor, for it was he who reroofed the chancel of the ruined church of Abbey Dore and installed the admirable Caroline woodwork we see there today. A High Churchman, and a bosom friend of Laud, he restored the tithes appropriated from the Church at the time of the Dissolution. This was the kind of work of reparation Laud struggled to achieve against mounting opposition and opprobrium.

It is to be hoped that Milton appreciated meeting the son of 'Sir Scudamour', the pattern of chivalry in Spenser's *Faerie Queene*, even if he did not the ambassador's chapel equipped in seemly fashion with altar and candles. This was not the end of the good works of the family, which for generations had been known for their horsemanship and improving the breed of horses. The delicious Herefordshire countryside owed much to Scudamore for his planting of orchards and cultivating the art of grafting; he introduced the redstreak apple into the county. In the confusion of the Civil War he suffered greatly from Puritan depredations upon his property. When under the Commonwealth Milton occupied a house in Petty France in St James's, it adjoined Lord Scudamore's, which had been sequestered and all his goods seized. Nevertheless, in retirement after the war, out of diminished resources – he had spent a fortune on the Church – he supported a number of eminent churchmen who had been thrown out by the triumphant Puritans.

Lord Scudamore did his best for the young man by introducing him to one of the foremost figures in Europe. Grotius had escaped from the prison to which he had been consigned by the triumphant Calvinists. To them the idea of toleration was as intolerable as it was to Catholics: each possessed the Truth, and the whole Truth, with mutual exclusiveness and contradiction. On a mission to England, Grotius had been impressed by the moderation and comprehensiveness of the English Church. He was now operating as Swedish ambassador in Paris; he and Lord Scudamore were together in wishing to see an ecumenical union of Protestant churches. Grotius was not only the greatest of European jurists but also an eminent classical scholar and Latin poet. He had written a drama on Paradise lost, *Adamus Exul*. No doubt this seed lodged in Milton's mind.

Milton always looked younger than his years, but it was not the poet's looks and accomplishments that opened to him all doors in Italy – though the Italians, even churchmen, had a sophisticated appreciation of male beauty. Sir Henry Wotton had been ambassador in Venice for many years; his recommendation went a long way. The Diodatis knew Galileo, whom Milton was thus enabled to visit in Tuscany – and the visit has left its flecks in *Paradise Lost*. Two years before, Galileo had received an Englishman of equal, but contrasting, genius: Thomas Hobbes. Later, Milton described the meeting in prose with 'a prisoner of the Inquisition for thinking in astronomy otherwise than the Franciscan and Dominican censors thought. And though I knew that England was then groaning loudest under the prelatical yoke [!], I took it that other nations were thus persuaded of her liberty.' Indeed, the clamour the Puritan opposition could arouse showed how light the yoke was.

In the literary society of the academies into which Milton went his admirable command of Latin made things easy for him; he read his own Latin poems, and later he recommended rightly, but in vain, that the Italian pronunciation of Latin should be followed in preference to the English. In Florence, Milton, at thirty, fell for a gifted young poet of nineteen, Carlo Dati; the friendship was returned, compliments and Latin poems exchanged. Later, Dati's tribute was prefaced to Milton's belated publication of his *Poems* (1645), along with another by Jacopo Gaddi. Another poet, Malatesti, dedicated to Milton a series of unsuitable sonnets, which remained, it is now known, in manuscript. We may be sure that these were not well received, and Malatesti's name was not mentioned. An Italian comment on the virtuous Englishman was that he was 'disliked on account of his too severe morals; and he would freely dispute about religion and inveigh against the Pope on any occasion'.

Nevertheless, in Rome he was hospitably received at the English College, where he dined in the company of Lord Falkland's brother. The courtesy was not rewarded by any politeness on the part of Milton later. Rome, however, has left its mark on *Paradise Lost,* where it is magnificently described – by Satan. On to Naples the poet went, where he was received by the eminent Manso, Marquis of Villa, who immensely appealed to Milton, for he had known Tasso; indeed, Tasso had dedicated his book on friendship to him. How these chords strike together and resound: Scudamore and Spenser, Wotton and Galileo, Manso and Tasso of the *Gerusalemme Liberata*!

The old nobleman was very kind to Milton, who acknowledged his courtesy in a Latin poem; and later 'he himself conducted me around the city and to the palace of the Viceroy, and more than once paid me a visit at my lodgings. On my departure he apologised that he had not shown me more civility, which he said he had been restrained from doing, because I had spoken with so little reserve on matters of religion.' He had intended to go on to Sicily and then Greece, but 'the melancholy intelligence I received of the civil commotions in England made me alter my purpose; I thought it base to be travelling abroad, while my fellow citizens were fighting for liberty at home'. However that may be, it was a good thing he turned homewards: from Sicily or Greece he might never have come back.

In Rome once more he had an honourable reception: he was invited to a musical entertainment at the palace of Cardinal Barberini, of the famous Papal family and a generous patron of the arts, and was apparently received next day. On one of the Roman visits he heard the famous Leonora Baroni sing. There followed no less than three Latin epigrams to her. From Venice he dispatched a chest of music books home: the works of Monteverdi, greatest of living composers, his opera *The Coronation of Poppaea* shortly to be written; Luca Marenzio, the prolific composer of madrigals; Orazio Vecchi; and Gesualdo, passionate and tortured spirit, innovator in chromatic effects. All of these wonderful expressions of the Italian genius were to be revived for us today.

Thus on to dreary Geneva, where Milton learned from the Diodatis the news of his friend Charles's death. It would be a sad homecoming. Milton commemorated him in the most moving of all his poems, the 'Epitaphium Damonis'. It is only the fact that it is in Latin that has prevented this poem from being as well known as 'Lycidas'. It is significant that it has more personal feeling, is a more poignant expression of grief: Milton felt freer to let himself go in the language in which they had often written to each other.

> Ah! certe extremum licuisset tangere dextram,
> Et bene compositos placide morientis ocellos,
> Et dixisse 'Vale! nostri memor ibis ad astra.'

He was now alone. Youth was over.

CHAPTER TWO

Milton and the Church

MILTON'S exact contemporary, Edward Hyde, later Lord Clarendon – both born in 1608 – has a famous description of Britain as it stood on the threshold of the Civil Wars. 'It was about the year 1639, when England enjoyed the greatest measure of felicity that it had ever known.'[1] Most of the Continent was at war: France and Spain with each other, while each had internal trouble – France the faction-fights of the Frondes, Spain the revolution of Portugal from her control. All Germany was locked in the Thirty Years' War, which ultimately ruined her chances of becoming a world power and made her so disastrously aggressive to redeem the time three centuries later.

'Of all the princes of Europe the king of England alone seemed to be seated upon that pleasant promontory that might safely view the tragic sufferings of all his neighbours. . . . His three kingdoms flourishing in entire peace and universal plenty, in danger of nothing but their own surfeits; and his dominions every day enlarged by sending out colonies upon large and fruitful plantations; his strong fleets commanding all seas, and the numerous shipping of the nation bringing the trade of the world into his ports. And all these blessings enjoyed under a prince of the greatest clemency and justice, of the greatest piety and devotion, and the most indulgent to his subjects, and most solicitous for their happiness and prosperity.

O fortunati nimium, bona si sua norint!

'In this blessed conjuncture . . . a small, scarce discernible cloud arose in the North, which was shortly after attended with such a storm that never gave over raging till it had shaken and rooted up the greatest and tallest cedars of the three nations;

blasted all its beauty and fruitfulness; brought its strength to decay and its glory to reproach and almost to desolation: by such a career of wickedness and rebellion as – by not being foreseen, or in truth suspected – could not be prevented.'

Note Clarendon's phrase *in danger of nothing but their own surfeits*. In the language of our own time – to adapt a notorious phrase – *They had had it too good for too long*. The country or, rather, its ruling classes felt themselves bottled up by the long intermission of Parliament, their institution and instrument. They were clamouring for a share in power. In the event, more – they collared power for themselves, and then fell out about it, as a prescient old Royalist had foreseen they would on their victory: 'you may now go play – unless you fall out among yourselves'. Which, of course, they did. But they had long been spoiling for a fight.

The occasion for it came from Scotland, with the Covenanting rebellion against the King's attempt to bring about some uniformity of religious observance between Scotland – his home country, where he had been born – and its more civilised southern neighbour, which he had come to rule. We must never forget that the King was a Scot, inclined to favour Scots, and not so well in tune with his southern subjects as the Tudors had been.

The historian Burnet – himself a Scot, but of a reasonable, tolerant temper, a charitable man – gives us a picture of how things were in the northern kingdom under the dominant Presbyterianism. In his *Memoirs* of the first two Dukes of Hamilton, both of whom died for the King, he tells us: 'the power the ministers had with the people was swelled to such insolence that it was more than necessary to limit it to just bounds. For nothing passed in the Court or Council but the pulpits did ring with it. . . . Neither did the King cherish any who was not devoted to them but they did represent him a favourer of Popery. Many of them being popular preachers and of insinuative tempers, they were much depended upon by the people, who looked on all their excesses as holy zeal. . . . The liturgy and ceremonies of England were held by the zealous of Scotland all one with Popery.'[2]

Burnet describes how the people hated the bishops appointed by the Crown to moderate and hold in check their fanaticism. As in Holland it was the populace, instigated by their preachers, that was mad for Calvinism. On the reading of the new Prayer Book in Edinburgh in 1637 tumults had been raised 'from women and the meaner sort of people'. The leadership was taken by the politic head of Alexander Henderson, a minister who had been balked of preferment when young, and now made himself the spearhead of the popular movement. He had a large hand in framing the Covenant and whipping up fervour and frenzy in support. With this irresistible motor-power behind him, he had no difficulty in defeating all attempts at compromise by the King's Commissioner, the Duke of Hamilton. In all these years full of trouble the fanatics never would compromise: only force could deal with them. They proceeded to raise a rebellion. Those who did not support the Covenant were forced by violence and mob-pressure to accede to it. It is a familiar pattern in all revolutions.

As to the temper behind it, we have a vivid pointer from the mother of the King's Commissioner, the Marchioness-Dowager of Hamilton, who was a violent Presbyterian. On the outbreak of war she raised a troop of horse and rode at their head. Her son commanded the King's ships in the Forth. She dared him to land, at the risk of being shot by his own mother – and she had silver bullets provided for the purpose.

The Civil Wars started with the rebellion in Scotland, which defeated the King. This was why, for a century afterwards, loyal Englishmen like Dr Johnson, or indeed Swift – who thought of himself as an Englishman – hated the Scots. Many Englishmen who were no supporters of Oliver Cromwell could not but be proud of the great man when he put the Scots in their place and an end to their interference in English affairs.

The judicious historian Gardiner – whose sympathies were with Parliament, was said to be a descendant of Cromwell, and in religion a Plymouth Brother – tells us that Laud, as the mainspring of Charles's government, always feared a conjunction of the discontented nobles and gentry in England with the rebellious Scots. It was a pattern for victory – and the conjunction came about. When Laud had been in Scotland with the King for his coronation in 1633, he had been shocked by the devastated appearance of the churches and the cathedrals in ruins, the amenities of the Reformation in its Calvinist form.

Laud stood for something better in England. He was really an Elizabethan, who upheld – with the great Queen and such figures as Jewel, Hooker, Whitgift, Bancroft – the Church of England as a genuine *via media* between Rome and Geneva with an ethos of its own. As Archbishop Whitgift had pointed out, why should the English Church be subject to the *ipse dixit*, the interference, of a Calvin? The Anglican Church had its own historic character and tradition, sealed by its own martyrs who had laid down their lives for it. Archbishop Laud was to become another, in succession to Cranmer, Latimer, Ridley, Hooper and all the others.

Laud may not have been the wisest of men, or indeed the best choice for the see of Canterbury, since he was a rather rigid man, not given to compromise on principles. Intellectually he was more tolerant than his Calvinist opponents; an adherent of Free Will, against their Predestination nonsense, he disliked doctrinal controversy. He well realised – like Queen Elizabeth – that, if people were given free leave to open their mouths about nonsense issues, they would shortly be at each other's throats. As for the mania for preaching, the insatiable thirst for sermons, the Queen had pertinently asked how many of the clergy were capable of preaching? Only 500, in a country of 9,000 parishes. This was not the only point in favour of an ordered liturgy. A liturgy was something impersonal, something all could equally share in without the personal excitements (and incitements), the antics and postures, of individual preachers in their pulpits. As Samuel Butler, who passed through the disillusionments of this sickening epoch with a clearer eye than anyone (except Selden or Hobbes), wrote in his character of 'An Hypocritical Nonconformist': 'He cries down the Common Prayer, because there is no ostentation of gifts to be used in the reading of it – without which he esteems it mere loss of time and labour in vain that brings him in no return of interest and vain glory from the Rabble: who have always been observed to be satisfied with nothing but what they do not understand.'[3]

Laud was a formalist, a stickler for adhering to the rules, dedicated to duty and the well-being of Church and State; a distinguished scholar and a most able brain, he was always overworked and had no relaxations. His father had been merely a Reading clothier. There was a class interest in the dislike of Laud among nobility and gentry: they could not bear that someone born so far beneath them should occupy power and place above them. One or two of them expressed precisely this attitude. For his part Laud was courageously determined to make grandees adhere to the rules as well as simpler people. Even Gardiner admits that underneath the Archbishop's rigorous application of principle personal kindliness was discernible. He was too much pressed for time by multifarious business to oil the wheels with a little tactful insincerity. When a Chief Justice himself interfered with the customary wakes down in Somerset, Laud treated him to a reproof before the Privy Council that made him say he had been 'almost choked by a pair of lawn-sleeves'. This kind of thing created dangerous enemies who could hit back – while the idiot people, for whom Laud was battling, so far from giving him any support, backed up his opponents by their hue and cry, mobbing him and hissing him in the streets.

Again there was this to be said for Laud's favouring churchmen in offices of state. He had pushed to have Bishop Juxon made Lord Treasurer. Juxon proved an admirable, even popular, administrator; and as a celibate churchman, with no family to provide for, he was financially beyond reproach. All previous Lord Treasurers had had their paws in the public purse one way or another – some of them made vast fortunes out of it. The clothier's son disapproved; but in keeping aristocrats out of a splendid office with all its perquisites he added the most powerful to his numerous enemies.

He was not the man to propitiate anyone – too upright, though he had his friends and disciples who admired him for the sincere and disinterested man he was. Clarendon has a story which brings home to us that, under the archiepiscopal dignity, there was more Christian humility than with many a Puritan. As a young lawyer with his way to make, Hyde once told the Archbishop to his face at Lambeth that he was too tactless, that he did not sufficiently consider people's susceptibilities. The Archbishop blushed for himself – and, so far from resenting it, ever afterwards treated the young lawyer with special confidence. It is a tribute to both men – both of them great men in their respective ways.

As a much older man, writing the history of the revolution to which these things led, Clarendon gives us the most perceptive and just character of the prelate, whom the Puritans made the most hated man in England and hounded to his death. 'He was a man of great courage and resolution and – being most assured within himself that he proposed no end in all his actions or designs than what was pious and just (as sure no man had ever a heart more entire to the King, the Church, or his country), he never studied the best ways to those ends.' He thought, apparently, that making up to individuals would tarnish his integrity. 'Let the cause be what it will, he did court persons too little; nor cared to make his designs and purposes appear as candid as they were by showing them in any other dress than their own natural beauty and roughness; and did not consider enough what men said or were like to say of him.'[4]

We should say that he did not care enough about his public 'image', in the jargon of today, when public figures think of little else. Nor did he consider 'public relations': he concentrated on the matter in hand. In short, Archbishop Laud was that very rare apparition in high politics and affairs of state – an entirely honest man.

We may note here, besides, some contrast in the way young Milton writes of these persons and affairs, having no first-hand knowledge or experience of them, and the grave, responsible way in which Clarendon writes – in the style, too, the one gnarled and sour, acrid and explosive, the other eloquent and controlled, actually more poetic and with far subtler discernment and insight into character.

The King's defeat in Scotland – he was forced to concede Presbyterianism to the fanatics and unscrambled episcopacy there – with the need to raise cash to buy them out and pay his own levies, forced him at last to call Parliament, first the Short and then the Long. At once the fat was in the fire, and did not cease burning until the Restoration of the monarchy in the King's son, Charles II. At once all the complaints and grievances against King and Church came to the fore – Ship Money (necessary to maintain the fleet), church courts (necessary to keep order in the nursery), the prerogative courts in the North and Wales (convenient for people not to have to make the journey to the courts in London) – and against his chief ministers, Strafford and Laud, whom Parliament were to run to the death. Neither of them could be found guilty of any crime against the state they had faithfully served – though the younger Sir Henry Vane, a doctrinaire fanatic, perjured himself to bring Strafford to the block. In the end Parliament brought in acts of attainder against both – i.e., to kill them by the decision of a parliamentary majority.

'We are all mad with joy here that his Majesty calls a Parliament,' a report went.[5] 'All men's hopes and prayers are upon the Parliament,' reported another. A third, 'a strong expectation of much ensuing good has possessed every man'. We shall see how these hopes were fulfilled. A revolutionary situation was in the making – the Puritan Revolution. It was the culmination of decades of campaigning, propaganda, misrepresentation, abuse of the Church and the bishops, from Cartwright and the scurrilities of the Marprelate Tracts onwards to the offensiveness of the hateful Prynne. The Puritans were in fact irrepressible, whatever anybody said or did. They were determined to have their way and get power. The fact that the Anglican Church had established a tradition of its own, a middle way between Rome and Geneva, was its very offence in their eyes. They wanted to complete the Reformation, as they put it; they regarded it as having been frustrated – i.e., themselves frustrated of power – as Parliament had been frustrated by the King's personal government. They were itching for power – the lesser gentry, the middle classes, the townsfolk, especially London which became ungovernable, and the Puritan clergy, their admired preachers with their frantic following, who expressed their ideology in its contemporary religious form.

They were now in a position to let loose their fulminations against the bishops and an episcopal church from hundreds of pulpits – the sounding-boards, the radio and television, and a good deal of the press, of the time. Not only without control, but with the support of Parliament. Gardiner states that, in reality, in spite of appearances, the Puritans were 'masters of the field'. A recent authority sums up: 'they bore a great share of the responsibility for the Civil War in England, and were "the chief causers and still are the grand incendiaries of our present miseries". . . . The division of the clergy into two factions split the country, and it was the divines that incited on both sides the people to fight, "with their preaching and noises, thumping and bumping the pulpit cushions", and crying, "Oh, rise! Oh, your lives, liberties and religion lieth at stake: thus were the poor men made murder each other." '[6]

This was more or less Thomas Hobbes's view of the matter in his analysis of the Civil War in *Behemoth*. Without illusions on either side, like a sensible man he left a country gone mad and stayed abroad for over a decade of the two devoted to revolution, disruption and destruction. I use the word 'mad' advisedly. An artist perceives much more than ordinary people do; and John Aubrey reports what the Czech artist, Wenceslas Hollar, observed: 'he told me that when he first came into England, which was in a serene time of peace, the people – both poor and rich – did look cheerfully'. But after the lunatic explosion was over, 'at his return, he found the countenance of the people all changed: melancholy, spiteful, as if bewitched'.[7]

How penetrating an observation! The whole experience of the Civil War is summed up in it. For, of course, people had been bewitched by the nonsense they were led to think – themselves incapable of thought – and the delusions that were fostered.

Gardiner considers that Laud never had the power people thought he had: his was a rearguard action in defence of the Church, and he was never sanguine that he could hold the line long. Now 'the order of bishops and the whole status of the Church were violently assailed in pamphlets: no less than 140 of these passed the press before the session was very far advanced'. Laud called upon the bishop who was least antipathetic to the Puritans – Joseph Hall, a good man, and an able writer – to defend the established order. This Hall did with his *Episcopacy by Divine Right Asserted*. In the excruciating theological atmosphere of the time the defence was couched in terms of 'divine' right. It should have been sufficient to defend the Church as established in practical terms, of working order appropriate to English circumstances. Towards the end of this mad period of revolution and war, confusion and endless insecurity, chops and changes, Cromwell's own brother-in-law, Wilkins – a founder of the Royal Society – advised Cromwell that religion could not be run in England without bishops.

Hall's defence was sufficiently close to the Puritans as to describe the Pope – after all, the traditional head of organised Christianity – as Anti-Christ. The ecumenical spirit of Laud deleted that insult; this charitableness was made a charge against him. Hall was at once set upon by five Calvinist divines, whose initials formed the rebarbative name Smectymnuus – and among them we find Milton's old Scotch tutor, Thomas Young. These Saints – the regular name in Puritan semantics for themselves, they were the 'godly', their opponents the 'ungodly' (they would have had nothing to learn from Hitler in the arts of propaganda and insinuation) – were, in order: Stephen Marshall, Edmund Calamy, Thomas Young, Matthew Newcomen, William Spurstow. They were all Cambridge men, as also was Hall.

Stephen Marshall was one of the most favoured preachers of the House of Commons. A swarthy, broad-shouldered man, he had 'a shackling gait' and rolled up his eyes in holy manner, not fixing them on his auditor. He was not a learned man, but essentially a political organiser and propagandist: 'he governeth the consciences of all the rich Puritans in those parts [Essex, a Puritan stronghold] and in places far remote, and is grown very rich'. He had once applied to Buckingham for preferment; his disappointment 'made him turn schismatic'.

His son-in-law surmised, 'if they had made his father a bishop before he was too far engaged, it might have prevented all the war.' As it was, he preached far and wide to influence the elections to Parliament on the Puritan side; he organised the petitions against bishops to Parliament, from his area, tampering with the signatures to give the impression of 700 who had signed different clauses, on the authority of only eighty who agreed with them all.

When the Commons arranged for seven morning lecturers a week at St Margaret's, Westminster, to preach in daily rotation, they received the very large salary of £300 a year each, their services were regarded as so useful. Marshall usually preached three times a week, to all the more approbation because a discriminating critic regarded them as 'uncouth rhapsodies'. He was particularly effective in pronouncing a solemn curse – his most famous sermon, 'Meroz Cursed', was preached over sixty times. An independent critic said that this cursing sermon 'ushered in, as well as promoted, the late bloody civil wars'.

Edmund Calamy, of Huguenot descent, would not 'read that wicked Book of Sports' in Puritan Suffolk. (We have seen how reasonable it was, providing for the average man.) Calamy developed a permanent giddiness – understandable enough – so that he could not mount a high pulpit but gave his eloquent diatribes from the reading-desk below. Hall had asserted the divine right of bishops, since he was a bishop; Calamy later asserted the divine right of ministers of the gospel, since he was a minister of the gospel. And that is about all there is to it.

Thomas Young was now in enjoyment of the rich living of Stowmarket at £300 a year (multiply by thirty or forty for contemporary value). In 1644 the Parliamentarian Earl of Manchester intruded him into the place of Master of Jesus College, Cambridge, which he held until after the execution of the King. Though the Presbyterians scuttled out of responsibility for it, they had been responsible for undermining the monarchy and bringing about the war.

Matthew Newcomen was a brother-in-law of Calamy, who described him as 'sanctified by divine grace'. Another brother-in-law preached Newcomen's funeral sermon: 'The Dead Saint yet speaking'. That master spirit of the opposition, John Hampden, was the patron of William Spurstow, who was his master's voice as chaplain to his regiment. He got the promotion of Master of St Catharine's College, Cambridge, for his services, in place of its properly elected occupant.

Such were Bishop Hall's opponents.

Into the attack on church order and the bishops yet another Cambridge man flung himself: this was John Milton, with no less than five publications in the next two years. The first of these was published in 1641: *Of Reformation touching Church Discipline in England and the Causes that hitherto have hindered it.* We can judge a man fairly only by his own words, so we must cite what Milton actually wrote. Most people do not realise what he said, for they have not read his prose works.

The argument of this first tract is that external forms have taken the place of inward spiritual grace. The Church has circumscribed worship: 'they hallowed it, they fumed it, they bedecked it, not in robes of pure innocency but of pure linen, with other deformed and fantastic dresses in palls and mitres, gold and gewgaws fetched from Aaron's old wardrobe or the Flamens' vestry. Then was the priest set to con his motions and his postures, his liturgies and his lurries [patter].' We see again: no appreciation of the beauty of ceremonial on the part of this aesthete – overborne by the doctrinaire in him – or even of its necessity or practical use. Deeper than that: everything in the experience of the next twenty years will prove – as the whole human record shows – that the ordinary sensual man cannot live by inner spiritual light alone. We may grant that a Milton may; but a Milton is very exceptional. It is characteristic not only of his egoism, but also of the blindness of doctrinaires, to suppose that the mass of men are like their exceptional selves.

In fact, average human nature needs external forms – a profound reason why Catholicism has survived, when Protestant sects have dispersed and all but disappeared: Catholicism is in keeping with human nature and rests on a truer reading of psychology. The Anglican Church, in retaining Catholic forms and organisation, has been proved by history to carry the character of the English people more comprehensively than any number of Protestant sects. And so the deplorable experiences of the next twenty years would show.

(A small point that appeals to a historian's imagination: one who realises what a seventeenth-century congregation would smell like would be grateful for a strong whiff of incense now and then.)

Milton had no patience with these uses. Baptism – a charming and touching ceremony, if nothing else – is 'thought little enough to wash off the original spot without the scratch or cross impression of a priest's forefinger'. The Anglican communion service, so moving in itself and for which such wonderful music had been written already in Milton's time, is 'a subject of horror and gloating adoration, pageanted about like a dreadful idol: which sometimes deceives well-meaning men by their voluntary humility'. A sensitive person can appreciate the prayer of humble access at communion, which bespeaks the spirit in which it is received. Not so Milton: it is merely 'servile crouching, sometimes lawful, sometimes idolatrous, under the name of *humility*, and terming the piebald frippery and ostentation of ceremonies *decency*'.

Not a spark of humility shows in Milton's make-up, or much among Puritans in general: he makes a reflection on St Peter's 'unseasonable humility' when Christ offered to wash his feet. Milton calls this show of humility 'stiff-necked' and 'arrogant'. Nothing like his own stiff-necked arrogance, which never found humility seasonable at any time.

The Reformation, 'bright and blissful, struck through the black and settled night of Ignorance and Anti-Christian Tyranny'. This was Milton's attitude to the Middle Ages throughout all his work, including his *History of Britain* later. No conception of what Europe owed to the Roman Church in civilising the barbarians, or its wonderful achievements in art and architecture, and the works of the mind. The medieval cathedrals are not only among the sublime achievements of man, but also monuments of the Catholic faith. And Dante – to whom the later Milton in defeat may be justly compared – was after all a more deeply, a more inwardly, religious spirit than ever Milton was.

'The pleasing pursuit' of contemplating the Reformation had often led him to debate with himself 'how it should come to pass that England – having had this grace and honour from God to be the first that should set up a standard for the recovery of *lost Truth* and blow the first evangelic trumpet to the nations – should now be last and most unsettled in the enjoyment of the peace whereof she taught the way to others'. Here we see that smug complacency characteristic not of Anglican England but of English Protestants, and especially English Nonconformists, which has naturally aroused so much dislike abroad (still more so with the New England mentality, the direct descendant of Milton's Puritans, which has attracted so much hostility to the United States in our time; the mentality of a Coolidge – 'Our charity girdles the earth' – or a John Foster Dulles).

Again, there is the paradox that Milton, who knew Catholic Europe and had imbibed so much of European classical culture, should have been so insular. We can only suppose that it was his doctrinairism, his intellectual certainty, his Puritan arrogance, that blinded him to more enlightened views. The English Church retained its 'senseless ceremonies only as a dangerous earnest of sliding back to Rome. And doubtless, whenever the Pope shall fall, if his ruin be not like the sudden downfall of a tower. . . .' Well, we still have the Pope with us, head of the greater part of Christianity – and where are the Puritans of 1641?

We are next given a very biased, Puritan reading of the course of the Reformation in England, with no sympathy for those bishops who died for it. 'But, it will be said, these men were martyrs. What then?' What a callous way to dismiss the sacrifice men like Cranmer, Latimer and Ridley made of their lives! It leaves a nasty taste in the mouth, like so much in Milton's prose writings. Again, how paradoxical in one so sensitive, the author of 'L'Allegro' and 'Il Penseroso', of 'At a Solemn Music' and the tribute to Shakespeare. There were obviously two sides to Milton; he gives the impression of being under strain. Was there something schizophrenic about him?

He has no good word for bishops, whether martyrs or not. 'They are not bishops – God and all good men [i.e., Milton and the Puritans] know they are not – who have filled this land with late confusion and violence, but a tyrannical crew and corporation of impostors.' The Caroline attempts to restore decency in the churches after so much depredation are thus described: 'stones and pillars and crucifixes have now the honour . . . the table of communion stands like an exalted platform upon the brow of the choir, fortified with bulwark and barricados to keep off the profane touch of the laics, whilst the obscene and surfeited priest scruples not to paw and mammock the sacramental bread as familiarly as the tavern biscuit'. Milton would reduce all bishops to an equality, 'elected by the popular voice, undiocesed, unrevenued, unlorded, and leave him nothing but brotherly equality, matchless temperance, frequent fasting, incessant prayer, continual watchings and labours in his ministry. Which, what a rich booty it would be, what a plump endowment to the many-benefice gaping mouth of a Prelate; what a relish it would give to his canary-sucking and swaneating palate, let old Bishop Mountain judge for me.'

Unfortunately for Milton, and for Puritans generally, this enables us to judge the truth of this vulgar abuse. Nothing ill is known of Bishop Mountain, Bishop of London in Milton's earlier days, except that he was born of poor parents, that he made benefactions to Cambridge, laboured hard and gave large sums for the repair of St Paul's, and that 'his benevolence left him poor'. Milton's reflection on him brings out the class prejudice there was among the Puritans at poor boys rising, through their abilities, in the Church. 'So that in this manner the prelates, both then and ever since, coming from a mean and plebeian life on a sudden to be lords of stately palaces, rich furniture, delicious fare and princely attendance . . .' – here is the envy of the aristocratic way of life among the middle classes, whose Puritanism was most strongly entrenched and for whom it provided an ideology, both defensive and offensive. No doubt it added an edge to the envy when the prelate came from poor parents, for Milton's father left 'a plentiful estate' from his *bourgeois* profession as scrivener and usurer.

If there were to be bishops at all, to square with antiquity to which they appealed, they should be 'elected by the hands of the whole church'. Milton favoured the Presbyterian view: 'he that, enabled with gifts from God, and the lawful and primitive choice of the Church assembled in convenient number . . . has his coequal and compresbyterial power to ordain ministers and deacons by public prayer and vote of Christ's congregation . . .'. He rejoiced in the present prospects of carrying the Reformation further forward, as all the Puritans did, in the spirit of the Old Testament they made their gospel: 'speedy and vehement were the reformations of all the good kings of Judah, though the people had been nuzzled in idolatry ever so long before'. He finished with a peroration which is a further blast on the trumpet of English patriotism. 'Then, amidst the hymns and hallelujahs of saints, someone may perhaps be heard offering at high strains in new and lofty measure [i.e., himself] to sing and celebrate thy divine mercies and marvellous judgments in this land throughout all ages. Whereby this great and warlike nation, instructed and inured to the fervent and continual practice of truth and righteousness, may press on hard to that high and happy emulation to be found the soberest, wisest and most Christian people at that day' – the Day of Judgment.

Here is the whole spirit of Puritan aggression, which found its strong right arm in Oliver Cromwell and its exponent in John Milton.

Shortly after this blast Milton produced a second: *Of Prelatical Episcopacy and Whether it may be deduced from the Apostolical Times.* This was a reply to Archbishop Ussher's moderate plea for the antiquity and divine sanction of episcopal order. Ussher was a prodigiously learned man, respected by all parties, by whose authority everyone was able to accept, until quite recently, that the precise year in which the world was created was 4004 B.C. A scholar rather than an administrator, the Archbishop of Armagh was of an ecumenical spirit, friendly with Puritans and Laud alike, much trusted by Charles I. Milton's treatment of him is not abusive like his first tract, though he has an offensive passage about Bishop Andrewes, on whom he had written an elegy in happier days.

What is remarkable about this tract is the extent of his reading in the Early Fathers – the fruit of those quiet years at Horton. It is an indication that he had seriously intended a calling in the Church. The argument was all about the sanction of episcopacy in antiquity. Milton was not moved by 'the offals and sweepings of antiquity'; he begins with the assumption that 'all men being born free and in the mistress island of all the British' had the right to retain or remove episcopacy according to convenience. If this were all there was to it, we need only say that removing episcopacy did not work. Events would show that the young man was wrong – as the young are apt particularly to be in regard to politics and society, for these demand experience and knowledge of the facts of life. Here Milton was sadly wanting. What was especially marked about him was that he would never take telling: he would not accept the lessons, from ill experience, that life brought home to him. His spirit remained erect and unbroken, though his world ultimately crashed about his ears. Never mind – he was right, not the world.

Hardly a month had passed before Milton was before the public again with an attack on Bishop Hall for daring to answer his opponents, the corporate monster Smectymnuus. Milton's American editor comments that he 'answers Hall in *Animadversions* by quoting him without concern for the context, then commenting satirically on it. The satire can hardly be called fair, and Milton himself was aware that his attack might seem improper to some.'[8] The tract was a return to abuse, and Milton defends his abuse of a 'convicted pseudepiscopacy of Prelates with all their ceremonies, liturgies and tyrannies, which God and man are now ready to explode and hiss out of the land'. It was better 'to handle such a one in a rougher accent, and to send home his haughtiness well bespirted with his own holy water. We know where the shoe wrings you: you fret, and are galled at the quick – and O what a death it is to the Prelates to be thus unvizarded, thus uncased, to have the periwigs plucked off that cover your baldness, your inside nakedness thrown open to public view.

' 'Twere hard if the freeborn people of England – with whom the voice of Truth for these many years hath not been heard but in corners, after all your monkish prohibitions and expurgatorious indexes, your gags and snaffles, your proud *Imprimaturs* not to be obtained without the shallow surview, but not shallow hand of some mercenary, narrow-souled and illiterate chaplain. . . .' We may comment fairly upon this: (*a*) that it is generally recognised now that the licensing of the press, customary in all countries, was exercised in a notably broad-minded spirit by the English Church; (*b*) that such is the irony of events that it fell to Milton to take part in the licensing which the Puritan commonwealth exercised after the overthrow of the Church.

Milton expresses his joy at the turn of events in which he was taking part, 'at a good time, our time of Parliament, the very jubilee and resurrection of the state. . . . The present age is to us an age of ages, wherein God is manifestly come down among us to do some remarkable good to our Church or state. . . .' We shall see. Liberal doctrinaires are often imbued with such illusions at the onset of a revolution. Charles James Fox said that the Fall of the Bastille was the best news he had heard since Saratoga. The French Revolution ended in a military dictatorship – as the Puritan Revolution was to do. Wordsworth, Coleridge and Southey learned from the deception of their early ideals. Milton never did.

As for Milton's abuse of Bishop Hall, we now know what kind of man he was. 'Personally well disposed to Puritans', at the beginning of the troubles he was translated from Exeter, where he was much liked, to the difficult diocese of Norwich where Puritans abounded. His preferment was meant as an olive-branch, but it was no use making concessions to fanatics. Whipped up by all the preaching, pamphleteering and abuse, the London mob – well organised by their preachers – came down to Westminster and prevented the bishops from taking their seats in Parliament. Their protest that they were an essential part of Parliament was voted treason, and they were sent to the Tower; condemned in *praemunire*, the episcopal estates were confiscated – which was what the Puritans had been after all along.

Samuel Butler said the last word on how things turned out in this regard later, when

> Rebellion now began for lack
> Of *Zeal* and *Plunder* to grow slack,
> The *Cause* and Covenant to lessen
> And Providence to be out of season:
> For now there was no more to purchase
> Of the King's revenue and the Church's,
> But all divided, shared, and gone,
> That used to urge the Brethren on.

At the beginning of these iniquities the mob at Norwich forced their way into the Bishop's chapel and destroyed the stained glass. They desecrated the Cathedral; Hall, confined in his palace hard by, could hear the miscreants at work. They then turned him and his family out of house and home. He and his family took refuge in a small house at Higham, which survived up to our own destructive time as the Dolphin Inn. There the old man gave himself up to devotional works for the remainder of his years, without expressing resentment in his plain narrative, *Hard Measure*.

Milton was more respectful to Archbishop Ussher in his next work, a reply to him: *The Reason of Church Government urged against Prelacy* (1642). This is a longer and more solid treatise to urge the argument, with much learning from the Fathers, about antiquity. The bishops had appealed to antiquity; very well, Milton tells them, presbyters were before bishops and exercised the right of ordaining. The bishops appealed to custom, Milton to reason. He hypostatised reason in all his works, the only court of appeal along with the Scriptures. Even with regard to the Scriptures reason must interpret – i.e., Milton's reason, not the accumulated reason, or tradition, of any church.

From the outset he tells us that 'persuasion certainly is a more winning and more manlike way to keep men in obedience than fear'. This is directly contrary to the view of the man of genius who saw most deeply into the nature of politics and society contemporaneously – Thomas Hobbes. The appeal to persuasion is based on the psychological delusion intellectuals are prone to – that men are rational, guided and motivated by rational considerations. This is belied not only by the findings of modern psychology but by the whole of human experience. Men are only *capable* of reason, and it is mainly in specialist and technical capacities – in their handiwork, in mechanics, engineering, etc. – that they use what reason they have. Few indeed are those men whose conduct of life is mainly governed by reason and, ironically, intellectuals are hardly more frequently to be found among these than others.

It is mostly when young and inexperienced that clever men fall for this rationalist delusion. Milton was no exception. 'If any man inclined to think I undertake a task too difficult for my years, I trust through the supreme enlightening assistance far otherwise; for my years, be they few or many, what imports it, so they bring Reason?' Again, 'if I hunted after praise by the ostentation of wit and learning, I should not write thus out of mine own season, when I have neither yet completed to my mind the full circle of my private studies, although I complain not of any insufficiency to the matter in hand. . . .' Of course not: he was always self-sufficient and right about whatever was in hand. His aggressive defensiveness is very revealing to a psychologist; he always has to stop up every loophole by which he may be faulted or found wanting. It is the regular pattern of defence by aggression; there must have been an inner insecurity to account for the overstrain and over-emphasis throughout his life and work.

As for completing his circle of private studies, it was not more book-knowledge that he needed to judge of political, social and religious affairs – 'the matter in hand' – but more knowledge of life and men. Precisely what William Shakespeare had – no man ever more so.

For once Milton recognised that this sphere of thought, to which he was devoting and was to continue to devote so much time and energy he could have better employed, was not rightly his. 'I should not choose this manner of writing wherein – knowing myself inferior to myself, led by the genial power of nature to another task – I have the use, as I may account it, but of my left hand.' Here he never spoke more truly: this was an insight which he should have acted on, instead of wasting his time and eyesight on matters that were not his proper sphere or in keeping with his genius. As to this last he never doubted: even in his early years, 'it was found that, whether ought was imposed me by them that had the overlooking, or betaken to of mine own choice, in English or other tongue, prosing or versing (but chiefly this latter), the style – by certain vital signs it had – was likely to live'.

What conceit, what unbreakable assurance – yet in the event justified. And how right he was! It was the *life* in his work, the recognisable living personality, that bespoke genius. In Italy his genius had been recognised, as by his friends at home; while his innermost nature told him that 'by labour and intent study – which I take to be my portion in this life – joined with the strong propensity of nature, I might perhaps leave something so written to aftertimes as they should not willingly let it die'.

Yes, indeed: this was to be *Paradise Lost* – not the kind of thing he was writing now and would continue to write, in fields where he was not well qualified to judge, let alone advise or instruct. Even into his own literary and artistic sphere he imported the blighting judgment of the Puritan. Here he is on the exquisite love-poetry of the Elizabethans and Carolines: he deplored 'the corruption and bane our youth and gentry suck in daily from the writings and interludes of libidinous and ignorant poetasters who – having scarce heard of that which is the main consistence of a true poem, the choice of such persons as they ought to introduce and what is moral and decent to each one – do for the most part lap up vicious principles in sweet pills and make the taste of virtuous documents harsh and sour'. Who would not prefer the poetry of Herrick and Carew, Lovelace and Suckling, to the 'virtuous documents' of the Puritans?

Milton goes on to inveigh once more against the tyranny of the Church and of subscription to proper discipline – 'that he who would take orders must subscribe slave' – when good men like Ussher and Andrewes, Hall and Laud and John Donne, with unnumbered others, had not found it so. Nor was he any more right in saying that under the prelates' 'inquisitorious and tyrannical duncery no free and splendid wit can flourish'. Simply untrue: the splendid wit of Donne had recruited itself to it; the wise and philosophic spirit of Hooker had expounded it; elect spirits such as Clarendon, Hales and Falkland, scholars like Ussher and Andrewes, Camden and Hakluyt and Spelman all found it sufficient and uninhibiting to their work. The Anglican Church proved a far better soil for culture and works of the spirit than Puritanism ever did. For that matter the Catholic Church was more propitious to the arts, if not to thought, of any – when at this very moment supreme creators in the arts, Rubens and Bernini, were carrying out its inspiration in glorious works.

So we do not need to take seriously the argument of the book. We might even accept it, with the contempt it deserves. Presbyters came before bishops – so what? 'We know Timothy received ordination by the hands of the presbytery' – so what? Church government is laid down in Scripture: 'God, whenever he meant to reform the Church, never intended to leave the government thereof to be patched afterwards and varnished over with the devices and embellishings of man's imagination.' We see throughout Milton's work that he always knew what God meant: living in the full certainty of Puritanism, long before modern psychology had undermined such innocent certainty, he would not have been aware that what God thought meant only what Milton thought; that 'God' was but a projection of his own ego.

At this time Milton gave vehement support to the Presbyterian attack on the Church, when the Presbyterian order was expected to take its place. In a couple of years he had reason to change his mind about the Presbyterians, not that this lessened his certainty that he knew best. He confidently contradicts the view of the Church that, but for its stand for a comprehensive uniformity, sects would proliferate and the country be distracted by their disputes, each man interpreting Holy Writ according to his own fancies and delusions. 'The prelates, as they would have it thought . . . forsooth, if they be put down, a deluge of innumerable sects will follow; we shall be all Brownists, Familists, Anabaptists.'

This was precisely what did happen – this doctrinaire wouldn't know, or take telling. The Church and the prelates were put down, and during the next twenty years of the Puritan Revolution sects proliferated; the air was rent by the prophesyings and upliftings, the delusions and lunacies not only of Brownists, Familists and Anabaptists, but Seekers and Quakers, Reevonians and Muggletonians, Fifth Monarchy men, and what not.

Milton came before the public with his fifth tract (1642) in defence of his old mentors: *An Apology against a Pamphlet called A Modest Confutation of the Animadversions upon the Remonstrant against Smectymnuus.* This, from its title, might well be thought more of the same indigestible chaff, but in fact it is more interesting for its information about the author. Milton had at last directed public attention to himself, and had been personally attacked in turn. So, without reluctance, he imparts a good deal of autobiographical information, telling us that he had not been sent down from Cambridge but had been highly thought of by the Fellows of his college, who would have been content for him to stay (though they never offered to recruit his permanent society as a Fellow).

The *Apology* is valuable for its description of his way of life, his devotion to study, the course he had followed and his intentions with regard to future work. It is illuminating about his literary principles and preferences – we might almost say his literary criticism, if that were not too stale a word. He had diligently studied the 'grave orators and historians' as well as the 'smooth elegiac poets'. What had inspired them would inspire him: 'what judgment, wit, or elegance was my share would herein best appear, and best value itself, by how much more wisely and with more love of virtue I should choose – let rude ears be absent – the object of not unlike praises'.

He was to be a virtuous, pure writer, and he applied these standards to writers of the past. 'If I found those authors anywhere speaking unworthy things of themselves, or unchaste of those they extolled – from that time forward their art I still applauded, but the men I deplored.' At this rate he deplored Shakespeare, Marlowe, Rabelais, Chaucer among moderns, and practically all amatory classical writers, Virgil, Ovid, Catullus, Theocritus, etc. For himself, 'he who would not be frustrate of his hope to write well hereafter in laudable things ought himself to be a true poem'. What a prig! Moral virtue has nothing to do with artistic achievement: look at Byron or Baudelaire, Dickens or Balzac or Proust, or for that matter Shakespeare or Marlowe.

But with Milton 'a certain niceness of nature, an honest haughtiness, and self-esteem either of what I was or what I might be (which let envy call pride) . . . kept me still above those low descents of mind, beneath which he must plunge himself that can agree to saleable and unlawful prostitutions' – i.e., to produce successful works. He insists once more upon the 'noble virtue of chastity' – and for how restricting this was we may contrast the unvirtuous Shakespeare, who was thereby enabled to depict the whole of life. Milton again congratulates himself on having avoided the temptations of the brothel – his 'moral discipline was enough to keep me in disdain of far less incontinences than this of the *bordello*'.

Here his self-approbation was superfluous, for with his refined feminine nature the brothel was no temptation to him. With his 'niceness of nature', his 'honest haughtiness', his 'self-esteem' – his own words – he could overcome greater temptations.

The argument of the pamphlet needs no further concern, for now the Church and its episcopal order were overthrown; as Milton kindly says, the prelates 'will soon be dumb and the divine right of episcopacy, forthwith expiring, will put us no more to trouble with tedious antiquities and disputes'.

The Church was down; it remained to be seen how much better a job the Puritans would do in maintaining and organising religion in England. In 1642 the Root and Branch Bill abolished the bishops; as the *Cambridge Modern History* comments, the very people who had campaigned against the bishops as innovators were now to become far more radical innovators themselves. 'Henceforward the extremists held the field: the moderate standard of ecclesiastical reform previously

proposed was thrown over.' All along there was collusion between Parliament and the Scotch Presbyterians to bring
pressure on the King. In 1643, to turn the scale in the war and
make victory certain, Parliament bought the Scots with a large
sum in cash and the promise of the establishment of Presbyterianism in England: the Solemn League and Covenant was
arrived at, negotiated by Sir Henry Vane, the perjurer who
betrayed Strafford.

The aim of the Solemn League and Covenant was to bring
about religious uniformity between Scotland and England on a
Presbyterian basis. Charles I and Laud had failed to achieve
this on an episcopal basis. We see that the Puritan aim was
uniformity all the same. To this end Parliament called into
being the Westminster Assembly: a large majority of divines, a
substantial lay representation (of which Selden was the most
eminent member), and a small body of Scots, led by Henderson
and Baillie, but with the more powerful voice in that they
claimed to be envoys from the sister nation.

It was a somewhat changed scene in the historic Abbey given
up to these people in these revolutionary years. All Laud's good
work was undone. The high altar was destroyed, the exquisite
medieval pavement mutilated; in Henry VII's Chapel, Tor-
rigiano's altar-piece was destroyed along with the magnificent
stained glass (similar to that at King's College Chapel in Cambridge – so we can imagine what we have lost). The thirteenth-
century tapestries, vestments, copes were sold; gold and silver
plate melted down, and later the regalia – crown, sceptre, orb
and all – broken up. Soldiers broke in at intervals, burning the
communion rails, smashing the organs. Choir and choirbooks
were alike dispersed, since Puritans hated the divine music of
the Church: 'nothing but roaring boys and squeaking organ-
pipes . . . and I know not what trash'. Paintings were defaced,
sculpture smashed; the place cluttered up with pews turned
towards a high pulpit for the preaching of the Word.

Seven powerful preachers had been appointed to lift up their
voices instead, in the desolate scene. On the sabbath, Mr Marshall would pray two hours; then Mr Arrowsmith preached an
hour, followed by a psalm (Milton's metrical versions of the

Psalms did not take on: those of Francis Rous did). Then Mr Vines preached near two hours, and Mr Palmer preached an hour. After that Mr Henderson for an hour; Dr Twisse closed, as he had begun, with prayer. 'Thus spending', Baillie tells us, 'nine to five very graciously.' These orgies of preaching, prayer and fasts served their purpose very effectively: they were propaganda exercises.

The clear brain of John Selden, who did not suffer from illusions and was the most brilliant intellect present, saw through it all. 'Preaching by the Spirit (as they call it) is most esteemed by the common people, because they cannot abide art or learning, which they have not been bred up in.'[9] And 'Preaching, for the most part, is the glory of the Preacher, to show himself a fine man. Catechising would do much better' – i.e., finding out by question and answer how much people know. As for the preaching of the Word, 'when the Preacher says, this is the meaning of the Holy Ghost in such a place, in sense he can mean no more than this: I . . . think this is the meaning of the Holy Ghost.' Q.E.D.

Selden, himself a Parliament man, says the last word about the Puritan mania about the Word of God. 'You say there must be no Human Invention in the Church – nothing but the pure Word. *Answer*: If I give any exposition but what is expressed in the text, that is my invention; if you give another exposition, that is your invention. And both are Human.' But of course. 'If we must admit nothing but what we read in the Bible, what will become of the Parliament? For we do not read of that there.' As for the Judgment of God, to which Milton constantly appealed, as Oliver Cromwell did too: 'we cannot tell what is a judgment of God; 'tis presumption to take upon us to know'.[10] From what Selden goes on to say, it is clear that he realised that what God thought was but an extrapolation of what the man holding forth thought – which is just what I have diagnosed in Milton. Selden diagnosed it better than any contemporary – along with Hobbes: 'the Puritan would be judged by the Word of God. If he would speak clearly he means himself. But he is ashamed to say so. And he would have me believe him before a whole Church, that have read the Word of God as well as he.'[11]

Q.E.D. That seems to settle the Puritans' hash.

All this hullabaloo arose from attaching too much importance to opinion – i.e., to what men suppose themselves to
think, when few men have the capacity to think at all. Their
thinking is but opinion, an irrational reaction to what they like
or dislike, the circumstances they find themselves in, or – as
Selden says – where the shoe pinches. 'Opinion is something
wherein I go about to give reason why all the world should
think as I think.'[12] This wise, sceptical intellect reflected that
'Man had something in him whereof neither gods nor beasts
did partake, which gave him all the trouble, and made all the
confusion, in the world: and that is Opinion.' It might be
Pareto speaking in our own time.

Selden, though no Laudian, realised as well as Laud the
trouble all those Puritan Lecturers, intruded by the disaffected
gentry, had been responsible for: 'if there had been no Lecturers, the Church of England might have stood and flourished
at this day'. And he understood perfectly – what historians
never sufficiently allow for – the personal factor of sheer envy
and aggressive jealousy in history. 'Missing preferment makes
the Presbyters fall foul upon the Bishops. Men that are in hopes
and in the way of rising keep in the channel; but they that have
none seek new ways.'

We have seen that the Scotch leader in the Assembly, Henderson, had been disappointed of preferment in Scotland. So
had Marshall, leader of the English Presbyterians, along with
Cornelius Burgess. Vicar of Watford, Burgess had been similarly disappointed, turned refractory and been accused before
Laud of 'being a continual vexer of two parishes with continual
suits of law'. The Puritan Revolution now gave much wider
scope to his drive for aggression. Opposed to bishops, he supported the Commons' proposal to suppress deans and chapters;
but he considered 'it was by no means lawful to alienate them
[i.e., their estates] from public and pious uses, or to convert
them to any private person's profit'.

What are revolutions for, if not to bring benefit to the
revolutionaries? In 1644 this leader of the Presbyterians in the
Assembly was made Lecturer at St Paul's Cathedral at £400 a

year (multiply by thirty or more!), with the Deanery to live in –
the Dean and Chapter having been suppressed. Burgess did
even better as Lecturer at Wells Cathedral, when in 1650 he
made a large purchase of the Bishop's lands – worth £12,000 by
1659 – but had some difficulty in explaining himself. He was
accused of stripping the lead from the Cathedral to use for
rebuilding the Deanery for himself and letting the gatehouses to
the Close as cottages. After all, Puritans had no real use for
cathedrals, and even if Burgess had become a rich man he had
advanced £3500 to Parliament to fight their war. At Wells,
Burgess objected to having to share the Cathedral with an
Independent congregation in Cromwell's time, when an open
rift between Presbyterians and Independents broke any pretence of uniformity among the Saints. The citizens showed
what they thought 'by walking up and down the cloisters all
sermon time, and the constables had to be called in'. When the
inevitable Restoration came about, to restore order in the
nursery, Burgess retired in comfort to Watford, though forced
to disgorge his gains from church property. He was the author
of innumerable sermons, like *The Necessity and Benefit of Washing
the Heart, The Vanity and Mischief of the Thoughts of an Heart
Unwashed* or *Prudent Silence* – which it would have been better if
he could have kept.

Of such were the Saints of God.

As the foremost classical scholar in the land Selden was able to
bait these humbugs on the exact meaning of the Hebrew and
Greek written by the hand of God in Holy Writ, and was often
able to fault them, to their annoyance. Much more serious was
the intention of Parliament – or that half of it which remained in
Westminster – to keep control of the process of godly Reformation. This dismayed the Scotch ministers, who had become too
much used to having things their own way in Scotland; Baillie
found the English very 'carnal' and 'fleshly' in the refusal of the
civil power to submit to the spiritual. Nor was this at all to the
mind of the Presbyterian majority in the Assembly, who
pressed again and again for the full powers of Calvin's ideal –
the entire discipline of lay folk by the clergy, their censure of

morals as well as beliefs, and authority to excommunicate, throw people out of their community. This was far worse than the bishops, because more effective, and not even a Puritan half-Parliament would submit to these outrageous demands, out of keeping with the native measure of English life.

Debates in the Assembly became acrimonious over this issue, since it was a struggle for power. It reflected the latent struggle, which came more and more into the open, between the Army, where the sects had freer run, and the Presbyterian ruling elements, with their stronghold among the moneyed men of the City. Parliament began the job of instituting presbyteries, especially in London, where the ground had been prepared by three generations of propaganda; elsewhere they found that for the most part it did not work. In all the confusion the traditional parochial organisation went on, Parliament taking care to keep power and preferment in its own hands.

Frustrated and soured, the Assembly was confined to the never-never-land of doctrine, and drew up its Confession of Faith in strict Calvinist terms, Predestination and the rest of it. On this nonsense issue, on both sides, Selden again said what should be the last word: 'the Puritans who will allow no Free-will at all, but God does all, yet will allow the subject his liberty to do or not to do, notwithstanding the King. The Arminians, who hold we have Free-will, yet say when we come to the King, there must be all obedience, and no liberty to be stood for.'[13] Each position was, of course, but the extrapolation of its own interests. To Milton, naïve as intellectuals usually are, these issues were real, and naturally he came round to the Free Will position of the Arminians, for it suited himself.

Already by 1645, while the issue between Presbyterianism and Independency was still in doubt, and the Westminster Assembly basked in full effulgence in the desecrated Abbey, he was affronted by the monstrous claims upon the individual conscience of the stiff-necked Presbyterians. He had now suffered from their calumnies upon his divorce tracts and their lying misrepresentations of himself; from these he had at any rate learned something. He now took up pen and wrote his scathing lines, 'On the New Forcers of Conscience under the

Long Parliament':

> Because you have thrown off your prelate lord,
> And with stiff vows renounced his liturgy
> To seize the widowed whore, *Plurality*,
> From them whose sin ye envied, not abhorred. . . .

This was true enough, as we have seen.

Within the Assembly there was only a handful of Independents to oppose the egregious majority, but their voices were strengthened by their relations with Cromwell and the Army outside – their *real* support being effectual force. A group of these men made an open protest, with which Milton sympathised, against the domineering majority. Among the dissenting minority was Thomas Goodwin of Milton's college, Christ's, who had left England for the Calvinist amenities of Holland and returned, at the beginning of the Long Parliament, to make trouble, with an Independent congregation at St Dunstan's-in-the-East. Upon the execution of the King he was made a chaplain to the Council of State at £200 a year, with lodgings in Whitehall, convenient for his frequent preaching duties. (When preaching, he wore two double skull-caps; he had a long hooked nose.) Next year, though a Cambridge man, the Commonwealth made him President of Magdalen College, Oxford. Talk about plurality! – but this was after Milton wrote his poem, and he was only talking about Presbyterian pluralists.

Philip Nye came next among these Independent dissentients. He had returned from Holland at the blissful dawn of the Long Parliament with its promise of revolution, to be presented to the good living of Kimbolton by the Parliamentarian Manchester. Sent commissioner to Scotland with Stephen Marshall, his sermon in Edinburgh did not please the censorious Scots. He returned to forward the Covenant, and got the fatter living of Acton, Middlesex. Besides this he held four lectureships in Westminster – one in the poor Abbey – and others in London. Talk about plurality! However, congregations must have got their money's value out of Nye, if somewhat ludicrously, for he insisted on wearing his hat as preacher, while the congregation had to be uncovered; at the sacraments the minister was to be uncovered, the communicants covered. This was evidently very important, but I don't know why.

Jeremiah Burroughes, of delightful Emmanuel, was another emigrant to Holland for God's sake, where at Rotterdam – according to Hugh Peters – he was 'the morning star' and one Greenhill 'the evening star' in the prevailing mania for preaching. He was another of those who dissented in turn from the Presbyterians dissenting from the Church. These would *not* concede to the Presbyterian 'classes' the coercive power they had objected to in the bishops. There followed a controversy in which they were attacked by Thomas Edwards of the *Gangraena* (they all suffered from that) and John Vicars; and they replied with equal acrimony.

Peter Sterry was another Emmanuel man, an intimate of Sir Henry Vane, whom Milton so unreasonably admired. The godly Baxter, of *The Saints' Everlasting Rest*, described Vane's admirers as Vanists, and queried 'whether vanity and sterility had ever been more happily conjoined'. Immediately after the King's execution, Sterry, as a follower of Cromwell, was voted another preacher to the Council of State – which must have wasted a lot of time in listening to sermons – at £200 a year, with apartments in the late King's palace. Sterry was a devotee of the new monarch, Cromwell – much more absolute than the King had ever been – and 'somewhat fulsomely' put forth his praises. Cromwell's death, Sterry assured the assembled ministers, was good news – for, if he had been so useful when in a mortal state, how much more so now when he was translated! The others were not so sure, viewing the abyss that opened before them. Richard Cromwell, 'Tumbledown Dick', was quite unable to fill the gap, for all that Sterry prayed that he might be made 'the brightness of his father's glory and the express image of his person'. Burnet thought this rather blasphemous.

Another of the group was Joseph Caryl, whom we shall meet again.

Such were the men whom Milton favoured against the

Presbyterians he now excoriated:

> Dare ye for this adjure the civil sword
>> To force our consciences that Christ set free,
>> And ride us with a *classic* hierarchy
>> Taught ye by mere A.S. and Rutherford?

Rutherford and Adam Stewart were two of the Scotch members of the Assembly who sought to impose the straitjacket of their Presbyterian 'classes' upon England.

>> Men whose life, learning, faith and pure intent
>> Would have been held in high esteem with Paul

– such as himself, for example –

>> By shallow Edwards and Scotch What-d'ye-call

– probably Baillie, thus contemptuously referred to for the sake of the rhyme.

>> But we do hope to find out all your tricks,
>> Your plots and packing, worse than those of Trent

– i.e., the Catholic Council of Trent: it must have gone against the grain to admit as much –

>>> That so the Parliament
>> May with their wholesome and preventive shears
>> Clip your phylacteries, though balk your ears,
>>> And succour our just fears
>> When they shall read this clearly in your charge:
>> New *Presbyter* is but old *Priest* writ large.

Well, what else could have been expected? He should have known beforehand. So much for the delicious hopes of 1640. The Revolution was revealing its true face.

CHAPTER THREE

Milton, Marriage and Women

WE NEED NOT doubt that Milton was an innocent virgin when he married – he has virtually told us so – and already getting on for thirty-four. This is exceptional for a normal heterosexual, but Milton was not an ordinary normal man, and it is fairly clear that he was not very heterosexual. It is also indicative that, when he did at last marry, he chose a young girl of seventeen, only half his age. (Was Mary Powell rather boyish?)

Everybody knows the story of Milton's disastrous marriage; it only remains for us to dot the i's and cross the t's. Mary Powell's father was the squire of Forest Hill, living in the manorhouse of which we see only a walled garden today, with gate looking down the slope towards Oxford. Richard Powell was the leading landowner thereabouts, with the fine Elizabethan house in Wheatley too, still there at the end of the village. But he was heavily indebted – one not inconsiderable debt being owed to Milton's father, the musical usurer. Milton went down into the country on business in June 1642, and within the month came back married to Mary Powell.

It looks as if the Royalist squire had taken the opportunity to provide for one of his numerous family, unloading her upon the unknowing Puritan. It is obvious to anyone with any social sense, especially in seventeenth-century circumstances, that the Powells would regard a marriage to the grandson of a keeper of Shotover Forest as a condescension. Milton brought his treasure back to the house in Aldersgate, and in a month she had left him. Not a successful honeymoon, evidently. Her excuse was that she would spend summer in the country, but she did not come back. Letter upon letter was sent summoning her to return. No answer. At last a messenger was sent, who was

69

dismissed with some contempt.

Milton had his sister's two clever boys, Edward and John Phillips, in the house to educate. We learn from Edward that Mary had been used to the jolly ways, the gay company, of a large Cavalier household. Nothing gay in her Puritan husband's house, with its frugal diet, its accent on temperance in every respect, her husband twice her age bent on scholarly pursuits, for ever reading and writing, trouncing the bishops and occasionally the boys. (Someone noted their cries, but beating was usual in seventeenth-century education.)

What is more noticeable to the perceptive is that Milton was not interested in sex. His conception of marriage, as of everything else, was very high-minded: marriage was an ideal relationship, a union of spirits, a mutual meeting of minds. He had come back from Italy to find his dear friend Charles Diodati dead; he had written his most moving poem in his memory. Evidently what he was looking for was a Diodati.

He did not attach importance to sex: that was the animal side of man. Marriage was not meant to remedy 'the mere motion of carnal lust: God does not principally take care for such cattle' (i.e., the average man). Marriage is not for 'the prescribed satisfaction of an irrational heat'; we observe no conception that the irrational heat gives pleasure – that would be an unworthy thought anyway – the pleasure issuing in 'the quintessence of an excrement'. With this state of mind in the bridegroom, is it to be supposed that poor Mary derived much pleasure from the marriage-bed? Is it likely, perhaps, that the scholar-poet, already rather middle-aged by seventeenth-century reckoning, was very adequate in bed? (Another contrast to William Shakespeare, more than usually keen on women.) The young bride certainly had some serious grounds for complaint, for she deserted her husband, and this was a very serious matter in the seventeenth century.

For Milton it was an appalling blow to his self-esteem, the very marrow of his being. 'If the love of God be the first principle of all godly and virtuous actions in men, this pious and just honouring of ourselves is the second, and may be thought as the radical moisture and fountainhead whence every laudable and worthy enterprise issues forth.' The two amount to the same thing – we may take the first for granted, since we see in everything he writes that what God thinks is what Milton thinks: God = Milton writ large. The poor girl must have found him insufferable.

For Milton it was an appalling revelation: everything shows that he was profoundly upset and suffered acutely. He had not known what ordinary people were like. Life would show him. His God was reason – i.e., his own reason – and he had expected rational conversation. From an ordinary girl of seventeen, God save the mark! But ordinary human beings are incapable of it – though, fortunately for themselves, they don't know it. (A Shakespeare wouldn't even expect it.) Milton knew that 'in God's intention a meet and happy conversation is the chiefest and the noblest end of marriage', not 'so necessarily implying carnal knowledge.... With all generous persons married thus it is that, where the mind and person please aptly, there some unaccomplishment of the body's delight may be better borne with.' Once more, one wonders whether the 'Lady of Christ's' was very adequate, really good at accomplishing the body's delight, which he depreciated.

He had been completely caught out by his ignorance of the facts of life – serve him right, for the irrational importance he attached to his own chastity. 'It may yet befall a discreet man to be mistaken in his choice: the soberest and best governed men are least practised in these affairs. . . . Many who have spent their youth chastely are not so quick-sighted.' He was one of 'those who have unwarily, in a thing they never practised before, made themselves the bondmen of a luckless and helpless matrimony'. 'The sober man may easily chance to meet, if not with a body impenetrable, yet often with a mind to all other due conversation inaccessible.' We are not to suppose, then, that the girl of seventeen was impenetrable, but just that her mind was closed to rational conversation, a pretty dumb creature. How maddening for so superior a person to be thus caught, when 'they who have lived most loosely, by reason of their bold accustoming, prove most successful in their matches'.

His wife did not and would not return; she had the backing of her family. They were Royalists, and in the first phase of the war – before Pym bought the Scottish Army, for that is what it came to – it looked as if the King might win in England. When the Royalists approached as near London as Turnham Green, and were held back only by the superior numbers of the trained bands, Milton wrote his sonnet, 'When the Assault was intended to the City':

> ·Captain, or Colonel, or knight in arms,
> Whose chance on these defenceless doors may seize,
> If ever deed of honour did thee please,
> Guard them, and him within protect from harms

– i.e., protect *him*, John Milton, the chosen one –

> He can requite thee, for he knows the charms
> That call fame on such gentle acts as these,
> And he can spread thy name o'er lands and seas.

There is the sublime self-confidence in his vocation, though the poet was hardly known as yet. Such is the irony of life that he was about to become notorious in England for the tracts he was now to write on divorce.

So shattering a blow to a man at once excessively proud and excessively sensitive, such a humiliation, inspired him to more eloquent and moving flights of indignation than against the bishops. In the next two years he put forth no less than four publications on the subject of divorce, of which the most important was the first, *The Doctrine and Discipline of Divorce, Restored to the Good of Both Sexes* (1643). Milton was impelled, as usual, by his own personal circumstances; his involvement is obvious at every point, and in his first tract he is for once anxious to persuade – not merely abuse, as with the poor bishops. He wanted to alter the law. Canon Law in England, under the Church, had remained Catholic; divorce was exceedingly difficult, and only for adultery, in accordance with Christ's words.

Egoistically inspired, as always, Milton wanted the law altered to suit his own circumstances; but he saw in the situation the opportunity to push forward reformation in a most important sphere. The Anglican Church had stuck to the old law and custom: the Puritan Revolution should change it, shake off its fetters here as elsewhere, extend liberty, the scope of the freeborn Englishman, in accordance with reason – i.e., Milton's reason – not antiquated custom. Milton was, however, caught in the toils of his own Puritan dilemma: he believed in reason, but Puritans were bound by the Word of God revealed in Scripture. Their Bible mania led Milton into increasing intellectual difficulties; the divorce tracts are notable for the considerable amount of casuistry Milton was reduced to, in order to square Holy Writ with his own interests.

For example, Christ had specifically laid down, 'Whoever shall put away his wife, except it be for fornication, and shall marry another, committeth adultery.' Very well: Christ cannot have meant fornication by the word fornication. The Mosaic prohibition of divorce was not so severe; it was impossible that Christ could have meant to be more severe than Moses. Milton knew better what He meant. St Paul had laid down that it was 'better to marry than to burn'. Milton argued that St Paul cannot have meant – what he obviously did mean – to avoid 'carnal lust . . . for God does not principally take care for such cattle'.

The physical side to marriage is virtually ignored, notably in its most important aspect, the procreation of children. The crucial importance of children in the business, the cardinal factor in family life, society's provision under safeguards for the continuance of the species – the kernel of the question – is never considered or once mentioned. Milton had no children at this time, so this aspect did not occur to the sublime egoist whom his wife had deserted. He treats the whole question of marriage from the point of view of his own bias and what *he* wanted out of it: not sex and children, but rational conversation, intellectual companionship, fit company to suit his needs and cheer him up.

Pure masculine egoism, of course. Though his title promised to consider the interests of both sexes, he was looking at the subject simply from his own point of view. The physical aspect, whether of sexual satisfaction or children, is discounted for spiritual and intellectual delights. As the law was, 'yet they shall, so they be but found suitably *weaponed* to the least possibility of sensual enjoyment [a revealing phrase!], be made, spite of antipathy, to fadge together, and combine as they may to their unspeakable wearisomeness and despair'. No doubt Milton had found the company of a dumb girl of seventeen unspeakably wearisome; but what had she found him? 'Who knows not that the bashful muteness of a virgin may ofttimes hide all the unliveliness and natural sloth which is really unfit for conversation?' Again, 'the freedom and eminence of man's creation gives him to be a law in this matter to himself, being the head of the other sex which was made for him'.

It is all very well to excuse Milton for this assertion of women's inferiority to men as being the customary attitude in his time; but I know no one else who so constantly and unwearyingly asserts it all through his work, not only in the divorce tracts, but also throughout *Paradise Lost* and *Samson Agonistes*. Why did he have so consistently to assert male superiority? Shakespeare, a much greater appreciator of women, didn't have to. Was it that Milton was unsure of himself? Normal and natural heterosexuals do not take this line: it is familiar enough with male homosexuals, expressed in Milton's time by James I, for example. We wonder whether Milton, the most honest of men, was emotionally honest with himself.

Milton's plea, underneath all the elaborate argumentation about Holy Writ, boils down to the simple one of divorce on grounds of incompatibility. He does not say mutual incompatibility – he is thinking only of a superior man yoked to a woman much his inferior. But very few women could have met the demands of this exceptional individual; there were a few, but they were chosen friends, not wives: the aristocratic Lady Margaret Ley, daughter of the Earl of Marlborough, a highly intelligent woman; Lady Ranelagh, of the intellectual Boyle family, for another; Mrs Thomason, well read and of a Christian conversation.

Milton considered that his case for divorce, on grounds of incompatibility, was a reasonable one; and so it was – in three hundred years' time, for it has taken us three centuries to arrive at it. In his own time it was – like his views on the Church and practically everything else, the monarchy, politics, society –

utterly impracticable. His rationalist view rested on the naïve assumption that men were rational, when actually his reason on the matter applied only to himself and a few like men. To the bulk of human beings in the seventeenth century, swaddled in unreason, superstition, religious mania, folklore, witchcraft, it was totally inapplicable. We see this in his disparagement of custom. He wants custom brushed aside: no idea that custom is immensely more important anthropologically than just one man's, or even a number of men's, reason. For custom is the necessary way by which societies cohere and exist; break it down, as revolutions threaten to do, and societies break apart. Custom is not the mere appearance but the real content of social life – to which reason may reasonably apply itself, and from time to time make useful amendments. That is all.

With the second edition of his work Milton appealed to both Parliament and the Assembly of Divines to undertake this urgent work of reform. He began with an onslaught on custom as being responsible, and custom was but the face of error. 'Hence it is that Error supports Custom. Custom countenances Error.' We see the superficiality of this doctrinaire's rationalism, and enjoy the spectacle of the response he got. Here was a God-sent opportunity for reform, a most urgent task to undertake, and now was the very time. 'Ye have now – doubtless by the appointment and favour of God – ye have now in your hands a great and populous nation to reform; from what corruption, what blindness in religion ye know well.' This was not the first time that England had been in the van. 'It would not be the first or second time since our ancient Druids – by whom this island was the cathedral of philosophy to France – that England hath had this honour vouchsafed from Heaven to give out reformation to the world. . . . Let not England forget her precedence of teaching nations how to live.'

Intolerable! In historic fact, it was Italy and France that had been the instructors of the barbarous northern peoples. This same spirit of self-righteous complacency inspired the Puritans in New England 'to build, as it were, a City upon an hill', for the enlightenment of others – a familiar note in later American pronouncements to the world.

Milton was proud of his proposal to free men's necks from the yoke; he thought that he was the first to propound his case for divorce. The superior intellect of Selden had already arrived there. 'Of all actions of a man's life, his marriage does least concern other people; yet of all actions of our life 'tis most meddled with by other people. Marriage is nothing but a civil contract.' All the reading and argumentation that went into Milton's divorce tracts were due to the necessity he was under to square his reason, and his interests, with Scripture. This kind of nonsense had no reality for Selden. 'We single out particulars, and apply God's Providence to them. Thus when two are married and have undone one another, they cry it was God's Providence we should come together; when God's Providence does equally concur to everything' – i.e., it means nothing. 'Marriage', concluded Selden, 'is a desperate thing. The Frogs in Aesop were extreme wise; they had a great mind to some water, but they would not leap into the well, because they could not get out again.' Neither would the wise Selden: he seems to have lived happily enough with the Countess of Kent. (He seems to have been well weaponed.)

The reception of Milton's divorce tracts was a further long step in his education: it proved a bitter deception. He had appealed to Parliament and the Assembly of Divines. Holy Mr Palmer, one of the Saints, a favourite preacher to the Commons, 'a kind of oracle', demanded in a sermon that they should suppress the book. Another cleric described the work as one in which 'the bonds of marriage are let loose to inordinate lust'. To others his views were 'licentious, new, and dangerous'; his book was 'lewd', he himself 'the deviser of a new and pernicious paradox', of 'a novelty of licence' and 'libertinism'. So his passion for liberty had become libertinism to his fellow-Puritans! Worst of all, the sanctified Prynne, whom Puritans venerated as Laud's victim, spitted Milton opprobriously as advocating 'divorce at pleasure', and this stuck. (But wasn't it what Milton's argument came to?) Milton's name to the general public became synonymous with divorce at pleasure; a little group was denominated Divorcers, or 'Miltonists'. A holy woman, Mrs Attaway, a preacher, went off with another woman's husband, pleading Milton on Divorce in justification, and now felt equal to setting up as mistress to the sanctified Baptists in Coleman Street.

The Assembly, for its part, cited him before the Lords, so we learn from the early biographer, probably Cyriack Skinner: 'The Assembly of Divines . . . instead of answering or disproving what those books had asserted, caused him to be summoned for them before the Lords. But that House . . . not favouring his 'accusers, soon dismissed him.'[2] Few enough of the Lords remained at Westminster now, but they were not likely to take their lead from the canting Assembly across the road.

Milton had been taken by surprise at the reception of his important book with its new message, its promise of a significant extension of freedom for men. (Was easier divorce in the interest of women, however, at that time?) He was shocked to find himself condemned by people who had not read his book: 'some of the clergy began to inveigh and exclaim on what I was credibly informed they had not read' (a situation familiar enough to writers who have anything new and original to say – about Shakespeare, for example). Milton was not the man to be discouraged by anything inferior brains thought, and when he shortly brought out a second edition he gave it a motto from Proverbs: 'He that answereth a matter before he heareth it, it is folly and shame unto him.'

So far from hauling down his flag he defied his critics by openly announcing his name, claiming proudly to be 'the sole advocate of a discountenanced truth'. In perplexing difficulties 'it is incredible how cold, how dull, how far from all fellow-feeling we are, without the spur of self-concernment'. He had that to spur him on well enough: 'what an injury it is after wedlock not to be beloved, what to be slighted, what to be contended with in point of house-rule who shall be the head – not for any parity of wisdom (for that would be reasonable) but out of a female pride. Is it not most likely that God in his law had more pity towards man thus wedlocked than towards the woman that was created for another?'

Once more this intolerable assumption of male superiority.

Milton made his appeal to Parliament and Assembly in the name of charity to both sexes. He really meant charity to the man – and he was not a very charitable man himself. When one thinks of the divine charity of Shakespeare towards women, for all that he had suffered from the Dark Lady:

> Why dost thou lash that whore? Strip thine own back:
> Thou hotly lust'st to use her in that kind
> For which thou whipp'st her.

Shakespeare was not only full of human sympathy but had that rarest of qualities – justice of mind.

Milton had been attacked for being singular – as indeed he was, in being sensible. Stirred up by the attacks he went further in his reading, to find that he was not alone. The wise Grotius took a broad-minded line on the subject; then Milton found that the Protestant reformers, Gagius and Bucer, who had been so influential in Edwardian England, were also of Milton's way of thinking. He proceeded to publish a tract, *The Judgment of Martin Bucer Concerning Divorce*: translation of passages from this big Protestant Bore backing him up, with another very characteristic appeal to Parliament. He pleaded that no one had answered his arguments: he had been treated merely with railing and abuse, when he had hoped for rational discussion. But now 'it hath pleased God, who had already given me satisfaction in myself, to afford me now a means whereby I may be fully justified also in the eyes of men'. Glad as he was of corroboration, nevertheless 'I may justly gratulate mine own mind with due acknowledgment of assistance from above, which led me, not as a learner but as a collateral teacher, to a sympathy of judgment with no less a man than Martin Bucer.' He insisted that he owed 'no light or leading received from any man in the discovery of this truth . . . and had only the infallible grounds of Scripture to be my guide'. Hence he could say (so like him): 'Not that I have now more confidence by the addition of these great authors to my party; for what I wrote was not my opinion, but my knowledge.' He could owe nothing to anyone.

He appealed to Parliament, 'confident, if anything generous, anything noble, and above the multitude, were left yet in the spirit of England, it could be nowhere sooner found, and nowhere sooner understood, than in that House of justice and true liberty [!] where ye sit in council'. In spite of this flattery, no notice was taken: the House of Commons – not notable for either justice or liberty – was more concerned to win its war against the King. The attacks on Milton continued, as a licentious person; some said that he favoured, if he did not practise, polygamy.

It was maddening for one who knew that he had written to free not only himself but others, and from the best of motives and purity of heart. Since Bucer had no more justified him in the eyes of men than before, he followed up with a further attempt to justify himself from Scripture. In *Tetrachordon* (1645) he expounded four cardinal passages from Holy Writ, according to his own sense of them. Once more we hear about woman's inferiority, and he has the Apostle Paul – an epileptic, and obviously no normal man – to support him. Milton allows that 'man is not to hold her [his wife] as a servant, but receives her into a part of that empire which God proclaims him to – though not equally, yet largely, as his own image and glory; for it is no small glory to him that a creature so like him should be made subject to him' (!). It is sometimes argued that this was the seventeenth-century view, but I do not know of any such constant harping upon it among Anglicans. The insistence came from the Bible mania of the Puritans, with its nonsense about Adam and Eve – to become the subject of Milton's epic. Their bloodthirstiness in the Civil War owed something to their odious cult of the barbaric Old Testament. One can hear it in Cromwell's language, as well as in action like the killing of the women camp-followers of the Royalists after Naseby, or the massacre at Drogheda. Here he is on the killing of Thomas Hobbes's brilliant pupil, the scientifically minded Charles Cavendish: 'he would fain have delivered himself', but 'my captain-lieutenant slew him with a thrust under his short ribs'.

Milton kindly allowed that, if the woman were the wiser and more intelligent partner, and the man was willing to let her, she might rule the household. This was no more than in keeping with contemporary practice, or indeed common sense at any time. He continued to denigrate the sexual side to marriage: 'we may conclude that such a marriage wherein the mind is so disgraced and vilified below the body's interest, and can have no just or tolerable contentment, is not of God's institution [i.e., of Milton's approbation], and therefore no marriage'. This is a very summary judgment, on far too idealistic a basis, out of keeping with the facts of human nature. However much anyone might sympathise with it today, or wish it more often realised, it was quite unrealisable in seventeenth-century circumstances and would have produced unutterable confusion. Hence the authorities took no notice of it and Milton was almost universally condemned.

It looks as if an attempt were made to suppress one of the tracts. This is what Palmer, of the Assembly of Divines, had advocated in preaching to both Houses of Parliament: 'If any plead for divorce for other causes than Christ and his Apostles mention – for which a wicked book is abroad and uncensured, though deserving to be burnt, whose author hath been so impudent as to set his name to it and dedicate it to yourselves – will you grant a toleration for all this?' All the Presbyterians hated the name and nature of toleration. Not only divines but also the Stationers' Company itself joined in the hue and cry, petitioning Parliament against 'the frequent printing of scandalous books by divers, as Hezekiah Woodward and John Milton' – one does not know who this person was, lumped together equally with John Milton.

Milton was not the man to take this lying down; furious, he responded in kind. He whipped out yet another tract, *Colasterion*, to which he gave the motto from Proverbs: 'Answer a fool according to his folly, lest he be wise in his own conceit.' (I rather agree with Milton on this point, and sometimes take a leaf out of his notebook.) 'Colasterion' means a place of punishment, and several people were for it. The horrible Prynne, whose mouth Laud had been quite unable to stop, though his ears were cropped, came out with his trumpet-voice against his fellow-Puritan. Milton dealt faithfully with him, as 'one, above others, who hath suffered much and long in defence of truth'; it was a pity that Truth should 'after all this leave him so destitute and so vacant of her defence as to yield his mouth as to be the common road of truth and falsehood, and such falsehood as is joined with the rash and heedless calumny of his neighbour'. It is nice to see these intolerable Puritans now going for each other.

An anonymous *Answer* had at last appeared; it had been licensed, and in part touched up, by – of all people – one of the sainted Five Independents who had protested against the tyranny of the Presbyterian Assembly. This was Joseph Caryl, and what he got from his fellow-Independent was this: 'you are reputed a man discreet enough, religious enough, honest enough – that is, to an ordinary competence in all these'. But when he had licensed 'a despiteful contumely upon a name and person deserving of the Church and State equally to yourself – and one who hath done more to the present advancement of your own tribe than you or many of them have done for themselves, you forgot to be either honest, religious, or discreet'.

Tempted as we are to say, 'See how these Puritans loved one another,' we may at least observe that John Milton's education was proceeding apace. He had attacked the prelates and churchmen for their pluralism; we shall now find him attacking the Saints themselves for accumulating livings, lectureships, chaplaincies and headships of colleges. We may also observe that, whereas there was a case for the historic Church to exert traditional and customary authority, by the Canon Law and the church courts, there was no reason for those who had usurped its authority to expect submission to its dictates. Milton did not omit to make the point: he did not expect, after his services to the cause, 'to be set on by a Junto of clergymen and licensers whose partiality cannot yet forgo old papistical principles'.

As for the anonymous opponent, Milton made play with the fact that he was not at all well educated: 'I mean not to dispute philosophy with this pork, who never had any.' He was too illiterate, 'an arrogant presumer in that which he understands not', unable to spell Greek or Hebrew. His 'ridiculous adversary' was 'an idiot', 'an odious fool', 'a most incogitant woodcock', 'a brainworm', 'an unswilled hogshead', a 'clod'. Amusingly enough, the clod, being no intellectual but an average man with some practical sense – no Milton – put his finger on the most important point Milton had omitted to consider amid all his learned argumentation: what was to happen to the children under his scheme of free divorce at will?

Milton wrote a couple of poems summing up his disillusioning experience over the past three years. One, in lighter vein, makes fun of the uncouth Scotch names precipitated into the forefront of events, but deploring the lack of learning he had encountered in the controversy. The other said what he thought of his detractors:

> I did but prompt the age to quit their clogs
>   By the known rules of ancient liberty,
>   When straight a barbarous noise environs me
> Of owls and cuckoos, asses, apes and dogs. . . .
>
> But this is got by casting pearl to hogs –
> That bawl for freedom in their senseless mood,
>   And still revolt when truth would set them free.
>   License they mean when they cry liberty.

But of course: this is what revolutionaries are apt to find out, after the first fine careless rapture. They had set the hogs on all right to come down from the City to Westminster to bawl for Strafford and Laud's deaths – and now intellectuals like Milton, nursing their illusions, were finding out what the mob meant by liberty. What had been gained by it all – the poems end with the query –

> For all this waste of wealth, and loss of blood?

The bloody victory of Naseby this year, 1645, crushed the Royalists; it remained now to be seen how the Puritans would settle Church and State – the game was theirs. Naseby crushed with it the hopes of the Royalist Powells at Forest Hill, indebted, impoverished, facing the fines imposed on Royalists to compound for their 'malignancy' – the choice piece of Puritan semantics for the cause of King and Church.

Milton's wife had remained away from him during the past three years and, so far as we know, there had been no further communication. He had given up thought of her returning, for – according to his nephew, Edward Phillips – he had proposed marriage to the daughter of a Dr Davis, 'a very handsome and witty gentlewoman'. An opinionated doctrinaire, he was prepared to act on his individual principle of free divorce: but it would have been a very rash step to take, for bigamy was against the law and would have incurred severe penalties. Fortunately Miss Davis had more sense than to risk such a thing; and now the intervention of Milton's relations combined with the circumstances of the Powells to save him from such a folly.

In the collapse of Royalist fortunes and their own, the Powells were glad to unload their daughter upon her husband once more, and no doubt this was really why she returned to his house. He behaved generously in receiving her – and not only her but her family, for all the Powells in their distress piled in on him. We may fairly say that this Cavalier family took advantage of him yet again and treated him in pretty cavalier fashion. It was a distressful time, the country was upheaved by the delights of revolution and civil war; some areas had been badly ravaged by it; there was poverty and want everywhere; in the North famine raged. London at least was safe.

Milton took his wife's family in, and also his quiet old father. The rest made havoc of his peace, as we know from a sad, nostalgic letter to Carlo Dati, his young Italian friend of better days. 'Those who are closely bound to me by the mere fact of proximity or by some other tie of no real significance, as by chance or legal claim – although they have nothing else to commend themselves to me – are with me all day. They deafen me with their noise and torment me as much as they please.' Such were the joys of family life. Then, with a touching memory of Diodati and his cultivated friends of blissful days in Italy: 'whereas those endeared to me by congenial ways, temperament and taste, are almost all separated from me by death or distance – and are usually snatched from me so swiftly that I spend my days in real and enduring loneliness'.

Milton's financial affairs were inextricably involved with the Powells, though he never received the £1000 dowry promised with his treasure. It is clear that he had no such practical business head as his father, and the times were hard, his investments difficult to manage. Mary Powell lived with him the rest of her short life – she was only twenty-seven when she died in 1652. She died in childbirth, leaving him with three daughters and a son. The eldest daughter, Anne, was lame and mentally defective; the other two were Mary and Deborah. Six weeks after his wife's death, his little son, another John Milton, died.

With three daughters to look after, one of them helpless, it was perhaps necessary to marry again, though it was well over four years before he did so, or could find someone to take on the assignment. For he was blind by 1656, when he married Katherine Woodcock. Already twenty-eight, she needed a home, for her widowed mother – about the same age as Milton – lived with her three children on the bounty of her Puritan relatives. Chief among these was a well-to-do alderman, Sir Thomas Vyner, the first knight to be created by Oliver Cromwell. Milton was now forty-eight.

After some fifteen months this wife, too, died in childbirth, and her baby five weeks after. It would appear that Milton found contentment with this wife, from the famous sonnet after a dream of her:

> Methought I saw my late espousèd saint

– the phrase indicates clearly that it refers to his second wife. She came from a Puritan background, hence the word 'saint': this regular term would not have been applied to the Royalist, Mary Powell. Moreover, she had died before her 'purification' from childbirth; Katherine after it, 'washed from spot of childbed taint'. Such was the old superstition – quite primitive, though some still continue to hold to it. 'Late espousèd' refers to Milton being well in middle-age at the time, and he was already blind, so that Katherine came to him 'her face . . . veiled'. He had never seen it; but he trusted to have

> Full sight of her in heaven without restraint.

It is a deeply touching personal poem, as rarely with Milton.

He needed to marry again, not only for his blind self but for his motherless daughters now growing up; but it was some five years before he did so. A friend introduced him to a young woman of twenty-four, Elizabeth Minshull, evidently of a lower class than her predecessors, for her brother was a framework-knitter in Cheshire. Perhaps she was more of a housekeeper to him – as such she filled the bill very well, looking after him, supplying his wants, considering his tastes.

With a young step-mother not much older than the daughters, there was disagreement and discord in the house. The eldest daughter was crippled, had difficulty with her speech and could not even write her name. The other two were very ordinary girls, who could not even learn the languages in which their father taught them to read to him, without understanding what they read. Milton, accepting their stupidity, would say, 'One tongue is enough for a woman.' So much for families, and family life, and the education of women. It must have been a strain for them, living with so very exceptional a father. Mary developed a dislike for him. On hearing the news of his intended marriage, she said 'it was no news to hear of his wedding; but if she could hear of his death, *that* was something!' A maidservant reported that his children would cheat him in their marketings, that they had made away with some of his books and would have sold the rest if they could.

Perhaps it is no wonder that Milton had rather a low view of womankind. He was not made for marriage, and should never have tried it. We shall see how he carried his view with complete consistency forward into his great poems, *Paradise Lost* and *Samson Agonistes*: they are continuous with the divorce tracts. The theme plays a cardinal part in both the epic and the tragedy, as the experience behind it was central in the poet's personal life. We need not doubt that, if he had not suffered this lasting deception, undergone this trauma, his view would have been somewhat different, at least. As it was, he never lets up in the line he takes about women, and goes on and on enforcing it.

We need not suppose that it recommends him to women today, after the revolution in the status of women, not the least of the revolutions of our time.

CHAPTER FOUR

Milton on Education and Free Thought

WHILE the fighting fools – as Hobbes considered them – rampaged over the country, ravaging some areas, destroying castles and country houses, pillaging cathedrals and churches, Milton returned to his private studies. As he wrote with some complacency, 'I again with rapture renewed my literary pursuits, where I calmly awaited the issue of the contest, which I trusted to the wise conduct of Providence.' Wise Providence ultimately rewarded all his hopes with the settled reaction of the Restoration of 1660 – particularly noticeable, by the way, in the field of education.

Meanwhile, he continued to educate in his house a few selected youths, much above average intelligence: his nephews, Edward and John Phillips, Cyriack Skinner, and Lady Ranelagh's son for a time (but he would not put up with the discipline). It has not been appreciated that these boys were rather exceptional, and that Milton's scheme of education, as laid down in the tractate of 1644, was geared to them, not to the average material of the public schools. His daughters were virtually ineducable; again there is nothing in his scheme about the education of women. Professor Hanford's criticism of it is precisely 'what is lacking is a recognition of the wisdom to be acquired from life itself and the need of taking experience as a starting point'.[1] But of course: that was what was lacking from the whole of Milton's outlook, bookish and intellectual, arrogantly self-confident while wanting in knowledge of life and ordinary human nature. 'He did not understand the actual workings of human personality, and therefore did not understand how the individual could be remade.'[2]

On the other hand, Professor Bush says, without any beating about the bush—rather roughly, in fact—'American readers... often recoil from Milton's heavy requirements; but these should be compared with the standards of the age and not with ours; Renaissance humanists did not believe in adjustment to life through the prolongation of infancy.'[3] We may take this for a tart Canadian's comment on the defect of American education – though in mass-society today education everywhere follows the social ideal of educating down to the level of the masses. Professor Bush's comment is, however, wanting in historical sense – as if schools in general in Renaissance England exemplified Milton's lofty ideal; while it misses the personal perception (Professor Bush is happier with mythology) that Milton's scheme – so like him – was really conceived in terms of himself and his own exceptional intellectual capacities.

Professor Parker considers that Milton believed that contemporary schools and universities 'failed utterly to instil *a love of learning* in youth'. As if one could, in ordinary folk. One can only comment in turn: Some hopes! Samuel Hartlib, a German busybody in England at the time, who asked Milton to set down his ideas on education, described him as 'full of projects and inventions'. Exactly: Milton was rather like another doctrinaire in the early stage of revolution, the Abbé Siéyès – a projector. Milton's project – his head stuffed with classical notions and learning – was the setting-up in every town of an academy of some 120 boarders, which should serve as both school and university, a kind of School of Pythagoras, as he says.

The project was, of course, totally unreal and impracticable in the circumstances of the time – like his other views on marriage and divorce, religion and the Church. And so was the curriculum, except for a few gifted individuals like Milton himself – we shall see how it worked out with the Phillipses, after years of indoctrination. Professor Hartmann asks sensibly, 'how can a twelve-year boy learn Latin and begin reading classical texts within one year? How can he, in the next three years, acquire a working knowledge of several more languages, Greek,

Hebrew, and – in his spare time – Italian? How can adolescents bear a fixed plan of studies from morning till evening for six days each week and then study Scripture in Greek on Sundays? ... The sheer mass of material to be taught sounds appalling.'[4] The Professor asks the question, 'how could Milton, so great an advocate of freedom, be so dogmatic?' But that is precisely what Milton was – dogmatic to his finger-tips, and about everything; dogmatic about freedom, in spheres which bore little relevance to the requirements and interests of the average man – freedom of thought, for one (as Communists well realise).

The divine common sense of Dr Johnson was far more relevant: 'nobody can be taught faster than he can learn. The speed of the horseman must be limited by the power of his horse.' No wonder Dr Johnson disliked Milton, not merely as a revolutionary and a doctrinaire ideologist, but because he was totally without humility. Dr Johnson, quite as able as Milton intellectually, a better moralist with a truer and more compassionate understanding of human nature, was a deeply humble man, an altogether better Christian.

Milton's self-confidence shines all through the tract as in everything else he wrote. It was inspired, like the rest, by his general aim of radical reform – now was the moment: Cromwell's army was winning the cause of Puritan Revolution. Milton had long nursed the idea, 'in silence, of a better education, in extent and comprehension far more large, and yet of time far shorter, and of attainment far more certain, than hath been yet in practice'. The first aim of all learning was to repair the ruins of our first parents by 'regaining to know God aright ... as we may the nearest by possessing our souls of true virtue'. We may take that as read, and go on to the second: the aim to educate for leadership in society. This had been the humanist aim all along for more than a century, notably with Dean Colet in founding Milton's own school, St Paul's, and his friends Erasmus and Sir Thomas More. More had carried it into practice by accepting office under Henry VIII – and it led him to the scaffold; Milton also carried out the principle in accepting subordinate office under Cromwell and wearing his eyes out in the service of the Puritan Commonwealth.

We need not go in detail into the exorbitant course of reading laid down, but direct attention to the admirable suggestions of a superior mind reflecting on what he found inadequate or deplorable in existing practice. Here Milton shows himself modern-minded, in a good sense, as over divorce. He was opposed to the long and tedious grind at Latin and Greek grammar as an end in itself. He proposed a shortened course of grammar – probably influenced by the ideas of Ramus, to the fore at Cambridge in his time – and then getting down to the substance of classical texts, learning more through them. Anyone who knows how the grind in Latin grammar and composition – Milton opposed both – stifled real appreciation of the classics among the great majority at the public schools over the next two and a half centuries will sympathise with Milton's progressive view on this point.

On the other hand, if we consider the exceptionally large syllabus of reading he proposed, quite beyond what was usual in the schools, we must remember that Renaissance education required a tremendous training of the memory. We see this in the astonishing verbal memory exemplified in Shakespeare, reinforced by his actor's profession; and again in Milton, further strengthened and developed by his blindness.

He made other progressive points. As against the English pronunciation of Latin, he favoured a Continental pronunciation close to Italian: this would enable English-speakers to understand and be better understood on the Continent, while it would be more in keeping with the nature of the Latin language. He was rightly contemptuous of the Norman French gibberish in which the law operated. Here the Commonwealth did enact a sensible reform. It was only temporary; at the Restoration the gibberish came back along with much else that was questionable. Even the traditional study of law he depreciated, the legal profession described as a trade (so much for stupid brother Christopher): 'grounding their purposes not on the prudent and heavenly contemplation of justice and equity, which was never taught them, but on the promising and pleasing thoughts of litigious terms, fat contentions and flowing fees'. (Milton was always a master of abuse.)

Contemporary English literature, for example, is depreciated. The pupils are to read Aristotle's *Poetics*, the Italian epics with the critical commentaries of Castelvetro, Tasso, Mazzoni! (Milton is thinking in terms of himself.) 'This would make them soon perceive what despicable creatures our common rhymers and playwriters can be – and show them what religious, what glorious and magnificent use might be made of poetry, both in divine and human things' – e.g., by the author of *Paradise Lost*. After such a course his pupils would come to see also what poor stuff their preachers were. 'There would then also appear in pulpits other visage, other gestures, and stuff otherwise wrought than what we now sit under, ofttimes to as great a trial of our patience as any other that they preach to us.' (One would not envy a preacher having to preach to John Milton – though the thought of Stephen Marshall lifting up his voice to curse Meroz before the perfectionist poet would make a good subject for caricature.)

One must sympathise with the perfectionist in deploring 'the preposterous exaction, forcing the empty wits of children to compose themes, verses, and orations, which are the acts of ripest judgment, and the final work of a head long filled by long reading and observing'. Nor was he wrong in disapproving of the universities' presenting 'their young unmatriculated novices, at first coming, with the most intellective abstractions of logic and metaphysics'. Francis Bacon had disapproved of that; but where Bacon's emphasis was the forward-looking, prophetic one of exploring nature, experimenting with the natural sciences and technology, Milton's was essentially literary and humanistic.

On top of the whole of classical literature, with Italian 'at any odd hour', and some instruction 'in the Chaldee and Syrian dialect', he was prepared to add agriculture, from the classical texts, then politics and economics. After this, they were 'to pass the principles of arithmetic, geometry, astronomy, and geography [what, no algebra?], with a general compact of physics, they may descend in mathematics to the instrumental science of trigonometry, and from thence to fortification, architecture, enginery, or navigation. And in natural philosophy they may proceed leisurely from the history of meteors, minerals, plants, and living creatures, as far as anatomy.'

After this, medicine and natural history, where they 'may procure the helpful experience of hunters, fowlers, fishermen, shepherds, gardeners, apothecaries; and in the other sciences, architects, engineers, mariners, anatomists'. We really cannot take all this seriously; it is the blueprint of an idealistic projector, a tract for the education of Milton himself.

'Sunday also and every evening may be now understandingly spent in the highest matters of theology, and church history, ancient and modern.' The pupils were thoroughly indoctrinated in the delights of Christian doctrine. Here, as elsewhere, Milton combined instructing the young with the continuance of his own education. He was painstakingly compiling his synthesis of Christian doctrine and, along with his teaching, a Latin grammar, an elementary text-book of logic, and a Latin dictionary. Some of the materials for this last later came in handy for a work of one of his nephews. For his own reading he had moved on to a conspexus of medieval and modern history.

In place of sport youths were to be taught 'the exact use of their weapons . . . the likeliest means to make them grow large and tall, and to inspire them with a gallant and fearless courage. . . . They must be also practised in all the locks and grips of wrestling, wherein Englishmen were wont to excel.' We observe again what a chauvinist this English Puritan was: 'nor shall we then need the monsieurs of Paris to take our hopeful youth into their slight and prodigal custodies, and send them over, back again, transformed into mimics, apes, and kickshaws'. Sympathetic as he was to Italy, he was always anti-French – no doubt reflecting the Puritan hatred of the French influence at Queen Henrietta Maria's Court, which was to prevail even more strongly, after the Puritan épopée was over, at the Court of the half-French Charles II.

The optimistic doctrinaire concluded: 'yet I am withal persuaded that it may prove yet more easy in the assay than it now seems at distance, and much more illustrious. Howbeit, not more difficult than I imagine, and that imagination presents me with nothing but very happy, and very possible according to best wishes – if God had so decreed, and this age have spirit and capacity enough to apprehend.'

It had not. The tractate had no influence whatever.

Milton's teaching of his clever pupils was, however, successful. Both his nephews became good linguists, and translators – no wonder, considering the course they went through: Edward Phillips was under his uncle's tuition for some eleven years. In his Life of Milton he bears out the curriculum, with its extraordinary range of authors not taught in the schools. He also confirms that, by teaching, Milton 'in some measure increased his own knowledge, having the reading of all these authors as it were by proxy'. Besides this, he was 'perpetually busied in his own laborious undertakings of the book or pen'.

As is the way with such high-minded pedagogues, the pupils turned out rather differently from expectations. Both Edward and John Phillips were literary right enough, but their literary productions were in some contrast to those of their stern unbending uncle. They were not only lightweight but rather indecent. In 1658 Edward produced *The Mysteries of Love . . . as managed in Spring Garden, Hyde Park and other eminent Places.* This was a work as entertaining as it was licentious – and we recall that Spring Garden was near the abode of the prophet himself. After the Restoration, Edward became tutor to the son of the pious Anglican, John Evelyn, who testified: 'he was not all infected by his uncle's principles, though he was brought up by him'. Edward loyally wrote the first critical tribute to *Paradise Lost*; but we can hardly suppose that the author of that work would have been gratified by his nephew's *Poem on the Coronation of his most Sacred Majesty King James II and his Royal Consort.*

The younger nephew, John Phillips, developed on very different lines too. In 1655 he published his *Satire against Hypocrites*, a scathing attack on Cromwell and his pious entourage. Next year John was summoned before the Council for a collection of scandalous poems, *Sportive Wit.* It had to be withdrawn, but was replaced by an equally naughty collection of poems by Davenant, Donne and others, *Wit and Drollery.* He next had a hand in ridiculing the anti-monarchical views of William Lilly, the astrologer, and – Aubrey thought – in a skit on the Republican General Lambert, *Don Juan Lamberto*. One sees that the rule of the Saints and hypocrites was making way for that of the cynics and satirists. Among his numerous translations John produced a spirited, but coarse, version of *Don Quixote*. He took an opposition line to James II, who patronised and promoted his uncle, Sir Christopher Milton. Aubrey commended John Phillips as 'very happy at jiggish poetry', and his muse as 'happy for a jiggish phancy and gypsies and ballads'.

It was all very unlike the domestic life and teachings of their sainted uncle.

Like the divorce tracts, the *Areopagitica* of 1644, the most famous of Milton's prose works – at least that most frequently spoken of, with reverence, if not read – has a personal point of departure. Attempts had been made to suppress his noxious views on divorce, and in 1643 Parliament produced a Licensing Order for the control of the press – a move towards a more effective Puritan censorship than the more tolerant Church had exercised. Milton was inspired to a fine flight of rhetoric, in a more convoluted style than usual – one cannot believe that those who profess to admire it so much have read it. It has been described as 'one of the great documents in the history of liberty'; but this rather contradicts the same authority's views that 'it was primarily a Protestant tract written for Protestants, with Protestant ends in view'.[5] The second judgment is more in keeping with the facts.

Areopagitica is a party tract, written in the hope of persuading Parliament to withdraw its Licensing Order, in favour of freedom to advance the cause of Protestant reformation, the Puritan Revolution, still further. What Milton feared was that the Revolution would be arrested at this point, instead of going forward to the discovery of further truth, especially Bible truths. The Presbyterians now in power knew, however, that Calvin had stated Bible truth once for all; it needed no further gloss. This was the stand of the Westminster Assembly, which Milton had already bruised his head against over divorce.

Milton appealed to Parliament again – that half of the Com-

mons with a small minority of the Lords that remained at Westminster – in terms of flattery that are hardly respectable in one
who was so hard on flattery of King and Court. He pays obei-
sance to 'your faithful guidance and undaunted wisdom, Lords
and Commons of England . . . after so fair a progress of your
laudable deeds and such a long obligement upon the whole
realm to your indefatigable virtues'. He wished himself 'to be
taught not so inferior, as yourselves are superior to the most of
them who received their counsel [the orators who addressed the
Greek assembly]; and how far you excel them, be assured,
Lords and Commons, there can be no greater appear than
when your prudent spirit acknowledges and obeys the voice of
reason' – i.e., the voice of Milton. To listen to it would 'show
both that love of truth which ye eminently profess and that
uprightness of your judgment which is not wont to be partial to
yourselves. . . .'

Really! Everything that they had done since 1640 had been
partial to themselves. This flattery from a partisan gives off an
unpleasant smell compared with the continued abuse of the
prelates, though now 'expired', and of Courts 'which had produced nothing worth memory but the weak ostentation of
wealth'. When one considers the magnificent collection of
works of art which Charles I brought to this country – the
greatest of its day – and which the Commonwealth was to dis-
perse; the patronage of Rubens and Van Dyck, the opportunities the Court gave to the genius of such as Inigo Jones and
Ben Jonson! One can excuse Milton's blindness only by concluding that he can have had no aesthetic sense, outside of
poetry and music – and he, who knew the Italy of Bernini!

His irrefragable and reiterated self-esteem is as much to the
fore as ever: his address proceeds 'from the industry of a life
wholly devoted to studious labours and those natural endow-
ments haply not the worst for two and fifty degrees of northern
latitude'. He ends as he began: in time of trouble 'God then
raises to his own work men of rare abilities, and more than
common industry, not only to look back and revise what hath
been taught heretofore, but to gain further and go on some new
enlightened steps in the discovery of truth.'

Here is the main argument of the tract: to allow virtually complete freedom of the press for the further advance of truth – i.e., the Puritan Revolution. To make this palatable to practical and self-seeking politicians Milton resorted to the regular tactic of Puritan insinuation, which must have been obvious to them, since they practised it themselves: censorship was a Popish practice, which savoured of the Inquisition, adopted by the prelates like other Popish ways of theirs. This debating point would have been seen through at once by a debating assembly – if they troubled to read the tract: there is no evidence that it had any effect. Power was what mattered in politics, and to politicians.

Nor – to be fair to them – was there anything practical in what Milton proposed. Milton suggested post-publication censorship: 'only *after* a work had been made *public* could action be taken to prove, in a public trial where they would have the right to defend themselves, that they and the publication had broken those known laws' – i.e., subverting law and order. In seventeenth-century circumstances this would mean utter confusion: 'hence Milton's vagueness', Professor Max Patrick concludes, 'about the nature, system, and enforcement of post-publication censorship that he envisages. . . . He can hardly have been unaware that many of his arguments against licensing were valid against post-publication censorship. Yet he is not precise about what kinds of publications would be outlawed.'[6]

The tract is nothing if not imprecise; it is wholly rhetorical, its argument self-contradictory, its assumptions, as usual, illusory. The argument is that freedom depends on reason. This might be well if men were capable of reason; but events were already showing Milton that people of more ordinary faculties – especially in the field of politics, whose practitioners were experts at exploiting the fact – that men in general had very little reason, and fewer still were those who exercised it. To persuade his readers, Milton flatters them as he had the Commons: to license books is an insult to the intelligence of the people, and assuming them to be ignorant and deluded. 'If we dare not trust them with an English pamphlet, what do we but censure them for a giddy, vicious and ungrounded people, in such a sick and weak estate of faith and discretion. . . .'

Everything shows that this was what he thought them to be; nor was he wrong, as the events of the Revolution were to bring home to him bitterly. Very well: then his political and social teaching should have been in keeping with his views of human nature – as Hobbes's was, or Shakespeare's. No one had more supercilious, or genuinely superior, views as to other people's inferior capabilities. Even in this tract, assuming the intellectual capability of the ordinary man, Milton has a contemptuous estimate of the capacity of his preachers and teachers. He has a derogatory description of the way they fadge up their sermons; if they cannot even do this for themselves, there is such 'a multitude of sermons ready printed and piled up, on every text that is not difficult', that they have 'vendible ware of all sorts ready made'.

If there is so little reason in the world, and few so capable of it, what becomes of freedom that depends upon it? Rational and reasonable direction, with flexible arrangements for change and internal criticism, is the utmost freedom appropriate to the facts of human nature.

With regard to both freedom and truth the argument is self-contradictory. At one moment we are told, 'Banish all objects of lust, shut up all youth into the severest discipline that can be exercised in any hermitage, ye cannot make them chaste that came not hither so. . . . Suppose we could expel sin by this means, look how much we expel of sin, so much we expel of virtue: for the matter of them both is the same: remove that and ye remove them both alike.' This is unexpected coming from a pure Puritan mouth: if this is so, what is the case for Puritan repression, Puritan discipline, the wicked Puritan act of Parliament making adultery punishable by death (wicked, even if not operated; and not operated because inoperable)?

Milton is in favour of leaving the choice to each man's discretion. We ourselves might be in favour of that (or again not), but it contradicts the Puritan, and especially the Calvinist, position with its view of depraved human nature after the Fall. 'How great a virtue is temperance . . . yet God commits the managing of so great a trust wholly to the demeanour of every grown man. God uses not to captivate under a perpetual childhood of prescription, but trusts him with the gift of reason to be his own chooser.' God appeared in a vision to Peter, telling him to kill and eat, 'leaving the choice to each man's discretion'. God . . . God . . . God: we have seen that this is a simple equation with Milton. 'And perhaps this is that doom which Adam fell into of knowing good and evil, that is to say of knowing good by evil. . . . What wisdom can there be to choose, what continence to forbear without the knowledge of evil?'

We may point out how contradictory this is with Milton's view of the Fall in *Paradise Lost*. In this prose passage he subscribes to what became Eve's argument for eating of the Tree of Knowledge, yet he cannot have approved of Adam's Fall. We see that the argument is no reasoned argument at all, mere rhetoric to serve Milton's turn and support what he wished, for his own purposes, to advance. To support himself, Milton cites Selden, with a very flattering reference since he agrees with him. Selden had shown 'by exquisite reasons and theorems almost mathematically demonstrative that all opinions – yea, errors – known, read and collated, are of main service and assistance toward the speedy attainment of what is truest'. That is all very well for Selden, who was a sceptic and knew what nonsense most opinions are. But this view was not open to Milton to advance, for a Puritan already knew what was true.

With regard to truth Milton is no less self-contradictory and confused. To license or prohibit is to misdoubt the strength of truth. There follows a reflection upon the Presbyterian possessors of truth: 'he who hears what praying there is for light and clearer knowledge to be sent down among us would think of other matters to be constituted beyond the discipline of Geneva, framed and fabricked already to our hands. Yet when the new light which we beg for shines in upon us, there be who envy and oppose if it comes not first in at their casements.' But of course – that is what is to be expected.

There follows a very un-Puritan thing to say of Truth: 'yet is it not impossible that she may have more shapes than one'. If so, why may the Church of England not be one, and the Church of Rome another? In all this freedom of discussion, 'I mean not tolerated Popery, and open superstition, which, as it extirpates all religious and civil supremacies, so itself should be extirpate, provided first that all charitable and compassionate means be used to win the weak and the misled.' On a point of fact he was mistaken. Since he was arguing in favour of free discussion he said that it would be hard to instance cases where people had been seduced by reading Papist books. In fact, there were people in the Elizabethan age who were converted to Rome by reading Roman controversialists, notably Father Parsons – as John Donne points out in a celebrated passage of his *Pseudo-Martyr*.

The time was at that moment disproving his contention also as to the proliferation of sects. Remove control and discipline, allow any and everybody to expound his idiot views of the Scriptures – to which Milton continued to appeal as the test, while they disagreed in what they said, and people disagreed as to what they meant – and naturally lunatic sects sprang up and proliferated. Once more Milton denied the danger. 'Under the fantastic terrors of sect and schism, we wrong the earnest and zealous thirst after knowledge and understanding which God hath stirred up in this City.'

God was stirring up at that moment Anabaptists, Quakers, Seekers, Soul-Sleepers, Ranters, Universalists, Reevonians, Muggletonians, Fifth Monarchy men. Their earnest and zealous thirst after knowledge and understanding led the illiterate and uneducated to some surprising manifestations. Holy Mrs Attaway, the woman preacher – a kind of Aimée Semple Macpherson of her day – had felt justified by Milton's divorce tracts to become the whore of the Baptists of Coleman Street. John Robins had no such excuse: he could not read Milton's highbrow books with their farrago of classical learning, their Greek and Latin. 'As for humane learning, I never had any; my Hebrew, Greek and Latin comes [sic] by inspiration.'

He was inspired to think that he was an incarnation of God, and that he had appeared before as Adam and Melchizedek. This was not enough for his followers, who deified him, or for his wife, who expected to become the mother of a Messiah.

Unbelieving folk called him 'the Ranters' God', or 'the Shakers' God'; himself claimed to raise the dead. He put forward a project of leading 144,000 to the Holy Land – the mystic significance of the number escapes me; Joshua Garment (one thinks of Bottom the weaver) was to be the Moses of the expedition. Volunteers prepared for it by a diet of dry bread, raw veg. and water, which proved fatal to some. Other fools set out, but never came back.

Later, in 1651, Robins was apprehended at a conventicle – since it had fallen now to the Republic to keep order in the nursery – and was whisked off to prison, where he modestly reduced his claims to being merely inspired. His followers insisted that he was an incarnation from on high. Next year Reeve and Muggleton, who had just received their commission from the same place, visited Robins in prison and, not content with upbraiding him, excommunicated him. Robins felt a burning in his throat and a voice telling him to recant. He did so in a letter to Cromwell, who received many such communications, was released, went into the country and was not heard of again.

One sees something of the consequences of allowing the people to read the Bible. Today Communists entertain no illusions about allowing the faithful to think for themselves, let alone interpret the Marxist scriptures.

Not that the people threw up the worst spirits. Milton has a glowing tribute – from which one sees what he admired – to the horrid fire-eater, Lord Brooke, who hated the Church. He had been killed by a bullet in the eye while directing the attack on Lichfield Cathedral on St Chad's Day, to whom the church is dedicated. (By the end of the war, it was a roofless ruin.) More interesting is to observe the signs of Milton's growing distrust of the Presbyterians whose attack on the Church he had vehemently supported. He was beginning to see that new Presbyter, after all, was but old Priest writ large: 'I hope that none of those were the persuaders to renew upon us this bondage which they themselves have wrought so much good by contemning.' Of course they were. 'And what do they tell us vainly of new opinions when this very opinion of theirs – that none must be heard but whom they like – is the worst and newest opinion of all others, and is the chief cause why sects and schisms do so much abound. . . .' This is another contradiction, and a mere debating point against the Westminster Assembly, which Milton did not now wish to see 'canonised'. If the Presbyterians could have had their way they would certainly have laid the sects by the heel.

In place of solid argument we are given revolutionary enthusiasm, passages of eloquent exaltation. 'For now the time seems come wherein Moses, the great Prophet, may sit in heaven rejoicing to see . . . not only our seventy Elders but all the Lord's people are become Prophets. . . . That our hearts are now more capacious, our thoughts more erected to the search and expectation of greatest and exactest things is the issue of your own virtue propagated in us. . . . What should ye do then, should ye suppress all this flowery crop of knowledge and new light sprung up and yet springing daily in this City, should ye set an oligarchy of twenty engrossers over it to bring a famine upon our minds again. . . ?'

We have witnessed some of the flowery crop of new light springing up, and shall see more. As for what the Commonwealth should do – after the extreme measure of the killing of the King, forced on by Cromwell and the Army – they appointed the extremist, Milton himself, who had defended their action, as a licenser of the press. Such is the irony of things.

'Lords and Commons of England [there would be few enough of them left at Westminster after the Army's Purge], consider what Nation it is whereof ye are, and whereof ye are the governors: a Nation not slow and dull, but of a quick, ingenious and piercing spirit, acute to invent, subtle and sinewy to discourse, not beneath the reach of any point the highest that human capacity can soar to.' Had not Agricola 'preferred the natural wits of Britain before the laboured studies of the French'? There is much more of this patriotic religious exaltation. 'Why else was this Nation chosen before any other that out of her, as out of Zion, should be proclaimed and sounded forth the first tidings and trumpet of Reformation to all Europe.'

'God is decreeing to begin some new and great period in his Church, even to the reforming of Reformation itself. What does he then but reveal Himself to his servants, and as his manner is, first to his Englishmen.'

Here is the very spirit of Puritanism, self-righteous and self-satisfied, self-confident and self-laudatory, arrogant and aggressive.

It was a nasty spirit.

CHAPTER FIVE

Milton as Historian

PURE literary scholars are apt to neglect the historical element in Milton, though he is one of those writers with whom it is of the utmost importance. His life and work were so bound up with the historical events of the Puritan Revolution that it is impossible to understand either without a knowledge of the time and its circumstances. And we have already seen that Milton was one of those writers with whom the personal and autobiographical element bulks largest, so that it is more than ever absurd to label this approach – with the unhistorically minded C. S. Lewis – 'the personal heresy'. A more discriminating judgment would be that this approach varies in importance from writer to writer; with Milton it is at its maximum, and is essential to understanding his work.

In addition to this, it is usual to dismiss Milton's interest in history as such. His reading in history was very wide, in Biblical and classical history, in European history as we have seen, and in English history. His interest was so great that he intended – what would have been a large work – to write a history of Britain up to his own time. His blindness prevented him from completing it. As it was, he wrote a *History of Britain* up to the Norman Conquest, a considerable quarto. Even Masson failed to appreciate it. But this dismissal neglects (*a*) the significance of history for the understanding of his poetry; (*b*) the value of Milton's historical work in itself; (*c*) his interest in history, the light it throws on his own mind, the morals he draws from it and the reflections it contains on his time.

We need not dally over his *Brief History of Moscovia, and of other less known countries lying eastward of Russia as far as Cathay* – i.e., Siberia – though he tells us that he read the accounts of travels thither 'with some delight'. It fell in with his patriotism that the first outside contacts with northern Russia had been opened up by Elizabethan Englishmen. 'The discovery of Russia by the Northern ocean made first – of any nation that we know – by Englishmen, might have seemed an enterprise almost heroic, if any higher end than the excessive love of gain and traffic had animated the design.' We may pardon the priggish qualification, revealing as it is of Milton's supercilious attitude towards commerce: the Elizabethan achievement in this field *was* heroic, and the accounts, which Milton read up with delight, make fascinating reading. He read them all, with his usual conscientious industry, but based himself principally upon Hakluyt – one more piece in common with Shakespeare, who certainly looked into the *Principal Navigations*.

Milton was much interested in geography, as we know from *Paradise Lost*, and even in his blindness he ordered the latest atlas for its information. He begins his account of Russia with a geographical description, based on the English voyages, noting where English traders had established their factories in the north. We need not traverse his account, but simply note a few touches that betoken him. The Russians were heavy drunkards, their Greek Church given to 'excess of superstition'; 'for whoredom, drunkenness and extortion none worse than the clergy'. When a couple come together, 'the man sends to the woman a whip, to signify, if she offend, what she must expect; and it is a rule among them that, if the wife be not beaten once a week, she thinks herself not beloved, and is the worse. Yet they are very obedient. . . . Upon utter dislike the husband divorces: which liberty no doubt they received first with their religion from the Greek church, and the imperial laws.' This must have had particular point for Milton.

Most of these two books was written during the four years from 1645 to 1648 when he retreated from publishing any more prose works. In the previous four years he had published no less than eleven tracts in the full spate of revolutionary ardour – and with no more effect than to be known opprobriously as the exponent of easy divorce. The Scotch Presbyterian leader, Baillie, a stiff-starched type, noted, 'Mr Milton permits any man to put away his wife upon his mere pleasure, without fault and without the cognisance of any judge.' The cantankerous Presbyterian Edwards, in his *Gangraena*, scored a bull's-eye with his description of Milton's doctrine in his syllabus of modern errors, concluding: 'and man, in regard of the freedom and eminency of his creation, is a law to himself in this matter, being head of the other sex, which was made for him, neither need he hear any judge therein above himself'. This was the long and the short of the matter.

In these years Mary Powell was back living with her husband – from what we know of both of them, we may suppose, not very agreeably; and their unfortunate children were born. Milton wrote little verse in this time of private burdens and public confusion. In the *History of Britain* his disillusionment with both Parliament and Westminster Assembly is plain for all to see. He chose to translate some of the more lugubrious Psalms, and his additions to the Hebrew express his mood. He conveniently italicised these for us:

> When trouble did thee sore assail,
>   *On me then* didst thou call,
> And I to free thee *did not fail*,
>   *And led thee out of thrall.*

Here is his familiar theme of the Puritan Revolution leading the nation out of thraldom.

> For thou wilt *grant* me *free access*
>   *And* answer, *what I prayed*. . . .

A note of dubiety as to how things would turn out sounds in this.

> *And life in us renew*. . . .

Here he is looking for a new inspiration, a new development, some reason to hope.

His increasing disillusion, looking for light in the dark way ahead, appears in his sonnet to Fairfax, after his bloody triumph at Colchester which ended the second Civil War:

> O yet a nobler task awaits thy hand;
>   For what can war but endless war still breed

– they should have thought of that when they started the madness –

> Till truth and right from violence be freed,
> And public faith cleared from the shameful brand
> Of public fraud. In vain doth valour bleed
> While avarice, and rapine share the land.

We shall see in detail what Milton thought of the contemporary situation in his *History of Britain*. Meanwhile Fairfax, on whom Milton's hopes were pinned at this time, would not take up the burden and, after complete victory against the Royalist cause, gave up and retreated from the ensuing chaos as hopeless.

On a lighter note Milton wrote a sonnet on the reception of his book with the unfamiliar Greek name, *Tetrachordon*. The eminent Puritan had not much sense of humour: what he had was a satirical turn in his conversation, according to Aubrey, emphasised by his rolling r's. Milton saw nothing wrong in the offspring of his genius, as usual:

> A book was writ of late called *Tetrachordon*,
>   And woven close, both matter, form and style. . . .

People's jibbing at the name gave him a chance to be satirical about the Scots, so much to the fore in the wars and in religion (after all, they had started it with their rebellious fanaticism):

> Bless us! what a word on
> A title-page is this! . . .
>   Why, is it harder, sirs, than Gordon,
> Colkitto, or Macdonnel, or Galasp?
>   Those rugged names to our like mouths grow sleek
>   That would have made Quintilian stare and gasp.
> Thy age, like ours, O soul of Sir John Cheke,
>   Hated not learning worse than toad or asp. . . .

Our prime authority on the seventeenth century, the historian Firth – who knew more about the period than any *littérateur* –

tells us that Milton's *History of Britain* 'elucidates both his political writings and his poems; like all that he wrote, it bears the
impress of his character and is, therefore, of some biographical
value; finally the book in itself is a work of learning and originality, worthy to be remembered in any account of the development of historical writing in England'.[1] Fancy neglecting it for
endless argy-bargy about nonsense theological issues, or
discussing what the sexual relations of Adam and Eve were
before the Fall!

Milton took himself seriously as a historian. He had long
been interested in the early period of British history and
contemplated the subject of Arthur for his British epic. Firth
suggests that we may take the *History* as a substitute for that, on
Milton's laying it aside for his poem. All the other British subjects that he considered for a possible tragedy related to the
period between the Roman and Norman conquests of Britain.
He was surprisingly more open-minded about the legendary
prehistory of Britain than might have been expected – in this
following the Elizabethans. The long and sympathetic account
of King Lear and Cordelia was, in a way, a tribute to Shakespeare.

Surprisingly, too, for such an extremist is to find that, when it
comes to prehistory, Milton took a middle-of-the-road line.
Modernist as he was in his critical sense, and vastly superior
intellectually to Elizabethan chroniclers like Holinshed, Speed
and Stow (not, however, to Camden) – all of whom he industriously read – he was willing to give the legendary element the
benefit of the doubt. 'That which we have of oldest seeming
hath by the greater part of judicious antiquaries been long
rejected for a modern fable. Nevertheless, ofttimes relations
heretofore accounted fabulous have been after found to contain
in them many footsteps and relics of something true.' No
professional historian could wish for a more judicious attitude.
If only he could have carried over this respect for antiquity and
openmindedness towards the traditional into politics and
religion!

He continues: 'that which hath received approbation from so
many I have chosen not to omit. Certain or uncertain, be that

upon the credit of those whom I must follow – so far as keeps aloof from impossible and absurd, attested by ancient writers from books more ancient, I refuse not as the due and proper subject of story.' This is a liberal attitude, more so than a modern historian would approve. Firth thinks that Milton's main attraction was in the story element, but his attitude opens up a more difficult question. How much of myth did Milton really believe to be factual when it came to religion and religious epic? The question is a subtle one, for undoubtedly he believed the Gospel narratives of the life of Christ – as they are drawn upon for *Paradise Regained*, for example – or the Old Testament history drawn upon for *Samson Agonistes*; but how much did he believe of what we may describe as Biblical prehistory, the stuff of *Paradise Lost*? It offers an interesting parallel to his treatment of the prehistory of Britain, and his indeterminate attitude towards it.

Sometimes, too, he cannot make up his mind as to what was historically true in the conflicting accounts of his authorities, and he confesses defeat, leaving the matter an open question. This is a more agreeable Milton; would there were more of this salutary historical scepticism in him! – as there was in Selden, whose scholarship he admired, and in Hobbes, whose intellect he respected but disapproved.

Milton was no less the moralist in writing history. All Elizabethans were agreed as to the didactic value of history, the lessons to be learned therefrom. This element was in the forefront of Milton's mind, but it is given a special urgency by the circumstances of those years in which it was written: the confusion and uncertainties, in spite of the Puritan victory, the disillusionment now complete with Milton – we note the personal reference, as always. 'Certainly ofttimes we see that wise men and of best ability have forborne to write the acts of their own days, while they beheld with a just loathing and disdain not only how unworthy, how perverse, how corrupt, but often how ignoble, how petty, how below all history the persons and their actions were. Who, either by fortune or some rude election had attained, as a sore judgment and ignominy upon the land, to have chief sway in managing the commonwealth.'

To bring home to the reader how pertinent this was to the circumstances of the time – between the crushing victory of Naseby and the 'judicial' murder of the King, a clarification indeed! – we may adduce a modern comparison. It is as if a modern historian took refuge in writing about the Elizabethan Age from the squalor and ignominy of ours – so rapid a descent from the heroic leadership of Sir Winston Churchill to that other Knight of the Garter, Sir Harold Wilson – or, to illustrate from America, the descent from Franklin Roosevelt to Nixon and Watergate. History has its lessons no less than war.

As a historian Milton is no more afraid of a personal reference or to make personal comments – as inferior spirits, perhaps appropriately, are – than as poet or writer of political tracts. He is writing, he says, 'for the good of the British nation'. The age was a revolutionary one, though for a moment the revolution was at a pause. And 'worthy deeds are not often destitute of worthy relaters – as, by a certain fate, great acts and great eloquence have most commonly gone hand in hand, equalling and honouring each other in the same ages'. Milton has himself in mind, as always – and so it worked out with historic propriety. The heroic spirit of the Puritan Revolution in action, Oliver Cromwell, would shortly be joined by the no less heroic spirit in the realm of the mind, John Milton.

His personal character, his gifts, his prejudices and defects, his superiority of mind, all appear as clearly in the *History* as in his other works. First, there is his intellectual grasp, so superior to the Elizabethan chroniclers, to whom he was much indebted for material, though he went to original sources wherever they existed. He even consulted a Danish chronicle for any light it might throw on the Danish invasions. Take the crucial case of the historicity of Arthur. Milton is very doubtful, and concludes: 'as we doubted of his parentage, so may we also of his puissance; for whether that victory at Badon Hill [the Mons Badonicus of ancient sources] were his or not, is uncertain. . . . Whether by Arthur won, or whensoever', that battle 'seems indeed to have given a most undoubted and important blow to the Saxons, and to have stopped their proceedings for a good while afterwards'. On this Firth comments: 'when we compare

Milton's treatment of this with that of Holinshed, Stow, and Speed, his superiority is evident. Alter the phraseology, and he might have been writing in the nineteenth rather than in the seventeenth century. For his conclusions are roughly those of modern scholars, and his reasoning practically that of a scientific historian.'[2]

In style he was no less superior to those rambling Elizabethans. A profound classical scholar, his model was Sallust; in his *History* he is not only more concise and brief than those, but notably more so than himself in argumentative tracts. Here he shortens the episodes, makes a point of his brevity, and sharpens the point with a summary, dismissive phrase. 'Of the Romans we have cause not to say much worse than that they beat us into some civility.' He was an admirer of the Romans and of their heroic virtues, as against the laxness of the Britons and their depravity, especially of the clergy – as to which he relied on Gildas, a denunciator of his time and age.

Milton rightly respected Camden, the first among Elizabethan historians; but it was a pity that he had no sympathy with the antiquarian scholarship Camden had inspired, which led on to the fine flowering in Milton's own time with such scholars as Cotton, Selden, Spelman, Dugdale. Milton was understandably impatient with tedious disputation about dates where there were no data, though when he came to later periods where there were sources of information in dispute he was careful to compare authorities and select the most probable. 'This travail, rather than not know at once what may be known of our ancient story, sifted from fables and impertinences, I voluntarily undergo, and to save others, if they please the like unpleasing labour – except those who take pleasure to be all their lifetime raking the foundations of old abbeys and cathedrals.'

Superior as ever, this is on a par with his Puritan Philistinism with regard to the contents of old abbeys and cathedrals, their stained glass and illuminated manuscripts, their monuments and sculpture, vestments and ritual. It leads us to his worst defect as a historian: his Puritan bias made him incapable of appreciating the marvellous achievements of the medieval

Church, intellectually and artistically, or even of the monastic chronicles upon which he had to rely for his material.

Of these he writes as ungratefully as blindly. 'Henceforth we are to steer by another sort of authors, near enough to the things they write, as in their own country, if that would serve . . . in expression barbarous, and to say how judicious, I suspend awhile. This we must expect: in civil matters to find them dubious relaters, and still to the best advantage of what they term the Holy Church, meaning indeed themselves [as Milton himself did too]. In most other matters of religion, blind, astonished, and struck with superstition as with a planet: in one word, Monks.'

This is indeed shocking, when we think of only one monk, Matthew Paris, of St Alban's Abbey, a man of genius among medieval chroniclers, an able diplomat, well versed in the affairs of his day, and no less of an artist. Art Milton evidently had no eye for. He did have some appreciation of St Dunstan; but little enough of the extraordinary intellectual achievement of Bede, a solitary Northern beacon across the wastes and waters of the Dark Ages. It is sad to think of his blindness to such superior spirits as Anselm or Aquinas; his hero was the arrogant and tiresome Wyclif, a good deal less of a saint if he had only known more about him. And shocking, too, not to admire the magnificence of medieval cathedrals, those expressions of medieval faith, among the grandest works of men's hands.

We recognise the familiar Milton in his comments about women all through the *History*. Cordelia's nephews revolt against her, 'not bearing that a kingdom should be governed by a woman'; Cartimandua is thrown off the throne by the Britons, not on account of her crimes, but because of 'the uncomeliness of their subjection to the monarchy of a woman'. (What about Elizabeth I?) The laws of Queen Marcia could not be supposed to be her own, 'for laws are masculine births'; they must have come from her sagest councillors, 'else nothing more awry from the law of God [= Milton] and nature than that a woman should give laws to men'.

The heroic Queen Boadicea is treated with contempt. A

feminist before her time, she brought the wives of her warriors to witness their victory: 'a folly doubtless for the serious Romans to smile at, as a sure sign of prospering that day: a woman also was their commander-in-chief. For Boadicea and her daughters ride about in a chariot, telling the tall champions as a great encouragement that, with the Britons, it was usual for women to be their leaders. A deal of other fondness they put into her mouth not worth recital: how she was lashed, how her daughters were handled, things worthier silence, retirement, and a veil, than for a woman to repeat as done to her own person, or to hear repeated before a host of men.' Here we see Milton the uncongenial prig.

Trenchant as always, and of the satirical spirit Aubrey denoted, Milton makes no bones about making contemporary reflections. One of his purposes in writing history was thereby to reflect on the present. The people are never well spoken of – any more than by Shakespeare: they knew too well their worth (the latter drew the correct conclusions). Vortigern, the British king who called the Saxons into the island, was 'of the people much beloved, because his vices so well sorted with theirs'. If we want to know what these were, he was 'covetous, lustful, luxurious, and prone to all vice; wasting the public treasure in gluttony and riot, careless of the common danger, and through haughty ignorance unapprehensive of his own'. We need not suppose Milton guilty of any of those vices – except perhaps a haughty ignorance of what ordinary folk are like.

The Scots come off no better. 'The Scots and Picts, in manners differing somewhat from each other, but still unanimous to rob and spoil. . . .' This is what the English of the time thought of the famished and fanatical Scots, crossing the Border again and again to intervene, living off the land as well as being supported by Parliamentary subsidies. Very well, the Puritans should not have brought them into the country by collusion and later purchased their alliance against the King. Even the sainted Buchanan, their prime historian, is treated with some superciliousness: he 'departs not much from the fables of his predecessor, Boethius'. He had no Gildas or Bede to rely on, 'authors to whom the Scotch writers have none to cite comparable in antiquity'. Buchanan had been a Presbyterian, and Milton was now sick of the Presbyterians: he has a tart comment about an early council to resolve the Arian dispute, which wrought no small disturbance in this island, 'a land, saith Gildas, greedy of everything new, steadfast in nothing'. Only three poor British bishops could afford to attend, though their colleagues offered to bear their charges: 'doubtless an ingenuous mind, and far above the presbyters of our age, who like well to sit in assembly on the public stipend, but not like the poverty that caused these to do so'.

This introduces us to the long digression Milton prefaced to Book III of his *History*, in which he summed up bitterly the frustration the Revolution had encountered, in both politics and religion, in spite of its complete victory in the field. He took off from a comparison with the confusion that prevailed in Britain upon the withdrawal of the Roman Empire. 'By comparing that confused anarchy with this interreign we may be able from two such remarkable turns of state, producing like events among us, to raise a knowledge of ourselves both great and weighty, by judging hence what kind of men the Britons generally are in matters of so high enterprise; how by nature, industry, or custom, fitted to attempt or undergo matters of so main consequence.' The aim was to estimate whether 'for want of self-knowledge' they were liable 'to enterprise rashly and to come off miserably in great undertakings': in other words, what would be the further progress of the Revolution.

Milton's summing-up of the progress so far attained – up to 1648 – is an embittered one. Victory after victory in the field had been theirs – Marston Moor, Naseby, Preston, Colchester; so it was not for want of force, superior military strength and resources that 'we must impute the ill husbanding of those fair opportunities, which might seem to have put liberty so long desired, like a bridle into their hands . . .'. Liberty, rightly used, might have made the ancient Britons happy. (What a hope! We can only gasp at such an illusion.) So, too, liberty had brought the British 'of late, after many labours, much bloodshed, and vast expense, to ridiculous frustration'. What else could have been expected? we may ask. Milton answers that all would have been easy, if men were reasonable and ready for freedom. Precisely. If we look around today, in the later twentieth century, and observe how little reasonable and capable of freedom, of governing themselves and their affairs, ordinary people are, even now three centuries later, we shall appreciate the better how silly Milton's expectations of them were in the seventeenth century. And all the more self-contradictory and absurd when he had learned by now what idiots they were. He had no illusions on that score – why, then, did he not draw the obvious conclusions?

Parliament had assembled in 1640 to redress popular discontents. This is what had happened – no Royalist could have been more scathing: 'Once the superficial zeal and popular fumes were cooled and spent in them, straight everyone betook himself – setting the commonwealth behind, his private ends before – to do as his own profit or ambition led him. Then was justice delayed, and soon after denied; spite and favour determined all. Hence faction, thence treachery, both at home and in the field; everywhere wrong and oppression; foul and horrid deeds committed daily.' Then supervenes Milton's snobbish feeling, belonging to the professional classes, about the merely commercial.[3] 'Some who had been called from shops and warehouses, without other merit, to sit in supreme councils and committees – as their breeding was – fell to huckster [i.e., buy and sell] the commonwealth.'

The uproar against Charles I's government had started with the campaign against Ship Money, of which agitation the popular John Hampden took the lead. Ship Money – necessary to provide for the fleet – had been paid by coastal counties: it was reasonable that inland counties should contribute, since they benefited also from the defence provided by the fleet. The amount of the imposition was inconsiderable compared with the heavy and general taxation imposed by Parliament when it usurped executive government, operating it far more effectively and severely, we may say, than the Royal government had ever managed to do, held up by so much obstruction and opposition. When men looked simply for the repeal of bad laws and their replacement by better, Milton says that Parliament 'resounded with nothing else but new impositions, taxes, excises – yearly, monthly, weekly'. (As it might be today, after the social revolution of our time.) And this is 'not to reckon the offices, gifts, and preferments bestowed and shared among themselves' – as again today with all the jobs created for those in the game, the bureaucratic jobs not only in Whitehall but all over the country – one out of ten employed are 'employed' in local government; the hand-outs to cronies, not only of so-called 'honours' (for a consideration); the lush appointments to government corporations; the rewards of public favour, or at least of publicity, in journalism, radio and television, with their official jobs.

We need not go on: Milton's comparison with a previous age suggests that of ours with his.

As usual he had been affected personally, and felt galled where the shoe pinched – in the complicated law-dealings in which he was now involved with the Powells: he could not recover the debts they owed to him, because they were under sequestration as Royalists. Hence the passage: 'they who were ever faithfullest to this cause and freely aided them in person . . . slighted and bereaved after of their just debts by greedy sequestrations, were tossed up and down after miserable attendance from one committee to another with petitions in their hands', yet failed to obtain their suit. Or, if it were at length granted, 'yet by their sequestrators and subcommittees abroad – men for the most part of insatiable hands and noted disloyalty, those orders were commonly disobeyed'.

This was what Milton personally was experiencing at this time – serve him right, for the illusions he had cherished. This is what ordinary people are – the circumstances of revolution gave them their chance, and brought the scum to the top in every field, in politics and administration as in religion. He goes on: 'thus were their friends confiscate with their enemies, while they forfeited their debtors to the state, as they called it – but indeed to the ravening seizure of innumerable thieves in office'.

Here was the language of someone who had been bitten personally: it should have taught him. As for 'that faith which ought to have been kept as sacred and inviolable as anything holy, *the Public Faith* [compare public credit today], after infinite sums received, and all the wealth of the Church not better employed but swallowed up into a private gulf [such types as Cornelius Burgess or Sir Arthur Haselrig, for example] was not ere long ashamed to confess bankrupt'. We may well compare the situation with Britain's today, after a generation of over-spending beyond resources, of astronomical waste with no return, expenditure of every kind on non-productive purposes, every kind of hampering imposition upon those engaged in any productive work, most people bent on doing as little work as possible. A society which gears itself to the slackest, a nation of parasites=National Bankruptcy.

A difference of ours from seventeenth-century Britain is that people did at least work – hence their recovery with the Restoration, and their prosperity in the later seventeenth century when the madness was over. (No such recovery for us today.) Another difference was the belief in religion. Milton turns to that: 'if the state were in this plight, religion was not in much better'.

To aid them in their work of spiritual reformation the Long Parliament had called into being the Westminster Assembly of Puritan divines – having overthrown the Church, imprisoned and dispersed the bishops, and were shortly to murder (I call things by their right names) the Archbishop by act of Parliament. Milton's expectations of the Westminster Assembly had been disappointed by their rigid attitude on the subject of divorce. He now describes them as 'neither chosen by any rule or custom ecclesiastical, nor eminent for either piety or knowledge above others left out, only as each member of Parliament in his private fancy thought fit'. This was rather hard on an assembly which brought together such preaching capacity, such lungs, that they could endure nine hours of it, in preaching and prayer, in the Abbey on the sabbath.

Milton describes them for us: 'the most part of them were such as had preached and cried down, with great show of zeal, the avarice and pluralities of bishops and prelates. . . . Yet these conscientious men – ere any part of the work done for which they came together, and that on the public salary – wanted not boldness, to the ignominy and scandal of their boasted reformation, to seize into their hands or not unwillingly to accept, besides one, sometimes two or more of the best livings, collegiate masterships in the universities, rich lectures in the city.' Thus they took their chance to become pluralists and non-residents themselves as quickly as they could.

The effect of this, he held, was to show people that their 'spiritual' pretences were as naught; the word 'carnal' was for ever on their lips to describe the 'ungodly', but they themselves were just as carnal. This was 'but to tell us in effect that their doctrine was worth nothing'. They were hypocrites – John Aubrey always referred to the years when they were in the ascendant as 'the hypocritical times', and we shall see the effects in the cynicism, scepticism and libertinism of the Restoration, after the rule of the Saints was over. Already the Presbyterian Assembly was losing its hold – hence its anxiety to impose the Presbyterian Discipline, an altogether more rigorous affair than the 'Bawdy Courts' of the traditional Church.

Milton exposed the hypocrisy of the Assembly's campaign to engross discipline, which was precisely what they had been complaining of against others not long before. The new tyranny was worse, 'setting up a spiritual tyranny by a secular power, to the advancing of their own authority above the magistrate, whom they would have made their executioner, to punish church-delinquencies, whereof civil laws have no cognisance'. This was now Milton's position, and it brought him into association, for a time, with the Independents. Once more, by the irony of history, when the great Independent, Oliver Cromwell, assumed dictatorial power by the force of the Army, religion in England became more Erastian than ever. The Protector interfered with church appointments and had things his own way, to a degree which the legitimate King had never enjoyed. Life must have been very disillusioning for innocent John Milton.

By this time he had no further hope of Puritan Parliament or Assembly. Their followers were no better than their leaders: 'their disciples manifest themselves to be no better principled than their teachers, trusted with committeeships and other gainful offices, upon their commendations for zealous and – as they sticked not to term them – godly men. So that between them the teachers and these the disciples, there hath not been a more ignominious and mortal wound to faith, to piety, to the work of reformation, nor more cause of blaspheming given to the enemies of God and Truth [=John Milton], since the first preaching of Reformation.'

Then why embark on it, with such delusive hopes? The consequences of the delusions of 1640 would be seen in 1660.

Now for the effect on the people. They were becoming alienated and disaffected, some conspiring, 'looking on the statists [politicians], whom they beheld without constancy or firmness, busiest in petty things, trifling in the main. . . . Then looking on the churchmen, whom they saw under subtle hypocrisy to have preached their own follies – most of them not the Gospel – timeservers, covetous, illiterate persecutors, not lovers of the Truth, like in most things whereof they accused their predecessors.' We might interpolate a correction here. The Church of Laud and the Laudians, of Charles I and Clarendon, was altogether more worthy of respect: their conception of it not wholly Erastian, they thought of it as having a certain spiritual independence; they were dedicated men, willing to lay down their lives for it, as both King and Archbishop did.

The upshot of the Revolution had been a vast deception. 'Thus they who of late were extolled as our greatest deliverers, and had the people wholly at their devotion, by so discharging their trust as we see, did not only weaken and unfit themselves to be dispensers of what liberty they pretended, but unfitted also the people, now grown worse and more disordinate, to receive or digest any liberty at all.' Here speaks the revolutionary idealist, disappointed in his hopes. The people never had been qualified for or capable of 'liberty' – Milton's mania for liberty was appropriate to himself, his own rationalism of mind (up to a point), his exceptional personality and gifts. That very fact shows how inappropriate it was for ordinary people. Nor was it even relevant to their needs: a proper direction in Church and State would take those into consideration, and that would be enough.

Hence, Milton concludes, as Britain is 'a land fruitful enough of men stout and courageous in war, so it is naturally not overfertile of men able to govern justly and prudently in peace. . . . Valiant indeed, and prosperous to win a field; but to know the end of reason and winning, unjudicious and unwise; in good or bad success, alike unteachable. . . . Hence did their victories prove as fruitless as their losses dangerous.' Milton was now so despairing that he fell back on a thought not like his usual self-satisfied patriotism, namely' that 'ripe understanding and many civil virtues be imported into our minds from foreign writings and examples of best ages'. I suppose he was thinking of himself again and the republican virtues of classical antiquity – the cult of which Hobbes regarded, with some reason, as so deleterious to order. Otherwise 'we shall miscarry still, and come short in the attempts of any great enterprise'.

So he was still expecting the Revolution to be carried a stage further. With more than republican pride, with all the old sense of superiority, this could not be expected 'unless men more than vulgar bred up, as few of them were, in the knowledge of ancient and illustrious deeds, invincible against many and vain titles, impartial to friendships and relations, had conducted their affairs'. Actually it would be a Puritan aristocrat who would carry the Revolution a signal stage further: we shall see how it worked out.

For the moment, 'from the chapman to the retailer, many whose ignorance was more audacious than the rest, were admitted with all their sordid rudiments to bear no mean sway among them, both in church and state'.

John Milton, in this mood and at this juncture, was awaiting a new inspiration.

CHAPTER SIX

Milton on the King and the Presbyterians

THE inspiration which gave a new phase to Milton's prose writings and brought him European notice was the 'judicial' murder of the King – the bringing of 'the Man of Blood' to judgment, as the small minority of militant fanatics put it. We must not be afraid of calling things by their proper names: the 'Fanatic party' was what contemporaries called it, and they used the word 'madness' to describe their state of mind.

The complete defeat of the King's party – the Royalists and the Church – by 1646 still left the King as the king-pin in the situation. It was a most complex and confusing one: it needs a historian to explain it, and it is his business not to make it more confusing for the reader, but to reduce it to its simplest elements. In each of the three kingdoms – England (with Wales), Scotland and Ireland – the balance of forces and their character differed. In the most powerful, the English nation, the struggle for power was now increasingly bitter between the Puritan Parliament (dominated by Presbyterians) and its Army (dominated by Independents, headed by Cromwell), with the King as the third factor, scheming to hold the balance between them.

Hence the complicated negotiations and manœuvres which occupied the next two years, 1647 and 1648. Parliament remained uncompromising, until too late. With the rigidity of Presbyterians they stood out for their own monopoly of power: Parliamentary control of ministers and of the Army, and the establishment of Presbyterianism. We need hardly point out that England was not a Presbyterian country, and never likely to be: the Church of England was in keeping with the character of the English people, and the King held to this position. This was what he believed in: as Gardiner says, Charles I was an intriguer, but he was not a hypocrite. He was a sincere and convinced Anglican.

To their impossibilism the Presbyterian magnates of Parliament added the stupidity of offending their Army, which had won the war for them. Parliament held up the payment of arrears to its soldiers, and obviously hoped to reduce the Army in numbers and to submission without paying up. The Army had no mind to be played with, refused to dissolve and, by a *coup*, got the king-pin, the King, into its own hands. Led by Cromwell, they offered him better terms – the 'Heads of the Proposals' – than the mean-minded Presbyterians had done. Charles I played with both – since he naturally did not agree with either – but eventually closed with the silly Scots to intervene again in England to restore him to power. With the characteristic folly of fanaticism they refused to allow any co-operation with anybody except Presbyterians – there were to be no experienced Cavalier officers, for example – and were deservedly cut to pieces by Cromwell at the battle or, rather, rout of Preston in 1648. Serve them right for their idiocy. (A great deal of human action is sheer idiocy.)

This invasion coincided with various Cavalier outbreaks, of which the most striking was the heroic resistance of Colchester. On its surrender Fairfax stained his record by the execution in cold blood of the gallant defenders, Sir Charles Lucas and Sir George Lisle. This piece of savagery was held at the time to be an act of vengeance: it was more likely intended *in terrorem*, to signal the Army's determination to crush all opposition and end the war.

Parliament, blind to the signals and yet alarmed at the Army's power, continued negotiations with the King, who naturally preferred a deal with Parliament – more constitutional, more representative, and offering the chance of a more permanent settlement. Even at this late hour Charles I nearly brought it off: he was alone, but he was the king-pin still, without whom the constitution could not be put together again.

But now both King and Parliament were up against Oliver

Cromwell at the head of the Army. On 4 December 1648 Parliament moved to come to terms with the King. Nasty Prynne, who had created so much trouble and hounded the Archbishop to his death, upheld 'the satisfactoriness of the King's Answers to the Propositions for the Settlement of a firm and lasting Peace', and deplored the 'supreme anarchical tyranny' of the Army. The Presbyterian magnates were too late. Two days later they were 'purged' by the Army – we have become familiar again with revolutionary 'purges' in our time. Only some ninety members were left on the rolls; of these a carefully sifted majority, about fifty, were the cat's-paw of the Army.

Such was the 'Rump' Parliament, which the Army kept in being as a civilian fig-leaf for its dictatorship, until it swept the cover away four years later for Cromwell to assume open power as Lord Protector in 1653 – far more absolute than ever Charles I had been at the height of his personal rule. And, of course, Cromwell was totally unrepresentative of the country. At any moment, if a vote of the nation could have been taken, the King would have been restored. Opposed to Cromwell was the whole of the Royalist party, itself a majority of the nation; the Church which was the religion of the majority; and now, the bulk of Parliament and the Presbyterians, who formed the core of the Puritans. Cromwell's rule was that of a small minority, resting upon naked force.

This was what Milton was now to defend; this was what all his palaver about 'liberty' had come to.

The Army – in a tumultuous state of excitement, political, social and religious, with Levellers, sectaries, fanatics seething within it – was pressing to bring the King to book. Cromwell, opportunist politician as he was, gave no sign but realised the dangers he stood between: from the Army, if he closed with the King; from the King, whom he could not trust. As to this last there is a clear hint in the tract Milton wrote at the height of the crisis, referring to historic persons who had been bumped off by tyrants when the chance came. Little as this has been noticed by historians with small perception how motives operate, especially unconsciously, the case is indeed obvious.

Charles I was unlikely to forgive all that he had endured at the hands of these rebels, once the tide had turned and reaction gave him the opportunity. The instinct of self-preservation, the prospect of ruin, sharpens a man's decision. Hitler was driven to murder his closest associates with Röhm in the blood-bath of June 1934 – and it turned out wonderfully for him. Cromwell settled for the King's 'trial' and public murder, and it succeeded wonderfully for Oliver Cromwell. His descendant, the Puritan historian Gardiner, admits that there was no shadow of justice in the 'trial', and that it was a crime to execute the King. Cromwell drove it forward with manic hysteria, forcing hesitant regicides to append their signatures – a sure sign psychologically of what it meant for him. It made possible his triumph and his famous place in history – for he made a far abler monarch than ever Charles I was. But it spelled out the term for Puritan rule in England, in the end: henceforward the martyred King's blood ran for ever between hateful Puritanism and the English people. Once Oliver's dictatorship and the rule of force were over they would see to it. . . . Never again.

Meanwhile, this was the case, the cause of a tiny revolutionary minority, that Milton drew his pen to defend.

After the end of the second Civil War with Fairfax's victory at Colchester, Milton hoped that he would take the state in hand, in a rather sycophantic sonnet:

> Fairfax, whose name in arms through Europe rings.

The concluding sestet suggests,

> O yet a nobler task awaits thy hand;
> For what can war but endless war still breed?

Yes, indeed; the question should be addressed to those who had been instigating rebellion for the past two generations. Here was the result; Milton wished the campaign carried further

> Till truth and right from violence be freed
> And public faith cleared from the shameful brand
> Of public fraud. . . .

We shall see how that worked out; for

> In vain doth valour bleed
> While avarice and rapine share the land.

They might have thought of that before taking to arms.

Fairfax refused to go on. He disapproved of the proceedings against the King; his wife protested openly at the 'trial' in Westminster Hall; he withdrew into retreat from public affairs. At the 'trial' the King himself protested that the liberty of the subject was endangered by the very same appeal to force by which his life was demanded.

The crisis aroused all Milton's revolutionary fervour. Only a matter of weeks after the ghastly scene of the execution outside the King's own Whitehall, which sent a shock through the nation, Milton produced his tirade, *The Tenure of Kings and Magistrates*. The argument of it is presented in the title – '*proving that it is lawful, and hath been held so through all ages, for any who have the power, to call to account a tyrant, or wicked king, and after due conviction to depose and put him to death*'. This is the argument that most commentators deal with, as if the tract were a contribution to political theory. In fact, the sting is in the tail – '*and that they who of late so much blame deposing are the men that did it themselves*'. For the pamphlet is sizzling with anger and vituperation at the Presbyterians, for withdrawing from the bloody business of executing the King, when they had been responsible for overthrowing him. In Milton's indignation he almost overlooks the King's misdeeds – those are assumed – to get at his brother Puritans. Nothing that anyone who detests them could utter equals what Milton said of his fellow brethren in Christ.

In essence he was right: they had dragged the monarchy down, vilified and reviled the monarch – and then, when they saw power slipping from their hands into the grip of the Army, washed their hands of the business and went over to the King's side, too late to save him. To anticipate events: it was eventually this alliance between Crown and Parliament, between the King's son and the Presbyterians, that restored the monarchy in 1660. It was the refusal of the Parliamentarians to carry the revolution a stage further, to go on with the business, that enraged the revolutionary doctrinaire. No tract that he wrote is so generally abusive or hits the target so squarely as this against his fellows who had betrayed the Revolution: it makes it a joy to read.

We can dispose of it briefly *qua* political theory. Most of what passes for political 'theory' is but the rationalisation of men's interests, prejudices or illusions. It does not conduce to the happiness of nations, but on the contrary does a great deal of harm. Milton starts from his usual rationalist assumption, 'if men would within themselves be governed by reason', instead of by 'custom from without, and blind affections within'. We see that the appeal to reason has become conditional now – he has learnt something from his experience over his rationalising about divorce, greeted with disgust and derision as it had been, driving him into silence until this renewal of inspiration and hope.

Again there is no understanding of the rationale of custom, that the very nature of human beings and of their grouping in societies necessitates custom as framework and regulation, though requiring pragmatic changes from time to time. As for 'blind affections within', who entertained them more than John Milton? Of this the sublime egoist was unaware. He continues, with his usual assurance: 'no man who knows aught can be so stupid to deny that all men naturally were born free'. On the contrary, a knowledge of anthropology tells us that men were *not* born free. The process of becoming free is a long and complex one, even in societies where conditions are favourable, and with persons who by their capabilities are qualified to profit from such freedom. A knowledge of history instructs us that such societies are few and far between; while a knowledge of men tells us that not only few qualify, but also that fewer value freedom than is popularly supposed. (Hence 'democratic' misunderstanding of Russia or China, India or Africa, South America or the Communist world, indeed most of the world as it is.)

Naturally, John Milton was one of the elect who qualify for freedom, like Rousseau ('Men are born free, but are everywhere in chains') or Thomas Jefferson ('All men are created equal and independent; from that they derive rights inherent and inalienable, among which are the preservation of life, and liberty, and the pursuit of happiness'). Each of these exceptional, elect persons is generalising from himself. It is not true that liberty is essential to happiness, nor is it true that the bulk of human beings find happiness in the pursuit of liberty. It is true only for the elect, like Milton, Rousseau or Jefferson – and they have caused much trouble by generalising from their exceptional selves to the human race as a whole.

Political theory, to be any good, must be based on a true view of human nature. Here we see why Americans in our time have such difficulty in understanding Russia or the Communist world, have experienced such a sad disillusionment in their expectations of China, have had a lovers' quarrel (shades of Lafayette!) with De Gaulle's France. Even more important: this is why it is so ludicrous that democracies – which in themselves are not all that exemplary – should expect the uncivilised peoples of Africa or South America or anywhere else to follow their 'democratic' example. This would be comic, if it did not lead to such tragic misunderstandings. It all comes from these universalising abstractions, generalising from very special cases to the human condition in general; they are put forward by intellectual egoists, like Milton, Rousseau and Jefferson; not by intelligent sceptics, not by Shakespeare or Montaigne, Machiavelli or Francis Bacon, Selden or Swift, Dr Johnson or Burke or de Tocqueville.

We can readily agree with Milton that there is nothing sacred about the person of a king, and that kings derive their authority from the consent of the people at large, i.e., the society. We do not need to believe any divine-right-of-kings nonsense any more than Milton did. The authority of a ruler was invested with a religious sanction because, people being the simpletons they are, this was the best way of giving authority some sanction, a religious sanction, to keep them in awe and to keep order in the nursery – in their own interests. Otherwise, they blow up into the explosions of civil wars, or succumb to breakdowns of society like Tsarist Russia or the Weimar Republic, with hideous consequences in loss of lives; or mur-

derous outbursts such as we have witnessed in our time in
Spain, Greece, Palestine, India, Cyprus, Northern Ireland,
and all over Africa. John Milton did not need a sacrosanct
authority, but ordinary humans did, for their own sakes.

Milton concludes from his premises, 'it follows that, since the
King or Magistrate holds his authority of the people, both
originally and naturally for their good in the first place, then
may the people as oft as they shall judge it for the best either
choose him or reject him, retain him or depose him . . . as seems
to them best'. Again, we do not have even to disagree – merely
ask, *who* was to say? For all this argy-bargy about the Tenure of
Kings and Magistrates, it was only force that said it in the case
of Charles I: the Army led by Cromwell. In the event it was only
one man who said it: it is highly doubtful if the execution of
Charles I would ever have been carried through but for Oliver
Cromwell. It is highly doubtful if the Soviet Revolution would
have been carried through but for one man, Lenin; the Chinese
Revolution but for Mao; the Nazi Revolution but for Hitler. So
much for the people in general in these historic events.

Milton was merely propounding and defending what others,
practical men, decided. He expounded it in terms of their
Puritan ideology, their Bible mania. The barbarity of the Old
Testament is called upon all through to illustrate and justify
God's (i.e., Milton's) condemnation of the King as a tyrant; the
divines are admonished to join together 'the vengeance of God
and the zeal of his people'. The Presbyterians of Parliament –
extruded by force by Cromwell in order to force on the King's
'trial' – are adjured 'not to fall off from their first principles', nor
'to dart against the actions of their brethren'. Unfortunately for
his argument, Milton defines with his usual clarity what he
meant by tyrant: 'a tyrant is he who, regarding neither law nor
the common good, reigns only for himself and his faction'. The
English monarchy was not absolute, it was bound by law and
custom; Milton's definition of a tyrant precisely described
Cromwell, who was bound by neither law nor custom, and
ruled as the head of a small faction over a passive people.

This tyranny the apostle of liberty was now to defend and
serve. Such is the irony that depends upon revolutions and

befalls revolutionary doctrinaires. (Cf. Marxist doctrine on 'the withering away of the state' with the facts of state-power in Soviet Russia!)

The Presbyterian majority among the Puritans, who had started the Revolution, having now failed to grasp power at the last moment, went into opposition against Cromwell's ascendancy. This infuriated Milton, who desired passionately that the new phase of the Revolution should carry it further. The hysteria of the time fostered Biblical hopes of a millennium, and Milton with his Bible mania (like some Marxists with their Gospel according to Marx) shared in these hopes. He burned with indignation at the majority-Puritans betraying them. Since we learn nothing from the lunacy of millenary hopes, it is more profitable to turn to this exposure of Puritan responsibility for what had happened.

He cited the Bible's curse on those '*that do the work of the Lord negligently*', after making a good beginning. They had 'bandied and borne arms against their King, divested him, disanointed him, nay, cursed him all over in their pulpits and their pamphlets, to the engaging of sincere and real men beyond what is possible or honest to retreat from'. Now they were not only retreating from, but also denouncing as disloyal, 'proceedings which are the necessary consequences of their own former actions – nor disliked by themselves, were they managed to the entire advantages of their own faction'. They now brandished statutes and laws 'which would have doomed them to a traitor's death for what they have done already. Others who have been fiercest against their Prince, and no mean incendiaries of the war against him', now protest against bringing him to 'the trial of justice, which is the Sword of God, superior to all mortal things'. 'As for mercy, if it be to a Tyrant, under which name they themselves have cited himself so oft in the hearing of God, of Angels and the holy Church assembled', then their plea for mercy is hypocrisy, or 'either levity or shallowness of mind'. We have no difficulty in seeing that 'the holy Church assembled' is Milton's semantics for the Puritan party, and God is Milton himself writ large.

And who were they to condemn their brethren for condemning the King? No Cavalier could have written of the brethren in Christ – as Queen Elizabeth used to refer to them – with more contempt. 'For how can their pretended counsel be either sound or faithful when they that give it see not, *for madness and vexation of their ends lost*', that the very Scriptures and statutes they cite 'against their friends and associates, would by sentence of the common adversary fall first and heaviest upon their own heads?' They were all in it together; they were equally responsible, Milton urges. But things did not turn out as he warned. The Parliamentarian Puritans, being politicians, managed to exculpate themselves from the murder of the King. When the chickens came home to roost in 1660, the crime was brought home to the regicides who had carried it through; John Milton was fortunate indeed to escape with mere imprisonment for defending it.

He cannot have foreseen this – he was thinking in terms of the millennium, the fulfilment of revolutionary hopes; perhaps even, for he was Bible-drunk, Christ's Second Coming. For things had certainly taken a most decisive new turn: there could not have been a more flagrant break with the past than the scene outside the palace of the long line of kings, a shock to the nation, a thrill to Milton. Who were these false brethren to betray such wonderful expectations, 'in the glorious way in which justice and victory hath set them: the only warrant through all ages – next under immediate Revelation – to exercise supreme power [i.e., the end justifies the means, success is the final test], in those proceedings which hitherto appear equal to what hath been done in any age or nation heretofore, justly or magnanimously'.

Let not 'any man be deluded by either the ignorance or the notorious hypocrisy of our dancing Divines, who have the conscience or the boldness to come with Scripture in their mouths, glossed and fitted for their turns with a double contradictory sense, transforming the sacred verity of God to an idol with two faces . . . and with the same quotations to charge others which they made serve to justify themselves'. So much for the Westminster Assembly, still sitting, though in a rather addled condition. Since Milton was as well up in holy

Scripture, the sacred verity of God, as any divine, he was able to bandy texts and to cite cases of Old Testament kings who had been brought to judgment.

Who were these Divines now charging with disloyalty and impiety those who had judged and sentenced the King?.'While the hope to be made Classic and Provincial Lords [i.e., rulers in the projected Presbyterian Discipline over the country] led them on; while pluralities greased them thick and deep, to the shame and scandal of religion, more than all the sects and heresies they exclaim against – then, to fight against the King's person and no less a party of his Lords and Commons was lawful, was no resisting of superior powers; they only were powers not to be resisted. But now that their censorious domineering is not suffered to be universal, truth and conscience to be freed, tithes and pluralities to be no more ... to bring delinquents without exemption to a fair tribunal by the common national law against murder is now no less than Corah, Dathan, and Abiram.'

We may leave these Puritans to dispute with each other the application of their rebarbative Biblical analogies. But we may reasonably comment that the Regicides' court that sentenced the King was no 'fair tribunal', nor was there any common law by which he could be 'tried'. As for tithes, they continued to be exacted – Cromwell as Lord Protector said that he could see no way to do without them. As for pluralities, his own favourite chaplain, John Owen, got the lush Deanery of Christ Church; others similarly – while the Lord Protector interfered more largely in church appointments than ever the King had done. Archbishop Laud, indeed, had stood for a measure of spiritual independence for the Church.

Milton went on: 'He who but erewhile in the pulpits was a cursed tyrant, an enemy to God and Saints [i.e., themselves], laden with all the innocent blood spilt in three kingdoms [we see what humbug this was], is now a lawful magistrate, a sovereign Lord, the Lord's Anointed, not to be touched, though by themselves imprisoned.' Good for Milton! No Cavalier could do better; nor, as an exposure of Puritan hypocrisy, could it be improved upon. Of course, the event itself was politics, practical politics, not the illusory hopes of a doctrinaire. The Presbyterians, cheated of power at the last moment – by their own ineptitude and meanness towards their army, and their inflexible opposition to toleration of any sects but their own – had switched horses to back the King. Too late – the Army got him by the neck. Now, 'their censorious domineering is not suffered to be universal, truth and conscience to be freed'; we must point out that this means only Milton's truth and conscience: the religion of the vast majority, the English Church ('Prelatists') along with the Catholics, was to be proscribed. So much for his idea of toleration! Humbug was not an exclusive possession of either side in the squabble between Puritans.

It was merely that hypocrisy was more flagrant on one side. For 'what need these examples to Presbyterians, I mean to those who now of late would seem so much to abhor deposing, when as they to all Christendom have given the latest and the liveliest example of doing it themselves? . . . And whether the Presbyterians have not done all this and much more, they will not put me, I suppose, to reckon up a seven years' story fresh in the memory of all men. Have they not utterly broke the Oath of Allegiance, rejecting the King's command and authority sent them from any part of the kingdom? Have they not adjured the Oath of Supremacy by setting up the Parliament without the King, and – though their Vow and Covenant bound them in general to the Parliament – yet sometimes adhering to the lesser part of Lords and Commons *that remained faithful, as they term it,* and, even of them, one while to the Commons without the Lords, another while to the Lords without the Commons?' We see very well what humbug all this was. On the other hand, bargaining and compromise are the essence of political action: of this the doctrinaire had no conception.

He was able, however, to bring home their clear responsibility. They had broken their oaths to the King, 'notwithstanding their fine clause in the Covenant to preserve his person, Crown, and dignity'. In short, this Puritan admitted that the Presbyterian Covenant was so much hypocrisy; but this we knew already. Had they not, 'in plain terms, unkinged the King, much more than hath their seven years' war, not deposed him only, but outlawed him, and defied him as an alien, a rebel to law and enemy to the state? Have they not levied all these wars against him, whether offensive or defensive, and given commission to slay where they knew his person could not be exempt from danger? Have they not hunted and pursued him round about the kingdom with sword and fire? Have they not formerly denied to treat with him, and their now-recanting Ministers preached against him as a reprobate incurable, an enemy to God and his Church marked for destruction? Yet while they thus assaulted and endangered it [the King's life] with hostile deeds, they swore in words to defend it with his Crown and dignity.'

They were hypocrites, of course; but then such people usually are, in anything that concerns their interest – what defence they put up is but a smokescreen. These persons were practical politicians; Milton was disqualified as such, since he called things fearlessly by their right names. The sheer intellectual power of this Puritan demolished the whole case of the Puritan majority. 'Nor did they treat or think of treating with him [Charles I] till their hatred to the Army that delivered them – not their love or duty to the King – joined them secretly with men sentenced so oft for reprobates in their own mouths.' Until then how often had they cursed him in their pulpits, 'with exhortation to curse all those in the name of God that made not war against him – as bitterly as Meroz was to be cursed that went not out against a Canaanitish king – almost in all the sermons, prayers and fulminations that have been uttered this seven years by those cloven tongues of falsehood and dissension, who now acquit him'. We see what charming people these devotees of the Old Testament were – this was a specific reference to the notorious sermon the canting Stephen Marshall had preached so often. Milton ended by praying that God would 'visit upon their own heads that *Curse ye, Meroz*, the very motto of their pulpits wherewith so frequently they have mocked the vengeance of God and the zeal of his people'.

The people had, as usual, been taken in. The political switch the Presbyterians had executed gave 'the most opprobrious lie to all the acted zeal that for these many years hath filled their bellies and fed them fat upon the foolish people. Ministers of sedition, not of the Gospel, who, while they saw it manifestly tend to civil war and bloodshed, never ceased exasperating the people against him', the King. This was exactly what the King and his supporters – a majority of the nation at any moment – claimed: it is as well to have it out of the mouth of a proclaimed Puritan, one who was not a hypocrite. If these Divines did their duty as good pastors, instead of 'mounting twice into the chair with a formal preachment huddled up at the odd hours of a whole lazy week . . . how little leisure would they find to be the most pragmatical sidesmen of every popular tumult and sedition?'

The late Archbishop, now four years in his grave – hounded thither by one of the worst of this lot, the dreadful Prynne – had never said anything so scathing, for all that he had had to put up with from them. 'It would be good also they lived so as might persuade the people they hated covetousness, which – worse than heresy – is idolatry; hated pluralities and all kind of simony [shades of Cornelius Burgess, Vice-Prolocutor of the Divine Assembly, up to his neck in church property!]; left rambling from benefice to benefice, like ravenous wolves seeking where they may devour the biggest.' But what had young Mr Milton written about the Anglican clergy in 'Lycidas', in similar terms? What the idealistic doctrinaire was in revolt against was average human nature, which he never understood, he had so little of it. 'Let them be sorry that, being called to assemble about reforming the Church, they fell to progging [prodding] and soliciting the Parliament – though they had renounced the name of priests – for a new settling of their tithes and oblations, and double-lined themselves with spiritual places of commodity beyond the possible discharge of their duty.' But of course. We need not take the protestations of the Westminster Assembly of Divines any more seriously than Milton did.

For himself, these were days of feverish expectation in which he lived, this was his greatest hour, in which he felt renewed and inspired to send out this trumpet-call, after the disillusionment and dejection, the silence, of the past four years. For 'God, as we have cause to trust, will put other thoughts into the people and turn them from looking after these firebrands, of whose fury and false prophecies we have enough experience . . . and will incline them to hearken rather with erected minds to the voice of our supreme Magistracy, calling us to liberty and the flourishing deeds of a reformed Commonwealth'.

We have only to reflect that 'liberty' meant the rule of the Army, inspired by Cromwell. The King had been 'tried' and executed in January 1649. In February, Milton's defence was published. In March, he received his reward: Cromwell's Council of State made him Secretary for the Foreign Tongues.

Milton was ambitious, and avid of fame: all his writings show that. So far he had achieved only notoriety – with his divorce tracts; even the splendid collection of his earlier poems in 1645 attracted little attention, where those of the Royalist poet John Cleveland went into ten editions. Anyway, the Royalists, cultivated people, read and wrote poetry; most of the poets (and all the musicians and artists) were Royalists – Milton and Marvell were exceptions again.

Now was his chance to win fame. The first job he was given was to answer the 'King's Book', *Eikon Basilike: the Portraiture of his Sacred Majesty in his Solitudes and Sufferings*. Milton can hardly have relished the task: he tells us that it was assigned to him, he did not choose it. He took months over it; his rebuttal, *Eikonoklastes* ('the image-breaker'), did not come out till towards the end of the year. It was in any case a hopeless task to overtake the King's Book, as it was called; and Milton's reply to it carries singularly little conviction.

The King's Book was a difficult book to reply to. Most people who have written about it seem not to have read it, they give one so little idea of its character. It is in fact an effective and plausible defence of the King's actions, chapter by chapter – all those most under attack or most to the fore: from the calling of the Long Parliament and the execution of Strafford, through all the vicissitudes of the war to the Vote of No Addresses and the King's meditations upon death. Each chapter ends with a prayer, the whole book with the King's private devotions.

No doubt the book was ghosted by John Gauden, who was himself a moderate. Hence the studied moderation of its tone, and this may well have represented the King's mood in adversity, nearing the end of his troubled course. He seems to have seen the draft of the book, made his emendations and suggestions, and approved it. So much of it seems too good to be untrue. Gauden must have received information from the highest source, for it clearly represents the King's own line, his reading of events, puts his actions in the most favourable light, and appeals in various ways to the sympathy of the reader. We are presented with a portrait of the King as a human being, in solitude and suffering, facing death. We are asked for our prayers. What reader could resist it?

Evidently the nation could not. It would be vulgar to describe it as a mere runaway bestseller, though some sixty editions of it sold in the year or so after the King's death – the book came out in the month after, along with Milton's little-noticed *Tenure of Kings and Magistrates*. The King's Book was almost equal to a final victory in the field. It fixed the sympathy which his death, and his unsurpassed dignity in his sufferings – his farewell to his children, his imprisonment, etc. – had won for him all over the country. The King's Book helped forward the myth, created the cult of the Royal Martyr which won through to final victory with the Restoration of his son in 1660.

Without going into disputed political issues, take only the question of religion. The Book begins reasonably enough from the position that 'no flames of civil dissensions are more dangerous than those which make religious pretensions the grounds of factions'. The King's position with regard to Church reform was a reasonable one: 'it is no news to have all invocations ushered in with the name of reformations in Church and State by those who, seeking to gain reputation with the vulgar for their extraordinary parts and piety, must needs undo whatever was formerly settled never so well and wisely'. This remark lands right on the target: the Puritans had been agitating all along for the undoing of the well-tried Elizabethan Settlement – the best consensus that could be obtained and the only one that would work.

The King continues – it so clearly represents his view as makes no matter whether he wrote it: 'As for the matter contained in the [Prayer] Book, sober and learned men have sufficiently vindicated it against the cavils and exceptions of those who thought it a part of piety to make what profane objections they could against it, especially for popery and superstition. Whereas, no doubt, the Liturgy was exactly conformed to the doctrine of the Church of England; and this by all reformed Churches is confessed to be most sound and orthodox.' However, 'some men, I hear, are so impatient not to use in all their devotions their own inventions and gifts that they not only disuse but wholly contemn and cast away the Lord's Prayer: whose great guilt is that it is the warrant and original pattern of all set liturgies in the Christian Church. I ever thought that the proud ostentation of men's abilities for invention, and the vain affectations of variety in public prayer merits a greater brand of sin than that which they call coldness and barrenness.'

All this is expressed with a regal dignity that bespeaks Charles I rather than Gauden; it makes a marked contrast with the vituperation and abuse of Milton. 'The Assembly of Divines, whom the two Houses have applied, in an unwonted way, to advise of Church affairs I dislike not further than that they are not legally convened and chosen, nor act in the name of all the clergy of England. . . .' Charles was well known to be a devoted son of the Church, and a chaste and pious man. During his long confinement, deprived of 'civil comforts and secular attendants, I thought the absence of them all might be supplied by the attendance of some of my chaplains: whom for their function I reverence, and for their fidelity I have cause to love. . . . The truth is, I never needed or desired more the service and assistance of men judiciously pious and soberly devout.'

He needed their help and their prayers. They were taken away from him. 'They that envy my being a king are loth I should be a Christian: while they seek to deprive me of all things else, they are afraid I should save my soul. I have sometimes thought the unchristianness of those denials might arise from a displeasure some men had to see me prefer my own divines before their ministers . . . who have (some of them at least) had so great an influence in occasioning these calamities and inflicting these wounds upon me.'

While the King was held at Holdenby, Parliament had obtruded its precious ministers upon him. It was not to be supposed that a cultivated king, accustomed to the moving liturgy of the Church, would welcome the nasal whine of these paragons, the occupational symptom of their profession. Deprived of his own chaplains, the King would take no notice of the ministers, say grace himself and proceed at once to dinner. These creatures obtruded themselves at the last upon his scaffold as they had upon Archbishop Laud's, and as Francis Cheynell did upon Laud's godson, the philosophic Chillingworth, on his prison death-bed at Chichester.

All that Milton has to say about the King's devotion to the ritual of the Church is this: ' "His glory", in the gaudy copes and painted windows, mitres, rochets, altars, and the chanted service-book, "shall be dearer to him" than in the establishing his crown in righteousness and the spiritual power of religion', i.e., Milton's idea of religion. It is probable that Charles I's religion had more of the spiritual in it, as certainly it had more Christian charity, than Milton's. Once more we are struck by the paradox that a poet, whose ear was so refined for music and poetry, should have so little visual aesthetic response: here was a real Philistinism, reinforced by doctrine, one of the worst aspects of all Puritanism – the denial of the works of art which redeem man from the slime.

Worse still was Milton's attack on the King as a dissembler in religion – like all tyrants, he says, and compares him with the murderous Richard III, who *was* a dissembler. Charles I was a dissembler in politics – needs must, and he was not a strong man, caught in the whirlwind of revolution; but everyone knew that he was no dissembler in religion. For all the pressures upon him, his wife's Catholicism (she was a terrible liability), the insistence of the Scots upon Presbyterianism for their support, etc., the King remained firm in his Anglican faith. Well read in Richard Hooker, intellectually he was eminently capable of defending his position – as the egregious Henderson found to his dismay, when he came face to face with the King against whom he had organised the Covenant.

The prosperous years of Charles's reign, the 1630s when he maintained peace and cultivated the arts, are described as merely 'voluptuous' and 'idle', 'without care or thought, as if to be a king had been nothing else but to eat and drink, and have his will, and take his pleasure'. How mean! Even the prim Puritan, Lucy Hutchinson, admitted that Charles's Court had been virtuous, the King given to encouraging scholarship, writing, taste. He has always received credit among the discerning for his patronage of Van Dyck, in whose art the Court is for ever romantically mirrored. Today we attach no less importance to the many-sided genius of Inigo Jones, most seminal of English artists, who created the masques that were superior to anything in Europe and gave their opportunity to the Caroline poets, Ben Jonson, Carew, Aurelian Townsend and others. Jones created the English version of classic Renaissance architecture with his grand works – brought to a halt by the Civil War. But for the financial stringency, we should have had a Whitehall Palace from him to bear comparison with the Louvre. This is to say nothing of the King's encouragement of music – which should have appealed to Milton – and his friendship for musicians, his grief when William Lawes, brother of Milton's friend Henry Lawes, was killed at Chester.

The King mourned for him. No words of sympathy escaped from John Milton. One cannot but think that life and Puritan doctrine were sadly embittering the young man who had charmed cultivated Italy. One is shocked to find Milton repeating the dreadful lie that Charles and Buckingham had poisoned the old King James – those three, James and 'Baby Charles' and 'Steenie', were all too closely bound together by ties of affection.

Enough of Milton's insults against the martyred King. Let us turn to what light *Eikonoklastes* throws upon himself.

The motto is from the Old Testament, of course: 'as a roaring lion and raging bear, so is a wicked ruler over the poor people'. One does not recognise Charles I; neither did the poor people: they recognised him in the King's Book. This infuriated

Milton, and *Eikonoklastes* is notable for its abuse of the people. They are the 'mad multitude', the 'silly people', the 'blockish vulgar', an 'inconstant, irrational and image-doting rabble'. 'The people, exorbitant and excessive in all their motions, are prone not to a religious only but to a civil kind of idolatry, in idolising their kings.' He is now disillusioned with the nation, for all his Puritan patriotism: 'now, with a besotted and degenerate baseness of spirit – except some few who yet retain in them the old English fortitude and love of freedom [e.g., John Milton], embastardised from the ancient nobleness of their ancestors, are ready to fall flat and give adoration to the image and memory of this man, who hath offered at more cunning fetches to undermine our liberties and put tyranny into an art than any British king before him'. One is inclined to say to this merely 'Chuck it, Smith!'

How to account for this 'low dejection and debasement of mind in the people'? Milton puts it down first to the prelates and their teachings – and he is off again with his gramophone record of abuse of the bishops and Anglican clerics, the justice of which we have already estimated. It is but repetition, for want of better, from the earlier tracts. There is fair agreement that Milton is not at his best in *Eikonoklastes*; his American biographer, Parker, concludes, 'he tried to be reasonable [!], and succeeded in being largely irrelevant'.

Supercilious as always, he had not wanted the job of answering a book so far beneath his notice: 'I never was so thirsty after fame, nor so destitute of other hopes and means, better and more certain to attain it.' This was true enough – in following his real inspiration in poetry; politics and prose were a misdirection of the spirit for him: he should have stuck to his last. It was his Republican enthusiasm, his revolutionary doctrinairism, that led him to grasp with both hands the chance to serve the Republic, to the sacrifice of his sight and the postponement of his real work in life, the last poems.

This first job for the Republic, it is generally agreed, was as inept in performance as it was totally ineffective in stemming the tide of sympathy for the Royal Martyr. For one thing, Milton was not really cognisant of the true inwardness of affairs

– as often with innocent intellectuals used by fly politicians to defend their doings. Take the crucial case of Strafford's execution, condemned quite unjustly of treason, and killed by attainder, i.e., by partisan act of Parliament. The King reproached himself for assenting to it, when he knew that his great minister was innocent; his hand had been forced, but it was against his conscience and he regarded his consent as a sin. The King argued, reasonably, that less than one-third of the Lords had been present when the act of attainder came before them; both Houses, and the King himself, had been subjected to organised mob-pressure and violence. 'For the House of Commons, many gentlemen, for their integrity in their votes, were exposed to the popular calumny, hatred and fury, which grew then so exorbitant in their clamours for justice – that is to have both myself and the two Houses vote and do as they would have us – that many were rather terrified to concur with the condemning party than satisfied that of right they ought so to do.' This was true, and it had opened the flood-gates of revolution. The King's forced assent was worse than a sin: it was a grave political mistake.

The young Sir Henry Vane perjured himself to bring Strafford to the block. He purloined the Council minutes from his father's cabinet, and then gave evidence that Strafford's proposal to use the Army to subdue 'that kingdom' meant England, when everyone present at the Council was agreed that Strafford meant no such thing – he was referring to Ireland or Scotland, both up in arms. This is that Vane to whom Milton addressed his admiring sonnet, another doctrinaire Republican, as heterodox in religion as Milton was, and as careless of truth:

> Vane, young in years, but in sage counsel old,
> Than whom a better senator ne'er held
> The helm of Rome. . . .
>
> besides to know
> Both spiritual power and civil, what each means,
> What severs each, thou hast learned, which few have
> done . . .
> Therefore on thy firm hand Religion leans

In peace, and reckons thee her eldest son.

They were in agreement about separating religion from the state, hence the admiration: Milton and Vane were in a minority of about two in this matter. Even today, three hundred years later, the Church of England is still the established religion of the state – so much for their views. It is arguable that the Church might not have succeeded in maintaining this position, if it had not been for the awful lesson of the rule of the Saints, and the nation's natural revulsion from it.

Milton has now to abuse not only King and Church, but the Presbyterians, who, we must remember, constituted the bulk of his own Puritans: 'they, who seemed of late to stand up hottest for the Covenant, can now sit mute and much pleased to hear these opprobrious things uttered against their faith, their freedom, and themselves in their own doings made traitors to boot. The Divines also, their wizards, can be so brazen as to cry Hosanna to this his book.' Actually, the striking thing about the King's Book is the moderation of its tone, its patience: there are no opprobrious things in it. We must give Gauden credit for this, a somewhat ambivalent man himself, who favoured Archbishop Ussher's plan of accommodating episcopacy to Presbyterianism. This suggests a new consideration: the Book appealed to Presbyterians as well as to Anglicans, and must have had an importance in reconciling them to the royal cause – which bore fruit in 1660.

This added to Milton's bitterness: 'none appearing all this while to vindicate church or state from these calumnies and reproaches but a small handful of men, whom they defame and spit at with all the odious names of schism and sectarism'. This was the fact: they were a tiny minority, totally unrepresentative of the nation, who had killed the King and forced forward the revolution. Milton had his usual self-satisfaction to fall back on: 'I never knew that time in England when men of truest religion were not counted sectaries; but wisdom now, valour, justice, constancy, prudence united and embodied to defend religion and our liberties, both by word [i.e., Milton] and deed [i.e., Cromwell] against tyranny, is counted schism and faction. . . .

Certainly, if ignorance and perverseness will needs be national and universal, then they who adhere to wisdom and truth [i.e., Milton] are not therefore to be blamed for being so few as to seem a sect or faction.' Milton concludes it to be 'a high honour done us from God, and a special mark of his favour, whom he hath selected, after all these changes and commotions, to stand upright and steadfast in his cause' (i.e., theirs).

A significant thing in the book is the doctrinaire's innocent admission of the Machiavellianism of the late proceedings. 'That is not always best which is most regular to written law. Great worthies heretofore, by disobeying law, ofttimes have saved the commonwealth; and the law afterward hath approved that planetary motion, that unblamable exorbitancy in them.' That was precisely Hitler's case in our time; it was then Cromwell's, with which the prophet of liberty and denouncer of tyranny identified himself. Indeed, 'a private conscience sorts not with a public calling'!

Politics has bitter ironies in store for revolutionaries, and history records them. Milton felt no need to give account of their actions to king or royalists, 'whom God hath made his conquerors'. 'We measure not our cause by our success, but our success by our cause. Yet certainly in a good cause success is a good confirmation. We are sure it argues not against us, but as much or more for us than ill success argues for them.'

That was all there was to it. In history it is the event, or the eventuality, that counts. This was what mattered to a practical politician like Cromwell: 'Look at circumstantials: they hang so together!' Victory, the way things had turned out, showed that God was with them. By the same token, 1660 showed that God was not with them. We may omit the intermediate term.

CHAPTER SEVEN

Milton on Monarchy and Himself

IN MARCH 1649 Milton had been given the job, by Cromwell's Council of State, of putting into shape their *Observations upon the Articles of Peace with the Irish Rebels*. With immense difficulty the King's representative in Ireland, the Marquis of Ormond, had brought about an alliance between some Irish Catholics, Anglican Royalists and Ulster Presbyterians against revolutionary England. The King had sought to bring Irish forces over to counter-balance the intervention of the Scots, but this had never been effective. His aim, however, had been one of the most damaging charges against him, for all Puritans hated the Catholic Irish, and indeed the Irish rebellion and killings of Scotch settlers in Ulster had fuelled the hysteria which led to the Civil War.

Where Ireland was concerned the Puritans were ruthless, and Cromwell expressed their views in action. The Irish have always blamed his ruthlessness upon the English in general – unfairly: they should ascribe it more properly to the Puritan mentality, which was inflicted upon the English too, though less inhumanly. The Puritans justified themselves by citing the Massacre. Irish historians minimise the event, and indeed Puritan hysteria greatly overestimated the numbers murdered. Milton says incredibly 200,000 – but 2000 or even 200 would be enough to set things off (though far less than those murdered in Ulster in our civilised day).

The King's lenity towards the Irish, his compromising attitude towards them, his civilised attitude towards Catholics opened him wide to Puritan misrepresentations, especially after Naseby, when his correspondence with them was found and published to incriminate him. But his attitude towards the

Irish was bound to be different from the Puritans': in his eyes the Irish were his subjects and he naturally wished to be humane and as sparing of their lives as of any other of his subjects.

The Puritans did not hesitate to charge him with connivance at the rebellion! The King's Book replies to this: 'some men took it very ill not to be believed when they affirmed that what the Irish did was done with my privity at least, if not by commission'. He returned the compliment, with more truth: 'certainly it is thought by many wise men that the preposterous rigour and unreasonable severity which some men carried before them in England was not the least incentive that kindled and blew up into those horrid flames the sparks of discontent. Which wanted not predisposed fuel for rebellion in Ireland, where despair being added to their former discontents, and the fears of utter extirpation to their wonted oppressions, it was easy to provoke to an open rebellion.'

This seems a fairer summing-up. Faced with superior force, the Irish resorted to their usual weapon of murder. If the English settlers objected, the reply of the native Irish was that Ireland was their island; and English uppishness has received its come-uppance only in our time.

At no point in his *Observations* does Milton consider the Irish point of view – as the King had done. We do not blame Milton, for he was merely carrying out the requirements of his job – though with complete conviction. Professor Max Patrick tells us that, in the letters Milton wrote for the Council of State to Hamburg at this same time, he wrote under the guidance of Henry Marten. A convinced Republican, Marten was a moving spirit of the new Commonwealth. We should add that, an addict of liberty in Milton's sense, he was also a libertine in others. He was a notorious whoremonger and atheist – pointed at as whoremaster by Cromwell when he sent his precious Rump of a Parliament packing four years later. No one regretted this action – on the contrary it was rather popular; but, truly, the irony of history makes queer bedmates, the virtuous Milton and the whoremongering Marten.

*

Driven into exile, the late King's son, now Charles II, called upon a scholar of international repute to put the case for his father before the public opinion of Europe. This was Claude de Saumaise, for many years professor at Leyden, most advanced and open-minded of universities; in November 1649 there appeared his *Defensio Regia*. Saumaise was an eminent Latinist, and the book, for European reading, was in Latin. The Council of State was highly perturbed; its summary execution of the King had shocked Europe, the new Republic was widely distrusted, its envoys liable to be murdered abroad. It tried to prevent copies of the book coming into England – liberty indeed! – its censorship was more effective than that of the Church had been; and during this very period, January 1651 to January 1652, the apostle of liberty, John Milton, was acting as censor. In January 1650 the Council ordered him to prepare a reply to the damaging strictures of Saumaise.

This was a proud moment in Milton's life. So far he had received little public attention, except as a notorious favourer of divorce, traduced indeed as a polygamist. His *Tenure of Kings and Magistrates* had attracted no attention from the public. Now was his chance to come on the European stage with a defence of the Republic he believed in, in Latin – and he was an even better Latinist than Saumaise. Milton loved controversy, and had been hitherto frustrated of fame: we can see with what joy he entered upon the conflict, ready to sacrifice his remaining eyesight for the sake of it. He regarded his *Pro Populo Anglicano Defensio* ('Defence of the English People'), which came out in 1651, as his chief public service.

God had given the English people victory, he begins; indeed, the way had 'been pointed out and made plain to us by God himself'. Nothing succeeds like success; we need hardly reiterate that military force had imposed the Republic against the will of the vast majority of the English people, and that if God had done it He reversed himself, and permanently, in 1660; the monarchy is still with us. We may exonerate the intermediate in the argument, God, from responsibility.

Milton himself rejoiced in the task that had now been allotted to him; 'as a single person he had but of late confuted and confounded the King himself – rising as it were from the grave – and with ease'. Now, 'my adversary's cause is maintained by nothing but fraud, fallacy, ignorance, and barbarity; whereas mine has light, truth, reason, the practice and learning of the best ages of the world, on its side'. It is hardly credible that anyone living in a free state – as Saumaise did in Holland – could censure the English for inflicting capital punishment upon a king; were they addicts of slavery, and what business was it of theirs, anyway, to interfere in English affairs? 'Nay, it is highly probable that all good men applauded us, and gave God thanks for so illustrious, so exalted a piece of justice – and for a caution so very useful to other princes.' Other princes indeed received the message, and opened their arms to Charles II; as for 'justice', few at the time had any illusions on the subject, and no one has today. Saumaise might well ask, 'by what law, by what right and justice?' Milton replies, 'by that law, I tell you, which God and nature have enacted, viz. that whatever things are for the universal good of the whole state are lawful and just'. But the point is: who is to decide? In 1649 it was merely force that had decided – certainly not the will of the people.

Milton found no difficulty over this, for he had no respect for the will of the people, any more than for their wishes or for what they were. 'I confess there are but few, and those men of great wisdom and courage [e.g., himself and Cromwell], that are either desirous of liberty or capable of using it. The greatest part of the world choose to live under masters.' We observe in Milton – no nonsense about democracy. The utmost he allows is that 'they would have them just ones'. And this is about right. It has its crucial application today. Democrats in countries like the United States and Britain make the mistake of for ever urging their models of democracy upon countries where they are totally inapplicable, Russia, for example, China, India, South America, Africa – in fact, most of the world. They would be more relevant to the facts if they accepted the necessity of authoritarian rule, people being what they are, and urged that such régimes should liberalise themselves a little.

Milton considered that 'a common wealth is a more perfect

form of government than a monarchy, and more suitable to the condition of mankind'. This is in contradiction to what Milton himself thought to be average human nature, of which he had a low view; events showed that monarchy was much more in keeping with it: the people preferred it. Milton, those genius was totally out of touch with ordinary human nature, asked: 'is there any people in the world that would not choose rather to live an honest and careful life, though never free from war and troubles, in the defence of themselves and their families, than under the power of a tyrant?'

The English people gave their answer, when freed from Cromwell and military dictatorship by his death. In 1660 they opted for the fun and frolics of the Restoration; Charles II was always popular, in spite of all his faults and failings. Never the Saints again! And such is the irony of history that Cromwell himself, Milton's hero, prepared the way for the return to monarchy by becoming Lord Protector in 1653, though himself would have preferred the title of king. The Army would not stand for it, and his rule rested upon the Army alone.

Twice, in the course of the book, the apostle of truth repeats again the wicked lie that Charles I had poisoned his father. 'Charles murdered both his prince and his father, and that by poison. For, to omit other evidences, he that would not suffer a duke that was accused for it to come to his trial, must needs have been guilty of it himself.' What an argument! We see what they had to put up with from odious Parliamentarians – Charles had refused to allow the indignity of such aspersions to be even discussed.

After this, it is difficult to take Milton's *Defence* seriously. Much of it is taken up by argy-bargy over the Old Testament and the treatment of their kings by the Jews, 'whom we suppose to have known most of the mind of God'. He gives full rein to the Puritan Bible mania – the book witnesses to his immense Biblical knowledge, as also of the classics. He is able to catch out the eminent French Latinist for several Gallicisms: this gives the English Latinist pedantic pleasure. He scores a debating point by quoting Saumaise' earlier views in favour of Presbyterianism. Better still, he scores over Saumaise' wife.

The poor fellow was under his wife's thumb; this gives Milton particular pleasure (which we can now appreciate psychologically) to rub in.

Professor Parker suggests that 'Milton never understood what another type of mind likes to call "avoiding personalities".' I suspect that he knew perfectly well, but enjoyed calling a fool a fool. The trouble was that Saumaise was no fool at all, even if he were a hen-pecked husband, and posterity may well conclude that he had the better case. Milton ended by calling upon Saumaise 'to make public repentance: I think the best course that you can take will be, for this long book that you have writ, to take a halter and make one long letter of yourself'. Milton, however, was incredibly pleased with himself and with attracting attention on the Continent. He was convinced that he had won a victory for himself and the Commonwealth.

He concluded his book with an eloquent address to the English people, whom he did not represent, which we may regard as a piece of Puritan chauvinism – the King, as a civilised person, had been more cosmopolitan in his tastes. God has 'gloriously delivered you, the first of nations, from the two greatest mischiefs of this life, tyranny and superstition'. We have seen what to think of Charles I's tyranny. With regard to superstition, we may say that under the tyranny of Charles I and Archbishop Laud there was, for example, no persecution for witchcraft – they were too civilised. With Puritanism in the ascendant the brutal and superstitious persecution of 'witches' received a boost, and scores of innocent old beldames were haled off for hanging.

Milton ends sublimely: God has endued the English to be 'the first of mankind' in putting to death their king. 'After the performing so glorious an action as this you ought . . . not so much to think of, much less to do, anything but what is great and sublime. You of all mankind are best able to subdue ambition, avarice, the love of riches, and can best avoid the corruptions that prosperity is apt to produce, which generally subdue and triumph over other nations.' Some hopes! as we shall see. Cromwell, in addition to his other large *traitements*, annexed to himself a large appanage in Ireland. John Milton said nothing about that, since the people 'have had larger experience of God's grace and favour than any other nation under heaven'.

For his work and his services Milton was awarded an apartment in the King's Palace of Whitehall, in Scotland Yard. This was convenient for supervising the government newspaper, under the editorship of Marchamont Needham. This sprightly young man, twelve years Milton's junior, needed watching, for he had been a Royalist. As a boy he had been a chorister at All Souls College, Oxford. Coming to London, he developed a marked journalistic talent, and started the *Mercurius Britannicus* on the Parliamentarian side to answer the King's *Mercurius Aulicus* edited at Oxford. In 1647 he changed to the Royalist side, to attack Cromwell with his large and potent red nose (he was a big fellow) as 'Copper Nose', 'Nose Almighty' and the 'Town Bull of Ely'. (Oliver, however, kept his favours for Mrs Cromwell.)

The Government pursued this irreverent young man, who lay hid with a Royalist clergyman, until he prudently changed sides again, was pardoned and given a salary to start the *Mercurius Politicus* and wage propaganda on behalf of the new government. Needham, with his record, was naturally in favour of toleration, and this drew Milton's sympathy to the apostate. Milton seems to have taken trouble with Marchamont; in any case, he found his most congenial companions among young men, from Charles Diodati and Carlo Dati onwards. Even in these bleak years there were not only his nephews, Edward and John Phillips, who remained close to him, but also young Edward Lawrence and Cyriack Skinner. Needham was attacked by the egregious John Goodwin, as 'of an infamous and unclean character, his foul mouth opened against the truth and mind of God', i.e., John Goodwin's.

Who was John Goodwin to talk? He was a brother Independent, which made his attack the more vexing. A Cambridge man, as vicar of St Stephen's, Coleman Street, he had given trouble to good Bishop Juxon. His inflammatory sermons had incited to war against the King. He went on to attack the Presbyterians as persecutors, which they were. In return

Goodwin was aspersed by the Presbyterian Edwards – the miscreant even went to bowls, if not on the Sabbath, at least on days of thanksgiving. As a good Independent Goodwin defended Pride's Purge, and the extreme measures of the army leaders. He had the insolence to offer his spiritual services to the King they had condemned to death. He was constantly engaged in controversy with everybody: Calamy, a fellow Saint, described him as 'a man by himself, was against every man, and had every man against him'. Goodwin claimed that he 'had to contend in a manner with the whole earth' – in consequence he left a large body of railing writings on nonsense theological subjects.

In one of these, a row with Obadiah Home, he expressed himself as a trifle uncertain whether the Trinity was a necessary truth. This was enough to earn from the dreadful Francis Cheynell the insult of 'sneaking Socinian', which meant that he was nearer to common sense on the subject. Common sense, however, was heresy in these matters, and Milton, as licenser for the press, got into trouble for licensing the Racovian Catechism, which expressed doubts about the Trinity and other such doctrines. Milton was had up before the Council, and could plead only that these were his own convictions. The Independents themselves brought the matter before Parliament, as much as was left of it. The protest was headed by Cromwell's chaplain, John Owen, whom he forked into the Deanery of Christ Church, in place of the Presbyterian Reynolds, who had been forked into it by the Long Parliament, in place of its proper occupant, Dean Fell. Even Cromwell's purged Parliament, a small assembly of less than a hundred, was horrified at such disbelief, and condemned the offending Catechism to be publicly burned as 'blasphemous, erroneous, and scandalous'. Nothing happened to Milton, whose services, especially in Latin, were useful; but he does not appear as licenser again.

This is the perspective in which to see his sonnet of this year, 1652, addressed 'To the Lord General Cromwell'. Much of what Milton wrote is personally motivated: he winced into print at what affected him. Disappointed of a career in the

Church, however conscientiously, he attacked the Church and
the prelates; disappointed in marriage, he erupted into the
divorce tracts; offended by the Presbyterians and the Westminster Assembly, he pursued them with insults.

Now his hope lay in Cromwell:

> Cromwell, our chief of men, who through a cloud
>   Not of war only but detractions rude,
>   Guided by faith and matchless fortitude
> To peace and truth thy glorious way hast ploughed.

We know by now that 'truth' means Milton's idea of truth; but
'peace'! . . . Cromwell had ploughed his way through shattering
campaigns, against the Scots, against the Irish, against the
King and lastly against the King's son, Charles II. These
decimating campaigns and bloody battles are celebrated by the
peace-loving Milton as

> God's trophies and His work pursued,
> While Darwen stream with blood of Scots imbrued,
> And Dunbar field resounds thy praises loud,
> And Worcester's laureate wreath. . . .

The victory at Worcester Cromwell regarded, in the religious
language of Puritans, as 'the crowning mercy', i.e., from God.
It was in fact an easy victory over inferior forces.

Milton now reminds his hero, in a phrase to become famous,
that

> peace hath her victories
> No less renowned than war.

There were the members of Cromwell's Parliament who,
though purged to make them pure (or, rather, to kill the King),
were still

> Threatening to bind our souls with secular chains.

Milton now called upon the great man to

> Help us to save free conscience from the paw
> Of hireling wolves whose gospel is their maw.

There was no need to; since Cromwell depended for his power upon the Army, which pullulated with Independents, he was bound, as a practical politician, to support toleration for the sects – though this did not include Anglicans, the majority of the nation, or (of course) Catholics.

The phrasing of the sonnet reminds us of 'Lycidas'. Then it was the Anglican clergy who

> for their bellies' sake
> Creep and intrude, and climb into the fold.

Well, clergymen have bellies to fill as well as anyone else. And then

> the grim wolf with privy paw

was Rome. Now it was the Presbyterians who were the 'hireling wolves'.

It was impossible to satisfy John Milton. I suspect that, unknown to himself, he was at war with the facts of life and his own nature.

Something of this, of the insatiable desire for self-justification, transpires through the second *Defence* he indited. There was no need for it. Saumaise had died in 1653, and was not there to carry on the controversy. Nor was there anything more to say on the subject – except what John Milton had to say about himself. The main interest, almost the sole interest, of the second *Defence* is autobiographical.

The first *Defensio* had made Milton's name known on the Continent at last, though by no means so favourably as he imagined. People were perhaps struck by the unexpectedness of a defence of such shocking proceedings, the daring and aggressive conviction behind it, let alone by so good a scholar, in eloquent Latin. Foreign visitors coming to London naturally

wanted to see the intellectual Secretary for the Foreign Tongues, now going blind. One of them saw him standing respect-
fully behind the seated Keeper of the Seal, the 'Lord'
Whitelocke. After all, he was a mere civil servant, who had no
part or lot in policy; his nephew reports that he was 'a stranger
to their private counsels'. Did he even know Cromwell? Milton
cannot have liked the war forced on the Dutch this year – 'peace
hath her victories no less renowned than war'! The Dutch were
a people both Protestant and free; but war with them was
popular with the commercial and maritime interests (in spite of
their Puritanism), and naval victories appealed to patriotism
on behalf of the revolutionary régime. War strengthened its
hold, as with the French Revolution in 1792 and the Bolsheviks
successfully repelling intervention after the Russian Revolution.

In April 1653 Cromwell sent what was left of 'Parliament'
packing. Having learnt nothing and forgotten nothing – in spite
of having been purged by Cromwell once before – this Rump of
a Parliament sought to perpetuate its own existence. They had
been there, those of them who had survived, since 1640. Cromwell had been a member through all vicissitudes, hence his
double power, military and political. He now descended on
them, listened to their nonsense for a while, then: 'The hour is
come, the Lord [i.e., Cromwell] hath done with you.' At their
protest: 'Come, come, we have had enough of this; I will end
your prating. Get you gone – you are no longer a Parliament.'
Stamping his foot, he called in his soldiers to clear the House.

Charles I had done nothing like it when he called on the
House to surrender the Five M.P.s in 1640. The last shred of
constitutional continuity – there never had been any legality in
the revolutionary proceedings – was gone. The Council of
Officers made Cromwell Lord Protector: sheer military
dictatorship. The apostle of liberty never made any protest.
Cromwell's *coup* was popular rather than not: the people had no
use for the Rump of a Parliament. But Milton, like other
revolutionaries, was now disillusioned with the people: 'an
ungrateful and perverse generation'.

There was no reply from Saumaise, for the poor man had

been in failing health and had suffered some loss of favour with his patron, Queen Christina. Milton was able to claim a victory and dance a war-dance over his dead body, when another opponent raised his head. This was an Anglican clergyman, Peter du Moulin, who wrote the anonymous *Regii Sanguinis Clamor* ('The Cry of the King's Blood to Heaven'). Since du Moulin was a Royalist he attacked Milton as bitterly as Milton had Saumaise: for once Milton got as good as he gave. But he never knew whence the blow came. Du Moulin had sent his manuscript to Saumaise who – ill and with no heart for controversy – turned it over to Alexander More to publish. More was a good scholar and practised theologian, half Scot, half French, living abroad; he published the *Clamor*, but he had not written it.

The real culprit was living quietly at Oxford. The funny thing was that Milton must have known his brother, Lewis du Moulin, a fellow Independent and Commonwealthman, who began a Latin translation of *Eikonoklastes*, but did not go on with it. Not a breath reached Milton as to the real author of the attack on him; he thought it was More, and replied in kind.

More exposed an Achilles Heel: unmarried, he had a weakness for women. This was mother's milk to Milton, who had no such weakness. Pages of the second *Defence* are devoted to More's ways with servant-girls, Latin jokes on the word *morus* ('mulberry') about giving the wife of a colleague a little mulberry, even a Latin couplet complete with word-play about her pregnancy, well translated by Parker:

> Who will deny, O Pontia expanded,
> You bear a little more than More demanded?

A great many insults were added – More was a goat of a pastor, a corrupter of maid-servants, a mass of impurity, a lecher, a scoundrel, a perjurer – all under the misapprehension that More had attacked him. The more the poor man protested his innocence and tried to defend his good name, the more Milton enjoyed pillorying his failings in regard to the fair sex. Even when the Dutch ambassador informed Milton that More was not the author, he took the line, according to Aubrey, that 'that was all one; he [Milton] having writ it, it should go to the world: one of them was as bad as the other', i.e., More was as bad as Saumaise. No doubt Milton was proud of his powers in vituperative Latin and unwilling to sacrifice what he had written. One can sympathise with his holding the claims of literature to be superior to mere human considerations, but it comes ill from an apostle of truth. Was it that the incursion of women into the argument diverted Milton, that it touched a special nerve in him?

The second *Defence* throws a good deal of light upon him. 'The praise of beauty I am not anxious to obtain' – he cannot have liked being called the 'Lady of Christ's', nor was the open admiration of his youthful looks by civilised Italians welcome to a Puritan prig. 'My stature is not tall, but it rather approaches the middle than the diminutive. Yet what if it were diminutive when so many men, illustrious in peace and war, have been the same? And how can that be called diminutive which is great enough for every virtuous achievement? Nor, though very thin, was I ever deficient in courage or in strength; and I was wont constantly to exercise myself in the use of the broadsword. . . . Armed with this weapon, as I usually was, I should have thought myself quite a match for anyone, though much stronger than myself.'

So we see, he was below average height and thin, a little man, still youthful in appearance: 'though I am more than forty years old, there is scarcely anyone to whom I do not appear ten years younger than I am, and the smoothness of my skin is not in the least affected by the wrinkles of age'. There is a suspicious note in all this: not only has Milton to be always right but he cannot bear to recognise that he is beholden to anyone. We have noticed that again and again; every cranny and crevice is stopped up. Psychologically the case is obvious: nothing more esoteric than an inferiority complex over-compensating itself aggressively. And this is particularly noticeable in regard to his attitude to women.

Though well equipped and practised with the broadsword, 'I did not participate in the toils or dangers of the war, yet I was at the same time engaged in a service not less hazardous to myself and more beneficial to my fellow-citizens; nor in the adverse turns of our affairs did I ever betray any symptoms of pusil-lanimity, or show myself more afraid than became me of malice or of death.' What exquisite priggery, worthy of a better aes-thete! 'For since from my youth I was devoted to the pursuits of literature, and my mind has always been stronger than my body, I did not court the labours of a camp, in which any common person would have been of more service than myself, but resorted to that employment in which my exertions were likely to be of most avail.'

No, indeed, the labours of a camp were good enough for any common person, though persons of gifts far above the common lost their lives in the senseless struggle: on the King's side, the philosophic Falkland; his friend Chillingworth, the philosopher-theologian; William Lawes, the most original genius among composers of the time; the best among English painters, Dobson; poets like Cartwright, who died of camp-fever at Oxford, for whom the sensitive King went into mourning, and Sidney Godolphin, more diminutive than Milton, who sacrificed his life nevertheless, in whose memory Hobbes dedicated *Leviathan* to his brother; and, on Parlia-ment's side, John Hampden, the great trumpet of liberty, who had done so much to bring the conflict on. We do not blame Milton for not fighting; though we may regard the action of Hobbes as still more sensible, leaving the silly country to fight it out, to return when it was over: 'I had a mind to go home' – between Milton's first *Defence* and the second.

The little man was inordinately proud of his achievement with the first, for which the Republic was sufficiently grateful. He was glad 'to be born at a time when the virtue of my fellow-citizens, far exceeding that of their progenitors in greatness of soul and vigour of enterprise – having invoked Heaven to wit-ness the justice of their cause and been clearly governed by its directions – has succeeded in delivering the commonwealth from the most grievous tyranny and religion from the most ignominious degradation'. Very well – and how long would this state of exaltation last? Long before 1660 the people had had enough of it – witness Milton's disillusionment with them and denunciation of their calumnies against the revolution's achievements, 'as is usual with the vulgar'.

He had been called upon to put this right: 'I, who was neither deemed unequal to so renowned an adversary [Saumaise], nor to so great a subject, was particularly selected by the deliverers of our country, and by the general suffrage of the public, openly to vindicate the rights of the English nation, and consequently of liberty itself.' We begin to sicken at the reiteration of the word 'liberty', when Milton identifies himself with military dictatorship. Facts are all in all in history, and only power decides. However, 'I did not disappoint the hopes nor the opinions of my fellow-citizens, while men of learning and eminence abroad honoured me with unmingled approbation, while I obtained such a victory over my opponent.'

We can only gasp at such assurance, and register that Milton was so remarkable an individual, so much of a doctrinaire, as to be completely out of touch with what humans are like. Though he had not fought in the war, he had had his own triumph against 'Salmasius or Salmasia, for to which sex he belonged is a matter of uncertainty': he had died in doubt and some disrepute. 'Hence, while I applaud those who were victorious in the field, I will not complain of the province which was assigned me, but rather congratulate myself upon it – and thank the Author of all good for having placed me in a station, which may be an object of envy to others rather than of regret to myself. . . . I experienced singular marks of the divine regard, that in topics of the highest concern, the most connected with the exigencies of my country and the most beneficial to civil and religious *liberty*, the supreme wisdom and beneficence had invigorated and enlarged my faculties to defend the dearest interests, not merely of one people but of the whole human race against the enemies of liberty.'

We must make some allowance for the absurd conventions of Latin rhetoric, but all the same this is insupportable. We can only think that, of the innumerable admirers of the Milton of the early poems, few can have read the Milton of the prose works – the other, and not less authentic, side to him. As to his service to the whole human race in propounding his kind of liberty, highly ethical and high-minded as it was, history seems to show that, by and large, the human race attaches less importance to liberty than to material welfare – witness Communist Russia or China, Mrs Gandhi's India or black Africa.

The second *Defence* is remarkable for its adulation of the dictator – this is what Milton's liberty had come to, this is what fanaticism and doctrinairism lead to. After a laudatory account of Cromwell's descent 'from a noble and illustrious house' (Laud had been a clothier's son), he became 'a soldier superbly trained in self-knowledge' – this is precisely what may be doubted of the great man, whether he was aware of his motives, since all was from the Lord, etc. He had 'first routed or forced into submission every inward enemy such as vain hopes, fears and desires' – this also may be doubted: Cromwell was a man of ruthless ambition who, like Milton, identified his own unconscious with God, and 'no man goes further than he who knows not whither he goes'. 'There bloomed in him such strength or will or intellect, or such control of discipline, applied not only to strategy but even more to Christian conduct and holiness, that from everywhere he drew to his camp, as to the finest training ground of military science as well as religion and piety, all the good and brave men – or he made them good and brave.'

We need not object to this – there is no doubt about the greatness of Oliver Cromwell. But what about the flattery of monarchs? There is no such flattery of anyone in those we can respect more – Hobbes, or Selden, or Samuel Butler. Cromwell was all Milton had left to repose hope in. 'Think how dear a thing is that liberty which the country gave to you [!] for protection and safekeeping. What it once expected from the choicest men of the whole nation, it now expects from you alone and through you alone hopes to pursue. . . . Go on therefore, Cromwell, in your wonted magnanimity – your country's deliverer, the founder of our liberty, and at the same time its Protector[!]'. This is what all the brave hopes of the Puritan Revolution had come to – as all the brave hopes of the 1917 Revolution, of international peace and the brotherhood of men, the 'withering away' of the state (according to Marx), have ended in a far more brutal tyranny than ever before, all geared to armaments for nuclear war.

Cromwell had yet one more war in prospect – against Spain, for imperialist expansion in the West Indies (the Puritans were the imperialists). All that 'liberty' had come to mean in Milton's mouth was the liberty of the individual religious conscience, for what that was worth to average humanity. It meant everything to Milton; but, then, he was so very far removed from average humanity. His hopes of Cromwell were thus expressed: 'I wish you would leave the church to the church, and would prudently relieve yourself and the magistrates from that burden which now constitutes one half of your power and is most incompatible with it.'

Cromwell was a practical politician who knew that power was indivisible – and he was not throwing away any of it. Personally more open-minded and politically more shrewd than Presbyterian stiffnecks, he made himself agreeable to individual sectarians like George Fox, but kept religion on as Erastian a basis as ever, continuing the tithe system in full operation as its support – he did not consider any other was practically possible, and rightly. Milton recommended him also to have particular care of 'the education and morals of our youth. I hope that you feel it unjust that the clever and the slow, the diligent and the idle, are brought up at the state's expense. May you rather put aside the scholar's rewards for those already earned and well deserving of them.' Milton, himself one of the clever and diligent, seeing things from his own point of view as usual, did not favour misdirecting the state's resources into the education of the not very educable, the great majority.

As the result of the Puritan Revolution, 'others, without labour or desert, got possession of honours and emoluments; but no one ever knew me soliciting anything myself or through the medium of my friends, ever beheld me in a supplicating posture at the doors of the senate, or the levees of the great'. As is apt to happen in the course of revolution, some people had made fortunes; not so Milton. 'I usually kept myself secluded at home, where my own property – part of which had been withheld during the civil commotions and part of which had been absorbed in the oppressive contributions which I had to sustain

– afforded me a scanty subsistence.'

Milton's father had made a decent fortune by his scrivening and usury, the son a bourgeois of independent means. But the Civil War had meant very heavy taxation: Charles I's Ship Money, about which so much fuss had been made, was chicken-feed compared with the far more efficient and heavy excise system imposed by 'King' Pym. Milton might have quoted Holy Writ on the matter: 'my father chastised you with whips, but I will chastise you with scorpions'. He must now have found his official salary, some £288 a year, a boon; when he was no longer able to fulfil his duties, he received a pension of £200 a year (multiply by perhaps thirty for contemporary value). He was well rewarded for his services. The Puritans rewarded themselves well – better than the King had been able to pay his servants, with funds withheld from him.

The misunderstanding with regard to More – which was of Milton's own making – continued. Milton shows up in a bad light, since he had known before publishing the second *Defence* that More was not the author of the *Clamor*. This was provoking, for it enabled the traduced More to score – in spite of his weakness for women. More's rebuttal, *Fides Publica*, according to Professor Parker, was 'an exasperating performance from Milton's point of view. Its tone was righteous indignation, and Milton was a convicted liar. . . . Having accused More of the authorship of the *Clamor*, Milton was unable to drop the argument.'[1]

Obstinate as ever – and rigid obstinacy of an almost psychotic character was a marked element in it – Milton indited yet a third defence, a *Defence of Himself*. It was quite unnecessary: all he had to say was that he had been wrong. This John Milton was unable to do about anything. Why? It offers an interesting psychological problem. Professor Mulder tells us that the second *Defence* 'was not nearly so widely read as the first', while the third, 'more than any other, reveals Milton's gift for venomous satire. . . . The *Defence of Himself* is largely *argumentum ad hominem*, an attack on the character of the opponent.'[2] Milton had got hold of more stories in the interim – the pamphlet was published in 1655 – about More's morals: his man-servant must have been talking. He describes 'with gusto a brawl between More and Pontia; he names the woman with whom More became involved' in the holy city of Geneva. Really, it is not worth going into.

It is true that other people equally misrepresented Milton. When the sainted Roger Williams of New England wrote recommending *Eikonoklastes* to the virtuous Mrs Sadleir, she replied: 'if I be not mistaken, this is he that has wrote a book of the lawfulness of divorce and, if report says true, he had at that time two or three wives living. This perhaps were good doctrine in New England, but it is most abominable in Old England.'[3] This was an unfair sally, and an uncharitable aspersion among Saints; for Mrs Sadleir was the aunt of Milton's young friend, Cyriack Skinner, and should have known better.

A foreign envoy, Henry Oldenburg, who was on friendly terms with Milton, had a more useful reaction than this feminine one. He questioned Milton's attribution of the scathing *Clamor* to More – rightly as we know – and criticised the argument of the second *Defence*. He ventured to suggest that Milton was wasting his time and had bettter things to do.

He had indeed. Not the least surprising thing about him is that he was prepared to take such a risk in postponing his great epic, not even yet making proper use of

That one talent which is death to hide.

Suppose if he had not lived on to fulfil himself and his genius in *Paradise Lost, Paradise Regained* and *Samson Agonistes?* What a loss that would have been to our literature, among its grandest works! We might even have had a projected Arthurian epic, or British tragedy, instead of the wastes of prose controversy.

The more attractive side of Milton is to be seen in the few sonnets he wrote in these years to friends; evidently he was responsive to young men, and they found him sympathetic. Here is Edward Lawrence, then about twenty or twenty-one (he was only twenty-four when he died, in 1656). Milton invites him one winter to 'help waste a sullen day' by his fireside, and

What neat repast shall feast us, light and choice,

> Of Attic taste, with wine, whence we may rise
> To hear the lute well-touched, or artful voice
> Warble immortal notes and Tuscan air?

Then the moralist steps in:

> He who of those delights can judge, and spare
> To interpose them oft, is not unwise.

Cyriack Skinner was another young man whom Milton chose to frolic with (temperately):

> Today deep thoughts resolve with me to drench
> In mirth that, after, no repenting draws;
> Let Euclid rest and Archimedes pause,
> And what the Swede intend, and what the French.

This was the nearest that Milton ever got to humour – and how pleasant a change it is! For one single day, 'when God sends a cheerful hour', they were to refrain from care.

The times were not cheerful, in those days of fanatic religious war, when theological foolery ran rife, and men killed each other for their mutually exclusive beliefs, each certain that his were absolute truth. In 1655 there came the massacre of the Swiss Protestants, the Vaudois, at the hands of Savoy. At this horror Milton's doctrine took wing and soared into poetry: for once doctrine and poetry fused into one, forecasting the grander glories to come:

> Avenge, O Lord, thy slaughtered Saints. . . .

In my day we all learned it at school. We did not appreciate the reference to medieval England:

> When all our fathers worshipped stocks and stones.

Nor did we reflect, any more than John Milton did, that this was the England that created Salisbury Cathedral.

CHAPTER EIGHT

The Puritan Collapse

PURITAN rule in England fell essentially with Cromwell's death on 3 September 1658 – the day of his 'crowning mercy' – though it took another twenty months before its visible bankruptcy brought back the King and restored the old order to the English people, after 'all the miseries that had overwhelmed them these twenty years'. These are the words of the poet Cowley – whom Milton *par exception* admired – and a perceptive observer of events outside the main stream, in retirement in the country.

In his penetrating *Discourse concerning the Government of Oliver Cromwell* Cowley diagnosed then, as historians have done subsequently, that Cromwell was fortunate in the time of his demise, as in practically everything he touched. It is doubtful if even he could have held up much longer, against the whole weight of the governing class, which had been so idiotic as to divide within itself and fight a civil war – with what results! It had ended in the rule of a small minority, supported by a large army, the expense of which was intolerable. What could have been sillier than 'to take arms against taxes of scarce £200,000 a year [Ship Money] and to raise them to above £2 millions? to quarrel for the loss of three or four ears [Prynne's, Burton's, Bastwick's – they should have been stifled rather], and strike off three or four hundred heads? to fight against an imaginary suspicion of 2,000 guards to be fetched for the King, and to keep up for himself [Cromwell] no less than 40,000? to pretend the defence of Parliaments, and violently to dissolve all even of his own calling and almost choosing?'[1]

What tragic lunacy it had been! and now the play was almost over, with the breath out of the dictator's body. But not quite, for he had left his throne to a son, Richard, as if he were sovereign of a dynasty – and indeed the hero of the republican Milton would have preferred to make himself king. Nor had the Puritan dictator favoured the separation of church and state so dear to Milton. In this Milton was disappointed in his hero, as he was disappointed in all his expectations – though he disingenuously kept silent: the Puritan cause was everything. Now it was falling about his ears.

Its rule could never in the nature of things have been permanent in England, whatever success it had in uncivil Scotland. Cowley saw – as indeed the few clear-eyed did, Clarendon and Hobbes above all – what a rôle chance had played in the catastrophe. In the common language of the day Cowley names this God: 'it is God that breaks up the flood-gates of so general a deluge, and all the art then and industry of mankind is not sufficient to raise up dykes and ramparts against it. . . . The valour and prudent counsels of the one side are made fruitless, and the errors and cowardice on the other harmless, by unexpected accidents.' Falkland must have felt this bitterly when he flung his life away – at thirty-two! – on the field of Newbury.

There had been no permanence, even when Parliament won so complete a victory. 'First, because he [God or Chance] has suffered nothing to settle or take root in the place of that which hath been so unwisely and unjustly removed. . . . For when the indisposed and long-tormented commonwealth has wearied and spent itself with the chargeable, various and dangerous experiments of several mountebanks, it is to be supposed it will have the wit at last to send for a true physician – especially when it sees that no usurpation can be kept up without open force, nor force without the continuance of those oppressions upon the people, which will at last tire out their patience, though it be great even to stupidity. They cannot be so dull, when poverty and hunger begins to whet their understanding as not to find out this no extraordinary mystery, that 'tis madness in a nation to pay £3 millions a year for the maintaining of their servitude under tyrants, when they might live free for nothing under their princes.'

The cost of the régime had gone up enormously with Cromwell's last imperialist war against Spain, and the unsuccessful attack on the West Indies. Charles I had – after his youthful mistakes – adhered to a peace policy: it was part of the furious Puritan case against him that he did not intervene in the Thirty Years' War on the side of Protestantism abroad. (He had sensibly left the undertaking to Gustavus Adolphus.)

Cowley was well aware of Cromwell's extraordinary achievement in taking the throne of his master. He put it down to a combination of dynamic energy and unwearied diligence, his courage and superior abilities, and to his dissimulation – when we should say his gifts as a politician. 'I know not what you can produce for the justification of his parts in this kind but his having been able to deceive so many particular persons and so many whole parties.' Hitler indeed made the motto of *Mein Kampf*, 'The German people have no idea of how they have to be gulled in order to be led' – which was dropped in 1932 when he was within sight, backed by the Army, of coming into power.

So with Cromwell. 'Good God! What have we seen? and what have we suffered? . . . To omit the whole reign of our late King (till the beginning of the war) in which no drop of blood was ever drawn but from two or three ears, I think the longest time of our worst princes scarce saw so many more executions than the short one of our blest Reformer.' Well before the end, people – even apart from the hostile majority of the nation – were weary of him and his antics. 'I believe his seasonable dying to have been a greater good fortune to him than all the victories and prosperities of his life. For he seemed evidently to be near the end of his deceitful glories: his own Army grew at last as weary of him as the rest of the people.'

Cowley regarded disingenuousness as simply dissimulation: 'if craft be wisdom and dissimulation wit [i.e., intelligence], assisted both with hypocrisies and perjuries, I must not deny him to have been singular in both; but so gross was the manner in which he made use of them that, as wise men ought not to have believed him at first, so no man was fool enough to believe him at last'. This was rather hard on Cromwell, but the circumstances of a revolution had so often put him in the position of having to break his word, though with 'his usual familiarity with Almighty God', as Clement Walker put it. Upon occasion Cromwell had protested to the House of Commons 'with his hand upon his breast "In the presence of Almighty God" before whom he stood that he knew the Army would disband and lay down their arms at their door whensoever they should command them' – and, instead, the Army had put through a purge of Parliament.

As a man of taste Cowley naturally detested Cromwell's Puritan language and posturings, which had been such a factor in his appeal to people who liked such things: 'I must confess that by these arts, how grossly soever managed, as by hypocritical praying and silly preaching, by unmanly tears and whinings, by falsehoods and perjuries even diabolical he had at first the good fortune to attain his ends. But it was because his ends were so unreasonable that no human reason could foresee them: which made them who had to do with him believe that he was rather a well-meaning and deluded bigot than a crafty and malicious impostor.' As for what a Cromwell might think of a Milton, Cowley has a remark much to the point. 'I am glad you allow me at least artful dissimulation and unwearied diligence in my hero. . . . But I see you are a pedant and Platonical statesman, a theoretical Commonwealth's-man, an Utopian dreamer.'

It is of more value and immediacy to cite the insights of men of genius at the time than academic discussion three hundred years later. Hobbes's diagnosis was wholly without illusions, since he regarded both sides as fools for fighting a war. (Even Clarendon, a participant, thought that the cause was 'too good to have been fought for'.)

Hobbes, like Cowley, allows a considerable element to chance and to mistaken estimates on both sides – so large an element in the causation of all wars. Parliament was so strong in 1641–2, the King so weak, that they thought that he could never raise a party to fight for him. Then there were the inexhaustible resources of London: 'but for the City Parliament never could have made the war, nor the Rump ever have murdered the King'. As for the people, 'there were very few of the common people that cared much for either of the causes, but would have taken any side for pay or plunder'. Here was one point on which Hobbes and Milton were agreed. (Myself, I should regard the people's attitude as rather sensible.) Milton respected Hobbes's intellect, though the idealist deplored the realist's conclusions. On 'liberty', for example, Milton's fixation: Hobbes drew the correct conclusion from their view of the people – as Milton did not – that 'to obey the laws is the prudence of a subject: for without such obedience the commonwealth, which is every subject's safety and protection, cannot subsist'.[2]

The Civil War proved that to be all too true; Hobbes regarded the whole period, 1640–60, as yielding 'a prospect of all kinds of injustice and of all kinds of folly that the world could afford, and how they were produced by their hypocrisy and self-conceit, whereof the one is double iniquity and the other double folly'. Neither Hobbes no Milton could be accused of hypocrisy, but we appreciate now to what folly Milton's Puritan doctrinairism led him.

Both were agreed as to the unbearable spirit of the Presbyterians and the incitement of the preachers – we have seen that Milton condemned their hypocrisy even more strongly than Hobbes. 'Presbyterians are everywhere the same: they would fain be absolute governors of all they converse with, and where they reign it is God that reigns, and nowhere else. . . . The mischief proceeded wholly from the Presbyterian preachers who, by a long-practised histrionic faculty, preached up the rebellion powerfully.' Milton had come to admit this, after his bitter disillusionment with the Westminster Assembly. This shows up in turn the hollowness, apart from the indecency, of his earlier attacks on the moderate prelates, Ussher and Hall, on behalf of the Presbyterians of Smectymnuus. Not that the Independents were any better, as Hobbes says: 'the Presbyterian ministers throughout the whole war instigated the people against the King; so did also Independents and other fanatic ministers'.

Hobbes perceived that 'it is easier to gull the multitude than any one man amongst them'. A single individual is liable to know his own interest, and even to recognise a small fact when he sees one. That genius of political propaganda in our time, Adolf Hitler, early grasped the fatal significance of this: tell a man a small lie and he may not believe you; tell the idiot people a big enough lie and there is nothing they will not believe (the Stab-in-the-Back lie, that Germany was not defeated in 1918, that everybody but Germany was responsible for the war of 1914 and again in 1939, etc., etc.).

Hobbes comments, 'the common people have been, and always will be, ignorant of their duty to the public, as never meditating anything but their particular interest; in other things following their immediate leaders. If you think the late miseries have made them wiser, that will quickly be forgot, and then we shall be no wiser than we were.' We see this to be no less true today, with the people at large, led by the trade unions, incapable of 'meditating anything but their particular interest', ruining what is now their own show, making it impossible to operate, while 'following their immediate leaders' (today shop-stewards). Milton was at one with Hobbes in his view of the idiocy of the people in general; from this Hobbes – like Shake-speare – drew the correct conclusion, that they were incapable of liberty, or, at any rate, much of it. Fortunately for them, they do not greatly value it; only to a Milton is it all in all. Very well, admit it for the Miltons of this world, but do not generalise from the elect to people in general.

Hobbes comments, 'what silly things are the common sort of people, to be cozened as they were so grossly!' He then asks pertinently, were their betters any better? 'What sort of people, as to this matter, are not of the common sort? The craftiest knaves of all the Rump were no wiser than the rest whom they cozened. For the most of them did believe that the same things which they imposed upon the generality were just and reasonable; and especially the great haranguers [e.g., for today, practitioners of political humbug], and such as pretend to learning', e.g., today's economic 'experts'. How, then, were people so misadvised? Hobbes pointed to the university educa-tion of the time which brought up the leaders of society in the classics, with their adulation of republicanism and antipathy to monarchy. 'And out of these men were chosen the greatest part of the House of Commons; or, if they were not the greatest part, yet by advantage of their eloquence, they were always able to sway the rest.'

We can appreciate the pertinence of this diagnosis today, when again we observe the protagonists of our society in dissolution brought up in theoretical discussion at still more universities, with little appreciation of productive enterprise or much capacity for operating anything. The sharp eye of Hobbes observed the part played by envy in the Puritan Revolution: 'that men of ancient wealth and nobility [e.g., Lord Saye and Sele, 'Old Subtlety'] are not able to brook that poor scholars [e.g., Laud, the clothier's son] should – as they must when they are made bishops – be their fellows'. Power was what they had fought for: there was no justice in the matter, especially no social justice, which Laud cared for more than any Puritan magnate. 'A great many gentlemen did no less desire a popular government in the civil state than these ministers did in the Church.' As for the commercial middle class, 'those great capital cities, when rebellion is upon pretence of grievances, must needs be of the rebel party: because the grievances are but taxes, to which citizens, i.e. merchants, whose profession is their private gain, are naturally mortal enemies – their only glory being to grow excessively rich by the wisdom of buying and selling'. But do they not set the working class on work? Yes, Hobbes answers, 'by making poor people sell their labour to them at their own prices'.

No wonder Hobbes, the poor clergyman's son, is more admired by Marxists than is Milton, the son of the successful scrivener who made a substantial fortune out of usury. Hobbes knew the facts of life better than the spoiled Benjamin who was given such a careful bringing-up by his adoring parent. Milton was left, and always remained, financially independent; it is not without significance that his foremost exponent today shares the background and mentality of the Nonconformist middle class.

In the end, out of his career of progressive disillusionments – after such exceptionally favoured beginnings – Milton emerged with hardly anything positive to offer but liberty to read and interpret the Scriptures. Here also he was not so much at fault as in contradiction, once more, with what he now knew to be the truth about human beings. Hobbes drew the logical conclusion: they were no more fit to interpret Scripture than they were for liberty. 'After the Bible was translated into English, every man – nay, every boy and wench – that could read English, thought they spoke with God Almighty, and understood what he said.' Hence the ludicrous absurdities of the sects that proliferated, like scum rising to the surface in the turmoil. Hobbes names some of these poor fools; 'others that held that Christ's kingdom was at this time to begin upon the earth were called Fifth Monarchy men; besides divers other sects, as Quakers, Adamites, etc. whose names and peculiar doctrines I do not well remember'.

Some of these men were dangerous to society. For example, Harrison the regicide, Cromwell's right-hand man in driving on the murder of the King, was a Fifth Monarchy man. Born a butcher's son, he had not much education but was very self-confident in interpreting Holy Writ. Baxter, who had after all the advantage of being in orders, observed with distaste Harrison's manic raptures in battle. He was a furious fighter. At the capture and destruction of wonderful Basing House – now but a tumbled mound – Harrison 'slew one Robinson', son to the door-keeper of Shakespeare's Blackfriars, and 'the Marquis's major, with his own hands, as they were getting over the works'. The story was that Robinson was surrendering, when Harrison shot him, saying 'Cursed is he that doeth the work of the Lord negligently.'

Harrison urged on Cromwell the calling of Praise-God Barebone's Parliament, after the model of the Jewish Sanhedrin. Roger Williams, who could hardly agree with himself for long – an acquaintance of Milton – described Harrison then as 'the second in the nation of late . . . he is a very gallant, most deserving, heavenly man. But most high-flown for the kingdom of the Saints, and the Fifth Monarchy now risen, and their sun never to set again.' Harrison went into opposition on Cromwell's becoming Lord Protector: 'Oliver P.' ('What if a man should take it upon him to become king?') The pragmatic Protector several times imprisoned his former friend. At the Restoration the regicide met with equanimity the fate he so richly deserved, justifying all he had done 'in the service of so glorious and great a God. I did it all according to the best of my understanding, desiring to make the revealed will of God in his holy Scriptures a guide to me.'

Such were the consequences, for some, of allowing uneducated persons to interpret Holy Writ; upon others the results were merely ludicrous. Hobbes summed up the effect in the political field: 'these were the enemies which arose against his Majesty from the private interpretation of Scripture, exposed to every man's scanning in his mother tongue'. The truth of the matter had been succinctly expressed before the Civil War by the admirable Anglican, John Hales, in his 'Abuses of Hard Places of Scripture': 'there are in Scripture of things that are seemingly confused, carrying semblance of contrariety, anachronisms, metachronisms and the like, which brings infinite obscurity to the text. There are, in Scripture, more of them than in any writing that I know, secular or divine.' This was the considered judgment of one of the best scholars of the age, in the best position to know. Many such passages 'the unlearned and unstable wrest, as they do other Scriptures, unto their own destruction'. He concluded, reasonably: 'Scripture is given to all, to learn; but to teach, and to interpret, only to a few.'[3]

This was very different from Milton, on both counts. Milton wrote, 'then we would believe the Scriptures, protesting their own plainness and perspicuity, calling to them to be instructed not only the wise and learned but the simple, the babes . . . attributing to all men, and requiring from them the ability of searching, trying, examining all things, and by the Spirit discerning that which is good'. This is, like much of what Milton *thought,* silly. Moreover, it is in contradiction of his own opinion of the intellectual incapacity of the ordinary man. Why did Milton hold on so obstinately to these contradictions? Saintsbury perceptively diagnoses his *intransigence*, his irreconcilableness, his 'strong separation from ordinary folk', his 'morose determination to be different, to be not like other

people' – in a phrase, his 'contumacy of spirit'. I suspect that
these tenacious contradictions, glaring as they are, these blind-
nesses, require no intellectual, but a psychological, explanation.

Milton's indefensible defence of the murder of the King was
worse than silly: it was criminal. Hobbes could not take it seriously. 'About this time came out two books, one written by
Saumaise, a Presbyterian, against the murder of the King;
another written by Milton, an English Independent, in answer
to it. They are very good Latin both, and hardly to be judged
which is better; and both very ill reasoning, hardly to be judged
which is worse: like two declamations, *pro* and *con*, made for
exercise only in a rhetoric school by one and the same man. So
like is a Presbyterian to an Independent.'

With Clarendon we come to the remarkable case of a professional politician who was capable of a more philosophic view of
events than anyone, at any rate a more just and reasonable one.
For he was a moderate, who had wanted an accommodation all
along, even into the Civil War, when he belonged to the peace
party among Charles's councillors. The unhappy King was
torn between these views and the extreme ones of the spirited,
but essentially stupid, Queen and her faction. The result was
that, wavering between the two, he could not be trusted.
Clarendon was capable of severe criticism of the King, but
came to have a real devotion to and sympathy for the man in his
trials.

Clarendon himself adhered to a consistent point of view and
followed a policy which made him, more than any other man,
responsible for the Restoration and the form it took. One
cannot but admire the firmness of principle and the steadiness
with which he maintained hope through all the disappoint-
ments and miseries of those two decades. Unlike Hobbes, he
had confidence in the long-term processes of history and the
sense of the English people; he was prepared to be patient,
leaving the Presbyterians and Independents 'alone awhile to
convert one another, till they do both mend'. (Paradoxically,
this rather pompous man had a sense of humour; Milton, who

was not pompous, had none: it did not go with Puritanism.)
After the shattering defeat of the Royalist cause Clarendon still
hoped for 'the resurrection of the English loyalty and courage';
his affection was for his native air, the soil and its inhabitants
rather than 'any abstracted notion of good and bad, right and
wrong, true and false'.[4] He was an English pragmatist, one with
the underlying 'nature of Englishmen', unlike Hobbes and
Milton.

Thus he was able to possess his soul in patience, convinced
that the temporary madness would wear itself out and the
country – or, rather, its governing class – would come to its
senses again. He had the magnanimity to appreciate the greatness that was in Cromwell, but, realising that the Cromwellian
régime necessitated an army with vast expense and taxation,
saw what the consequence would be. He would wait on the
obvious divisions among opponents, who could never unite on
a constructive system without monarchy. 'A firm peace can
never be established but by the old' model, a constitutional
settlement of King and Parliament working together as he had
hoped after the reforms of 1641, which Charles I had accepted.
Mr Wormald, in his admirable book, considers that Clarendon's 'sense of the deeper causes of English events was superior
as political thinking to Hobbes, precisely because he was
thinking historically', and of course he was immeasurably
superior to Milton, who was just a fanatical doctrinaire.

When the inevitable Restoration came about it took the form
Clarendon had adumbrated; and it was his conception of the
constitution that prevailed in 1660. He had preached during
the years in exile that there should be no revenge; his view,
sympathetic to that of the majority of Englishmen, was that the
tragedy had been brought on by the extremists on both sides.
Thus, when the time came, except for the just punishment of
the regicides, the Restoration was astonishingly non-violent
and marked by extraordinary clemency. This fitted well with
Charles II's easy-going nature, but owed more to Clarendon's
principles.

Another man of firm principle and constancy was Sheldon:
the Church was restored along with the King. One cannot

withhold a tribute of admiration to the man who – amid defeat and discouragement in these appalling decades of destruction and loss of valuable lives, or irreplaceable treasures of art, religion and culture – maintained his faith that all would yet be well and made himself the organising centre of the Church, when the defeated and dying bishops failed. Sheldon raised the funds and kept going a vast correspondence with numerous clergy ejected from their livings. At Great Tew it had been said that he was 'born to be archbishop of Canterbury'. At the Restoration, Juxon was old and frail, who had been on the scaffold with the King and had broken down weeping at the silent burial at Windsor on that snowy February day of 1649.

In 1660 Sheldon was ready and prepared to take over the leadership of the Church. It was essentially Laud's Church that was restored; the martyred prelate had not, after all, died in vain. His conception of the English Church was justified, and his persecutors answered, by the fact that – in spite of all the temptations of poverty and actual want in exile – hardly a churchman went over to Rome. Laud had not only made the case unanswerable but set an ideal for which he had laid down his life. There was indeed a difference made in 1662. Laud's Church included the whole nation; the Puritans had campaigned to capture it as such, the whole concern. In 1662 many accepted defeat and accommodated themselves. Moderate people like Cromwell's brother-in-law, Wilkins, who had already seen that the Church could not be run without bishops, sensibly accepted to become one. Pernickety types like Baxter refused all the offers made to them – Archbishop Sheldon must have been glad to see them go, after all the trouble they had caused – and went out to tread the dreary corridors of Nonconformity.

We anticipate a little; but we are now in a position to evaluate the spate of writing into which Milton erupted once more, with the disturbed state of affairs upon his dictator's death and the set of the tide towards the Restoration.

Twist and turn as he might, Oliver Cromwell could never cover the fact of his military dictatorship with the trappings of constitutionalism. During the eight months of his son Richard's Protectorate, September 1658 to May 1659, all the rifts and splits within the Puritan régime came into the open. It could never last, for even with the Army in power it represented a small minority of the nation. Now the Army, increasingly unpopular, was dividing within itself. The grandees had done well for themselves: they 'had feathered their nests successfully from the public offices they had held; their affluence, which contrasted ill with the poverty of the lower ranks, was the more unpopular because partly acquired at the expense of the common soldier. Some of them, like Lambert, were said to have made fortunes by purchasing from necessitous soldiers, at a heavy discount, the right to receive their arrears of pay.'[5] Even more important than the cleavage within the Army was that between the Army and Parliament. The Cromwells were forced to summon these unrepresentative, and unco-operative, assemblies to provide a fig-leaf of justification for taxation – the kernel of the matter. The situation could not last: all the Cromwells in the world could not square the circle. Richard Cromwell's Parliament was of the usual Puritan complexion, i.e., dominantly Presbyterian, with a few leading Republicans like Haselrig and Vane. Such a body did not provide support for a Protectorate; it proceeded to attack the régime, while doing nothing to provide for the arrears of army pay mounting up the while. Richard was losing control of the Army, while his Parliament was alienating it. It was in this not very hopeful posture of affairs that Milton returned to the fray with his *Treatise of Civil Power in Ecclesiastical Causes: showing that it is not lawful for any power on earth to compel in matters of religion*, which appeared in February 1659.

It was addressed to Parliament 'in a season wherein the timely reading thereof, to the easier accomplishment of your great work, may save you much labour and interruption'. Some hopes! Parliament, the poor badgered Protector, the nation at large had more important things to think of. Parliament particularly, in spite of Milton's pertinent reminder that 'in regard that your power being but for a time, and having in yourselves a Christian liberty of your own, which at one time or other may be oppressed, it will concern you while you are in power so to regard other men's consciences as you would your own should be regarded in the power of others; and to consider that any law against conscience is alike in force against any conscience, and so may one way or other redound upon your-selves'. This straight talk was hardly likely to commend itself to the Presbyterian majority, whom Milton had come to dislike quite as much as he had the Prelatists – and with more reason.

He appeals recognisably therefore to Vane in what follows: 'some of whom I remember to have heard often for several years, at a Council next in authority to your own, so well joining religion with civil prudence and yet so well distinguishing diffe-rent power of either. . . .' We notice how anxious he was, as always, to direct attention to his participation in public affairs, subordinate as that was. He concluded that the commonwealth could flourish, 'if ever, when either they who govern discern between civil and religious, or they only who so discern shall be admitted to govern'. Here is once more that 'contumacy of spirit', that irrefragable egoism: only those who agreed with Milton were fit to govern! Even today, three hundred years after, it is generally considered that some association of religion with the state, in the form of the established Church, is a good thing, even by those who do not believe any of its tenets; in seventeenth-century circumstances to divorce religion from the state would have plunged society into chaos. It was utterly impracticable: only a lunatic fringe of such people as Quakers – and Milton – held such views.

It may be said in his defence that he had the remote future with him in urging the separation of Church and state and freeing men's consciences – though there is no sign of it in the New Jerusalem, the Communist pattern of future society, where there is no room for the individual conscience. And Milton argued for it in the regressive terms of his Bible mania: 'what I argue shall be drawn from the Scripture only; and therein from true fundamental principles of the Gospel, to all knowing Christians undeniable'. This has no authority for us today, and even at the time no one took any notice.

The tract is argued simply in inapposite, anachronistic

Scriptural terms, and even in those may well be incorrect, if the point were worth considering. More worth notice is the debating point Milton makes, that it is particularly improper for Protestants to persecute on grounds of conscience, when the basis of Protestantism had been its revolt of conscience against the claims of the Catholic Church. Once more this advocate of toleration and of freedom of conscience excludes Catholics, i.e., the majority of Christians, from it; again he describes Catholicism as 'heresy', when it is virtually synonymous with Christianity. There was a case for excluding Catholicism from power in seventeenth-century England, simply on grounds of secular expediency: its claims were totalitarian, and if it had got hold of power there wouldn't have been any toleration for anybody else. That was sufficient to exclude it, without any Puritan nonsense about 'heresy'.

Finally, Milton urges a consideration which is usually accepted without thought, simply taken for granted. 'Force', he says, 'is no honest confutation, but ineffectual, and for the most part unsuccessful, ofttimes fatal to them who use it.' But is it true that force, in matters of conscience, is ineffectual and unsuccessful? The Inquisition succeeded in burning out Protestantism in Spain and Italy; Austrian arms, in Milton's own time, succeeded in suppressing Protestantism in Bohemia and most of southern Germany – as the Puritans themselves complained. In our time Hitler succeeded in stamping out a great deal of the resistance to the nonsense he inculcated – only extraneous force overthrew him; and Communism is still more successful in repressing deviation from its orthodoxy by force. We are impelled to conclude that Milton was wrong on this point too: Hobbes knew better. Milton may well be more right in the consideration that force is not a good thing – rather than 'fatal' – for those who use it; but we are not concerned with the spiritual well-being of politicians.

All was not well with the poor Protector, who was decidedly not a chip of the old block; he had nothing of his father's prestige and sleight of hand, and was now falling between the two stools. We cannot go into the complicated manœuvres that took place; but that April the Army grandees, the Wallingford

House clique of officers, forced Richard to dissolve his Parliament, whereupon he quietly withdrew, much relieved. The Protectorate was at an end, and shortly the old Rump of the Long Parliament was recalled, as before Oliver's contemptuous dismissal of it. The Rump had no more support in the country than Richard had had. It was dominated by Presbyterians and, having learned nothing and forgotten nothing from its experience at Oliver's hand, they spent their time attempting to perpetuate themselves, or at least to control the membership of any new Parliament, and in alienating the Army they sought also to control. In October the Army kicked them out, and then, finding itself equally unpopular, brought them back again. Milton's admired politician, the egregious Vane, was dismissed for intriguing with the Army. There was no stability or security, things were breaking down into anarchy. But we anticipate.

In August this year Milton had brought out his *Considerations touching the Likeliest Means to remove Hirelings out of the Church* – meaning by the rather insulting term 'hirelings' ministers who were provided for by tithes, not voluntary gifts from their flock. He addressed himself to the Rump, a body hardly likely to listen. 'Owing to your protection, supreme Senate, this liberty of writing which I have used these eighteen years on all occasions to assert the just rights and freedom both of Church and State, and so far approved as to have been trusted with the representment and defence of your actions to all Christendom against an adversary of no mean repute. . . .' This was the third time he had referred, with his usual egoism, to his defence of the King's murder, exaggerating its importance and his own; and with unrepentant, obtuse pride, for he proceeded to repeat it: 'if I have prosperously, God so favouring me, defended the public cause of this Commonwealth to foreigners, ye would not think the reason and ability, whereon ye trusted once, either grown less by more maturity and longer study [!] . . . but that if it sufficed some years past to convince and satisfy the unengaged of other nations in the justice of your doings [!], though then held paradoxal [it was, indeed], it may as well suffice now against weaker opposition'. Really, the arrogance, the conceit!

He was becoming a bore. The tract was received, like its predecessor, with complete indifference: the little man was totally unaware of his own unimportance.

By way of making up to the resuscitated Rump, Milton disagreeably dismisses the Protectorate of Richard Cromwell – son of the man to whom Milton had owed his place – as 'a short but scandalous night of interruption'. Rather ungrateful, all things considered; however, Milton was really a Commonwealth man and can hardly have approved of the Protectorate he served, though he said nothing. Now he is ready to recognise, rather sycophantically, in the tattered remnant of the Long Parliament, 'a new dawning of God's miraculous providence among us, revolved upon your shoulders'.

Most of the tract is taken up by his tedious Bible mania, numerous citations from the Scripture, on which we need waste no time. A few practical points, more relevant, relieve the tedium. He is on target when he complains that, if the ministers insist on keeping their tithes, they might as well 'bring back again bishops, archbishops and the whole gang of prelatry' – as indeed, unsuspected by the prophet, they were on their way back. Much of the pamphlet is taken up with abuse of the ministers, as eighteen years before he had insulted the prelates. 'Certainly it is not necessary to the attainment of Christian knowledge that men should sit all their life long at the feet of a pulpited divine – while he, a lollard indeed over his elbow-cushion, teaches them scarce half the principles of religion; and his sheep ofttimes sit the while to as little purpose of benefiting as the sheep in their pews at Smithfield, and for the most part, by some simony or other, bought and sold like them.' Here we see the very spirit of Nonconformity in its embryo beauty. To be just, if there is something in what Milton says, he is only quarrelling again, as throughout the whole of his life, with the facts of human nature, the way men are made. What was the source of his perennial discontent?

Ministers should have 'the same faith which those disciples had to trust in God and the promise of Christ for their maintenance as they did'. We are reminded of Cromwell's recommendation to *his* ministry, his soldiery, 'Trust in God;

and keep your powder dry' – the powder was the effective term in the proposition, as tithes were to the ministers: we may discount the intermediate term in both propositions, trust in God; it would certainly not have supported the establishment. Milton puts forward his alternative. He suggests a handbook of divinity, 'without school terms and metaphysical notions', such as he was himself compiling at this time for his book on Christian doctrine. 'Thus taught once for all' – as he of course would teach them – 'under the government of their own elders performing all ministerial offices among them, they may be trusted to meet and edify one another whether in church or chapel or, to save them the trudging of many miles thither, nearer home, whether in a house or barn.' It is the very pattern of dreary Nonconformity – we see Milton on his way to becoming a mentor of the Dissenters shortly to issue forth in 1662.

Not that he had any exaggerated idea of the qualifications for the ministry. 'Our ministers think scorn to use a trade, and count it a reproach of this age that tradesmen preach the Gospel. It were to be wished they were all tradesmen: they would not then – so many of them – for want of another trade, make a trade of their preaching. And yet they clamour that tradesmen preach – and yet they preach, while they themselves are the worst tradesmen of all.' Nor had he any very high opinion of universities or what the ministers learned in them – or, for that matter, of the intellectual capability of those who went there. A year's revenue from a benefice was enough to defray the expense of those who fly 'from the government of their parents to the licence of a university. If they had then means of breeding from their parents' – as Milton had had, living on a *rentier* income – 'it needs must be mechanic and uningenuous in them to bring a bill of charges for the learning of those liberal arts and sciences which they have learned – if they have indeed learned them, as they seldom have.' The whole passage is sizzling with superciliousness, however much justified.

He had never thought much of universities either. 'What learning, either human or divine, can be necessary to a minister may as easily and less chargeably be had in any private house' – no doubt in Milton's house: once more we see him generalising from his own perspective, incapable of viewing things from any other. He has a point, however, in saying that 'those theological disputations there held by professors and graduates are such as tend least of all to the edification or capacity of the people, but rather perplex and leaven pure doctrine with scholastical trash than enable any minister to the better preaching of the Gospel'. That was just what Laud and Hales had thought about disputatiousness, though they put it less offensively; it was the Puritans above all who loved disputing, under the name of 'Christian warfare'.

No one exposed his fellow Puritans in a less amiable light than this Puritan, 'hating that they who have preached out bishops, prelates and canonists, should, in what serves their own ends, retain their false opinions, their Pharisaical leaven, their avarice and closely their ambition, their pluralities, their non-residences, their odious fees, and use their legal and Popish arguments for tithes'. The Independents were no better than the Presbyterians – 'that Independents should take that name . . . and seek to be Dependents on the magistrate for their main-tenance! which two things, Independence and State-hire in religion, can never consist long or certainly together'. This was all very well for a *rentier* like Milton, who enjoyed also a regular salary from the state for his services, but ministers too needed the assurance of regular payment for their services. As for the Puritan Commission of Triers, set up to eject 'malignant' (i.e., Royalist) and 'scandalous' (i.e., un-Puritan) clergy – Puritan semantics, of course – Milton tells us, what we might have guessed: 'magistrates at one time or other will pay none but such whom, by their committee of examination, they find conformable to their interest and opinions. And hirelings will soon frame themselves to that interest and those opinions which they see best pleasing to their paymasters.' This passage might have been written by Marx or Pareto, or by Hobbes – but he would have expected no other. What else, after all, could one expect of humans? Humans are but human; as a *rentier* Milton could afford to be above these considerations.

However, at these yelps not a dog barked.

That October 1659 the Army kicked out the Rump, but could not produce a government of its own. At the centre there was a hiatus, a virtual suspension of government, the people caring no more for Parliament than the Army. This confused autumn was a heyday for the doctrinaires proposing all sorts of projects and constitutional schemes, totally irrelevant to the crisis and the inevitable solution. Aubrey describes for us the nightly discussions organised by Harrington, the Republican author of *Oceana*, whom Parliament had placed about Charles I in his confinement at Holdenby in 1647. 'Mr Harrington and the King often disputed about government. The King loved his company, only he would not endure to hear of a Commonwealth; and Mr Harrington passionately loved his Majesty. He was on the scaffold with the King when he was beheaded; and I have at these meetings [of the club in 1659] oftentimes heard him speak of King Charles I with the greatest zeal and passion imaginable, and that his death gave him so great grief that he contracted a disease by it: that never anything did go so near to him.'[6]

How much more agreeable and human was this Republican doctrinaire than that other, John Milton! What made the difference – for evidently Milton was personally a decent man? Clearly the difference was made by his ghastly Puritanism.

Harrington's meetings were held in New Palace Yard, and Milton would have been cognisant of them through Cyriack Skinner, who took the chair at them. Milton would have known the Republican doctrinaire Henry Nevill, if not the profiteering Leveller, Wildman, or the Fifth Monarchy man, Major Venner, who eventually went up in smoke. (Shortly after the Restoration he led an insurrection in the City, with the watchword, 'The King Jesus, and the heads upon the gates' – and was very properly hanged before the gate of his own meeting-house in Coleman Street.) Aubrey tells us that among these 'virtuosi, the discourses in this kind were the most ingenious and smart that ever I heard, or expect to hear, and bandied with great eagerness. The arguments in the Parliament house were but flat to it.' Just like the amusing chatter of intellectuals, of course

– smart, impracticable and totally inapplicable to the realities of the situation.

This is the background in which to see Milton's October *Letter to a Friend concerning the Ruptures of the Commonwealth*. 'Upon the sad and serious discourse which we fell into last night, concerning these dangerous ruptures of the Commonwealth, scarce yet in her infancy, which cannot be without some inward flaw in her bowels. . . .' There was indeed! The unknown friend had desired Milton to set down his thoughts on the situation; I suggest that the friend was Cyriack Skinner, the more so in that only a young man would value Milton's opinions on such a matter.

Milton had been 'overjoyed when I heard that the Army, under the working of God's Holy Spirit – as I thought, and still hope well – had been so far wrought to Christian humility and self-denial as to confess in public their backsliding from the Good Old Cause, and to show the fruits of their repentance in the righteousness of their restoring the old famous Parliament, which they had without just authority dissolved'. Now the Army had kicked it out again: 'it amazes me that they, whose lips were yet scarce closed from giving thanks for that great deliverance [the usual humbug] . . . should now dissolve that Parliament which they themselves re-established and acknowledged for their supreme power in their other day's humble representation.' Milton might well be amazed, but in politics there is nothing easier to eat than words.

He considered their action 'to all other nations most illegal and scandalous, I fear me, barbarous or, rather, scarce to be exampled among any barbarians, that a paid army should, for no other cause [relieving nine leading officers of their commissions], thus subdue the supreme power that set them up'. He knew of no such examples with those barbarian powers, France or Venice or even the United Provinces: 'why not, being most of them held ignorant of true religion? How grievous will it then be, how infamous to the true religion which we profess! how dishonourable to the name of God, that his fear and the power of his knowledge in an army professing to be his, should not work that obedience, that fidelity to their supreme magistrates that levied and paid them!' – when lesser breeds without the law, without the knowledge of true religion, should set so much better examples.

It is delightful to watch his amazement and indignation – it never occurred to him that there might be something wrong in his 'true religion', or that 'God's Holy Spirit' might have erred. The Holy Spirit was to carry them a great deal further yet, back along the paths they had trodden with so much bloodshed and destruction – Marston Moor and Naseby, Carlisle and Lichfield cathedrals unroofed, the sack of Basing and Raglan and Lathom, the scene outside Whitehall so much more 'barbarous to all other nations'. Now in view was 'approaching ruin, being now in anarchy, without a counselling and governing power'.

What remedy was there, but for which, 'in my fear, which God avert, we instantly ruin? . . . If the Parliament be again thought on, to salve honour on both sides, the well-affected party [of course] of the City and the congregated churches may be induced to mediate by public addresses and brotherly beseechings: which, if there be that saintship among us which is talked of, ought to be of highest persuasion to reconcilement.' The people of England, however, were sick of their saintship on all sides. A soldier said that 'he hoped never a true Englishman would name the Parliament again, and that he would have the House pulled down where they sat, for fear it should be infectious'. When one thinks of the magic the name of Parliament had commanded in the 1640s! As for the Army, they were so unpopular that officers dared not wear their swords in the City for fear of being insulted, while common soldiers went in danger of being rabbled. No wonder the religious General Fleetwood considered that 'God had spit in his face'!

We need waste no time considering Milton's remedy for the situation, it was but a counsel of despair. He proposed that, having reconciled Parliament and the army leaders – by 'brotherly beseechings of the congregated churches' – both Parliament and the generals should take an oath to keep each other in place in perpetuity! This is what all his palaver about liberty had come to, along with, we may conclude, an entire sacrifice of principle. For he says, 'whether the civil government be an annual democracy, or a perpetual aristocracy, is not to me a consideration for the extremities wherein we are, and the hazard of our safety from our common enemy, gaping at present to devour us.'

Milton's anxiety receives further expression in his 'Proposals of Certain Expedients for the Preventing of a Civil War Now Feared, and the Settling of a Firm Government'. This remained unpublished; though it represents a change of direction, he could not keep up with the speed of events. He now looked to the restoration of the Rump alone; the Army having disgraced itself in his eyes, he discards his previous proposal of permanence for its leaders. What matter what he thought anyway? Placing his hope in the restored Rump – 'the senate being the basis and foundation of government, which cannot be movable without great danger to the whole building' – reminds us that he had not thought this when he applauded Cromwell's removing them as sinful, self-seeking and arbitrary. When it came to politics he was hardly more consistent than others – and much less sensible.

In the prevailing chaos at the turn of 1660 the dominant factor was General Monk and the army, united under his control, which he had marched slowly south from Scotland. Monk, of West Country Royalist background, was a completely honest and able professional soldier, notoriously reserved and taciturn. This served him well at this juncture, for all sections looked to him for a way out; a slow but wise man, he imposed no view of his own but waited on events to see how the general will of the country shaped itself. The Rump turned somewhat mistrustfully towards him, as he was their only hope. A commission as commander-in-chief in both England and Scotland made him the determining factor; but he did not make up his mind prematurely, he waited until the country gave a clear call.

The Rump, like the Bourbons they were, were still bent on perpetuating themselves and their authority – a mere fifty – and keeping out the members who had been excluded in 1653. 'To Monk and his men alike, the Rump was revealed in its true colours, and it suddenly became hateful to those who had

risked all to restore it.'[7] The man in the street, who had played
such a part in the mob support for the Long Parliament in the
beginning, cared nothing now for the goings-on at Westminster. The City of London, determined on the recall of the
excluded members, who would form a majority, refused to pay
taxes. 'Just as their support had enabled the Long Parliament
to triumph over Charles I, so their opposition to the Rump
made it certain that Charles II would be restored.' Monk
ordered the admission of the excluded members, the filling-up
of vacancies in the House and preparation for dissolution and
free elections. Everybody recognised the signs, and that they
meant the Restoration of the King. That March night Pepys
saw the City 'from one end to the other with a glory about it, so
high was the light of bonfires . . . and the bells rang everywhere'.
Praise-God Barebone's windows were broken for good measure; the rule of the Saints was over.

One blind inhabitant of the City could not see the bonfires,
but he heard the message. That same March he addressed an
open letter to Monk, *The Present Means and Brief Delineation of a
Free Commonwealth, Easy to be Put in Practice and without Delay.*
Free elections were approaching, for the first time in twenty
years: they would express the will of the nation, or the sentient
part of it. They would inevitably produce a Parliament that
would welcome back the King. Free elections were anathema to
this protagonist of freedom: the first condition he propounds is
that 'the ensuing elections be of such as are already firm or
inclinable to constitute a free commonwealth – according to the
former qualifications decreed in Parliament – without single
person or House of Lords'. The doctrinaire enjoined upon the
General 'the danger and confusion of readmitting kingship in
this land – especially against the rules of all prudence and
example, in a family once ejected and therefore not to be trusted
with the power of revenge'. Certainly he had reason to fear for
himself if revenge were exacted.

He favoured a grand council of the nation, 'whose office must
be to dispose of forces both by sea and land, under the conduct
of your Excellency, for the preservation of peace both at home
and abroad'. What was this but to propose another Protector-

ate? Monk, however, was thinking of the well-being of the country, and had by now made up his mind that only the Restoration of the King could guarantee it. The Royalists had only to wait a few weeks, when a silly Welsh clergyman, Dr Griffith, with typical Celtic temperament, threw fat in the fire with a vehement Royalist sermon anticipating revenge.

This gave Milton the text for his *Brief Notes upon a Late Sermon*, and a last chance of a kick at the Church, ridiculing the uninstructed theology of 'a pulpit mountebank'. At last there is a note of resignation to the inevitable: 'despairing of our own virtue, industry, and the number of our able men, we may then – conscious of our unworthiness to be governed better – sadly betake us to our befitting thraldom; yet choosing out of our own number one who hath best aided the people, and best merited against tyranny, the space of a reign or two we may chance to live happily enough, or tolerably'. It was a contemptuous way of putting it, and he suggested who better than Monk, 'the General who hath so eminently borne his part in the whole action'.

Monk, however, had other and more patriotic ideas; he had waited and watched, until he was certain that only the restored monarchy would satisfy the nation.

That April, on the very verge of the Restoration, General Lambert – whose army in the North had deserted him on Monk's approach, while Fairfax emerged from retirement to take him in the rear, and he had been sent to the Tower – escaped to make a last desperate throw. He sent out his emissaries to make a rendezvous at Edgehill of evil memory – the first battle in the Civil War. Again his soldiers would not fight for him. The jeering crowds on his being brought back to London reminded him of the time when Cromwell and he had been given a magnificent send-off, when they set forth against the Scots. The great man, who had no illusions about the people, had said: 'Do not trust to that: these very persons would shout as much if you and I were going to be hanged.' Lambert thought that Cromwell had the spirit of prophecy and that himself would be hanged when the King came in. He was not.

Milton hoped against hope, and against his expressed principles, from Lambert's forlorn gamble. He put out his last writing on the whole Puritan *épopée*, *The Ready and Easy Way to establish a Free Commonwealth, and the Excellence thereof compared with the Inconveniences and dangers of readmitting Kingship in this Nation*. It had probably been written in March; but, uncompromising and obdurate as ever, Milton put forth a second edition in April while the King was on his way. We need pay no attention to what the hopeless doctrinaire advocated, even at this last moment – a perpetual oligarchic council of the 'well-affected' (i.e., the few who thought like himself). Of more interest is his state of mind, the anguish and despair, the indignation that gives this prose work a sharper edge than any. After the endless cant and hypocrisy we have had to put up with from the Puritans, for so long, it is delicious to read.

The tract gives us Milton's summing-up of the experience of the past twenty years. He had no hope of the people: 'if their absolute determination be to enthral us, before so long a Lent of servitude, they may permit us a little Shroving-time first, wherein to speak freely and take our leaves of Liberty'. He runs through events from the Irish Rebellion, which he puts down to Charles I's 'occasioning, if not complotting, as was afterwards discovered, the Irish massacre'. This, as we know, was an unscrupulous lie. The Parliament left in London – minus one-third of its Members, a majority of the Lords, and the King himself – 'made up in outward formality a more legal Parliament of three estates against them'. Anyway, they were 'not bound by any statute of preceding Parliaments, but by the law of nature only, which is the only law of laws truly and properly to all mankind fundamental': i.e., it was no law, but mere resort to force..No wonder Hobbes did not think highly of Milton as an arguer: this was to admit the unconstitutionality of everything that Parliament had done on its own, and all that had flowed from that. Clarendon based himself on the constitutional position agreed between King and Parliament in 1641, with its reforms, and went on from there. This was where the Restoration took up in 1660, as if the intervening aberrations had never been.

These aberrations had never had the majority of the nation with them. Little did Milton care for that: 'the best affected also and best principled of the people stood not numbering or computing on which side were most voices in Parliament, but on which side appeared to them most reason', i.e., what *they* thought. No nonsense about majority rule: 'in matters of nearest concernment all men will be judges, nor easily permit that the odds of voices shall more endanger them by corrupt or credulous votes'. Then who was to judge? Milton, of course. 'A great, though not the greatest, number of their chosen patriots might be more in weight than the others in number, there being in number little virtue.'

A commonwealth 'shall retain the best part of our liberty, which is our religion'. So this is what it comes down to: his bloody (I use the word literally) Puritanism. We hear the trumpet sounded yet once more. 'Nor was the heroic cause unsuccessfully defended to all Christendom against the tongue of a famous and thought invincible adversary; nor the constancy and fortitude that so nobly vindicated our liberty . . . unpraised or uncelebrated in a written monument, likely to outlive detraction, as it hath hitherto convinced or silenced not a few of our detractors, especially in parts abroad.' This was Milton blowing his own trumpet again – there really was something psychotic about his fixation.

The people were willing to throw away the delights of a Puritan Commonwealth, 'regardless of deliverances vouchsafed from heaven, to fall back or rather to creep back so poorly, as it seems the multitude would, to their once abjured and detested thraldom of kingship: to be ourselves the slanderers of our own just and religious deeds – though done by some to covetous and ambitious ends, yet not therefore to be stained with their infamy, or they to asperse the integrity of others', e.g., Milton. Their enemies now would be able to triumph over them, who will now think they 'justly censured both us and all our actions as rash, rebellious, hypocritical and impious' – as they were. They had fallen apart into as many factions as the Tower of Babel – he might have added, had he not detested the Book of Common Prayer, 'and there is no health in us' – leaving 'no memorial of their work behind them remaining but in the common laughter of Europe'.

This must have been particularly bitter to a man without a sense of humour – it was the nonsense of their religious beliefs that had led them to this pass, all their labour lost, their victories and endurances in vain. It had all been for nothing. Where they might have had a 'free' commonwealth, 'most cherishing to virtue and true religion, but also plainly commended or rather enjoined by our Saviour himself . . . what government comes nearer to this precept of Christ than a "free" commonwealth, wherein they who are greatest are perpetual servants and drudges to the public at their own cost and charges; yet are not elevated above their brethren, live soberly in their families, walk the streets as other men, may be spoken to freely, familiarly, friendly, without adoration'. We see the ghastly Nonconformist ideal, *bourgeois* and lower middle-class, which has at last come to prevail in a society run by his spiritual descendants – and what a society, without pride of ancestry and all too much hope of posterity!

However, it has taken three hundred years to get there. In his own day, in a matter of weeks, Milton could envisage a king 'adored like a demi-god, with a dissolute and haughty Court about him, of vast expense and luxury, masks and revels [not *Comus*!], to the debauching of our prime gentry both male and female – not in their pastimes only, but in earnest by the loose employments of Court-service, which will be then thought honourable. There will be a Queen also of no less charge, in most likelihood outlandish and a Papist, besides a Queen Mother such already, together with both their Courts and numerous train.' Actually the country was put to the further expense of repairing the Queen Mother's Somerset House, which the Puritan mob had sacked and thrown the altarpiece of her chapel (by Rubens!) into the Thames. Cowley wrote a poem on what these Philistine hooligans had wrought:

> Nothing remained to adorn this princely place
> Which covetous hands could take, or rude deface.
> In all my rooms and galleries I found

The richest figures torn, and all around
Dismembered statues of great heroes lay:
Such Naseby's field seemed on the fatal day.
And me, when naught for robbery was left,
They starved to death; the gasping walls were cleft,
The pillars sunk, the roofs above me wept,
No sign of spring or joy my garden kept,
Nothing was seen which could content the eye,
Till dead the impious tyrant here did lie.

Cromwell had kept Whitehall and Hampton Court in use, but other royal palaces which fell victim were Theobalds, Holdenby, Nonsuch, while Windsor, used as a prison, needed large reconstruction by Charles II.

Milton cared for none of these things: his nasty Puritanism inhibited his natural taste. All he could think about was the moral consequences of Court service, the nobility and gentry brought up 'to be stewards, chamberlains, ushers, grooms, even of the close-stool'. But this was what they liked, and what the people welcomed – we still have these offices at Court, even the last, covered by the more decent appellation of Groom of the Stole. All this that Milton envisaged, and worse, was shortly to come about; it was not to the taste of the Nonconformist middle class, but nobility, gentry and the people at large welcomed it. 'Certainly then,' the sourpuss went on, 'that people must needs be mad or strangely infatuated that build the chief hope of their common happiness or safety on a single person', a monarch and his Court, when they might have the ravishing delights of a Puritan commonwealth. 'And what madness is it, for them who might manage nobly their own affairs themselves. . . .' This is well said; the only thing is that people are not like that, are not made like that, are not so many Miltons or Hampdens: few such exist.

'How a people, and their leaders especially, can do who have fought so gloriously for liberty, how they can change their noble words and actions, heretofore so becoming the majesty of a free people, into the base necessity of Court flatteries and prostrations, is not only strange but lamentable to think. . . . Can the folly be paralleled, to adore and be the slaves of a single person for doing that which it is ten thousand to one whether he can or will do, and we without him might do more easily, more effectually, more laudably ourselves?' Milton simply could not understand ordinary people's preferences and tastes. 'If there be a king, which the inconsiderate multitude are now so mad upon, mark how far short we are like to come of all those happinesses which in a free state we shall immediately be possessed of.'

Alas for Milton, the country was sick of all those happinesses over the past twenty years. But he was not one to bend his neck to what the vast majority wanted: he belonged to 'that part of the nation which consents not with them, as I persuade me of a great number [in fact they were few], far worthier than by their means to be brought into the same bondage'. This raises a still living issue, as much alive in Communist societies like Russia as in our own delightful variation upon the same theme. What is the discerning individual, one of the elect, who loathes what the vast majority prefer to do when they come into their own? Solzhenitsyn has his answer: *mutatis mutandis*, it is not unlike Milton's in his own day. If there was to be a king, he would wait 'if God favour us, and our wilful sins provoke him not, even to the coming of our true and rightful and only to be expected King, only worthy as he is our only Saviour, the Messiah, the Christ, the only heir of his eternal father, the only by him anointed and ordained since the work of our redemption finished, Universal Lord of all mankind'. We see that he was as mad as other contemporary millenarians. Can one imagine William Shakespeare thinking such nonsense?

Milton's hopes were nonsense; his despair was on target. 'Let our zealous backsliders forethink now with themselves how their necks yoked with these tigers of Bacchus, these new fanatics of not the preaching – but the sweating – tub, inspired with nothing holier than the venereal pox. . . .' How mad with anger he was – and how right! The Court of Charles II scintillated with whores: Barbara Palmer, made Lady Castlemaine, then Duchess of Cleveland for her services; Louise de Quéroualle, made Duchess of Portsmouth for hers; Nell Gwynne, Moll Davis, Arabella Churchill, Catherine Sedley, all the rest of the 'Beauties of Windsor' whose lush charms we can still appreciate as portrayed by Lely. The French pox was ripe at the Court too, just as Milton said. But who would not prefer Rochester and Kenelm Digby with the pox to Stephen Marshall and Cornelius Burgess without?

Indomitable as ever, Milton was courageous to the point of foolhardiness to issue the challenge of a second edition (at his own expense, for no one would publish it), at the moment when the King was about to land. 'They who, past reason and recovery, are devoted to kingship perhaps will answer that a greater part by far of the nation will have it so; the rest therefore must yield.' Milton was not the one to yield, however great the majority: 'I reply, not so much to convince these, which I little hope, as to confirm them who yield not.' This was direct incitement to armed uprising such as Lambert's. Milton cared not a whit what the nation opted for: 'this greatest part have both in reason and the trial of just battle lost the right of their election what the government shall be'. That is to say, he would force his minority views, his egregious religious fanaticism, on the country by force, if he could: so much for his idea of 'liberty' and 'reason'! It is the creed of the revolutionary minority at any time, his spiritual descendants in Boston in 1776, or Robespierre in 1792, Lenin in 1917.

Milton had reason to fear what he foresaw. 'Let them but now read the diabolical forerunning libels, the faces, the gestures that now appear foremost in all public places . . . let them but hear the insolences, the menaces, the insultings of our newly animated common enemies crept lately out of their holes, their hell, I might say, by the language of their infernal pamphlets, the spew of every drunkard, every ribald. . . .' This upright Christian, who set such store by the virtue of temperance, was a good hater; but indeed the pamphleteers were beginning to point the finger at him, the defender, the exponent, of regicide. He was in danger. 'What will then be the revenges and offences remembered and returned, not only by the chief person but by all his adherents; accounts and reparations that will be required, suits, indictments, inquiries, discoveries, complaints, informations, who knows against whom or how many?' – including, of course, himself.

*

The country was in the grip of a general election, free at last – not in Milton's sense of the word. There was immense excitement and competition everywhere to get seats in Parliament, but it was noticed that the nasty ministers, who had been such powerful election-agents in 1640, had little or no influence. Even the son of the sainted Hampden could not get a seat in his own Buckinghamshire, once at his father's command. The country's reaction against the rule of the Saints was gathering momentum, but the Presbyterians still hoped to impose conditions upon the King's Restoration. When he stepped ashore at Dover in May, the Anglicans kept discreetly in the background, while the Presbyterian mayor handed His Majesty a ponderous Bible. Charles II said it was 'the thing that he loved above all things in the world'.

His father would never have said it. Trevelyan comments that, with the son, the Comic Spirit had landed on the coast of Britain. We might say, rather, the Spirit of Cynicism: Charles II was giving the humbugs some of their own back. And who can wonder that he was a cynic, after all the horrors and dangers, the humiliations of exile he had endured? The wonder was that he had come back so good-tempered a cynic. When he entered London on his thirtieth birthday, there were such expressions of universal joy that he said it was no doubt his own fault that he had been so long away, everybody was so glad to see him. John Evelyn was in the crowd in the Strand, amid all the bell-ringing and acclamations. 'And all this was done without one drop of blood shed, and by that very Army which rebelled against him.' It was indeed very remarkable, and – more to the point – had been well managed.

'The Restoration of King Charles II released the English people from the fears and repressions of nearly twenty years. All over the country the maypoles were set up again, loyal toasts were drunk immoderately, Puritanism was repudiated and derided.'[8] The reaction against it was so strong that the Presbyterian magnates found that they could not impose their conditions on the restored monarchy. In the course of the next year they gave way all along the line; in 1661 the Church was restored in full power as the church of the nation, the magnates sacrificed their ministers, who in 1662 went out into the twilight for good. The fact was that the governing class had learned its lesson – whatever happened, not to divide its ranks again to the point at which inspired cobblers and jumped-up butchers and tailors could take their place. The Puritan régime had all along operated against the bulk of the nation, latterly – under the Army – against the whole balance of social forces in the country. Now the ruling classes, backed by the people at large, had served notice on the small middle-class minority to carry their minority-mindedness outside into their venerated Nonconformity. All over the country, in every parish the alliance between squire and parson, manor-house and parish church, Church and state, held good – right up to the social revolution of our time. From the point of view of society the Restoration represented a real reaction, which might never have come about if it had not been for the Revolution the Puritans tried but could not maintain.

Prominent Republicans began to abscond, others remained to await their fate. Milton was in danger, he could not know what to expect. The *rentier* had invested most of his salary from the Council of State in excise bonds, some £2000. On the day of the King's proclamation in London, 5 May, he transferred one of the bonds to Cyriack Skinner and with the money went into hiding (the rest was lost). He lay hidden in a house in Bartholomew Close during those hot summer months until his fate was decided.

The astonishing thing about the Restoration was the degree of its clemency. An Act of Indemnity and Oblivion was passed pardoning all who had taken part in the rebellion, except for a number of named individuals, regicides who were responsible for Charles I's murder. Poor Cavaliers who had suffered so much for his cause called the act one of indemnity for the King's enemies and of oblivion for his friends. This clemency represented the joint spirit of Charles II and Clarendon, neither of them a vindictive man.

Parliament, however, kept adding names to the schedule of those excepted from pardon. In June the case of Milton was discussed, and the King was asked to call in his *Eikonoklastes*, against Charles I's Book, and the defence of his murder, to be burned by the common hangman. It was a miracle that Milton escaped – Hugh Peters was hanged for less – and no one knows *how* he escaped. His nephew, years later, said that Milton had been saved 'through the intercession of some that stood his friends both in Council and Parliament. Particularly in the House of Commons Mr Andrew Marvell, a Member for Hull, acted vigorously on his behalf, and made a considerable party for him.'[9] Another story was that Milton earlier had interceded for the Royalist Davenant, poet and dramatist, and now Davenant repaid his debt by interceding for Milton. It would be nice if this story were true, for Sir William Davenant liked to think that he was Shakespeare's by-blow, and there is nothing against that either.

However it was, it was by a close margin that English literature acquired *Paradise Lost* and the rest. At the end of August the bill of pardon passed in its final shape, and Milton's name was not among those excepted. In September he was able to come out of hiding, to take a lease of a house in the parish of St Giles-in-the-Fields. At the end of the year he was briefly imprisoned, presumably on the mistaken action of the Commons' Serjeant-at-Arms on the warrant of the House prior to the pardon. Soon released, Milton characteristically pursued the Serjeant for the exorbitant fees he had demanded. An official pardon was granted in December, and there the matter ended.

We may observe, however, that if Clarendon, who had the last word in these matters, had chosen to add Milton's name to those excepted from pardon, he might have perished with those regicides whose action he had defended with such conviction. (Hugh Peters was hanged for just that – but he had no one to defend him.) Clarendon, a man of principle and conviction quite equal to Milton's, but a Royalist and Anglican, was a magnanimous man. Magnanimity was not a characteristic of Puritanism.

CHAPTER NINE

Milton's Christianity

WE HAVE now seen what a fool this doctrinaire intellectual was about politics. Was he any better in his religious beliefs and doctrines?

I am well aware that these are not gentlemanly terms. But this age of revolutionary egalitarianism is not a gentlemanly age, and I deliberately call things by their right names – rather than adhere to academic categories more dead than alive – in order that people may understand in contemporary terms.

We must put Milton's religious beliefs in perspective. This does not mean that we are being anachronistic in regarding most of them as nonsense, quite as much as his political doctrines, if not more so. For he did not *have* to believe nonsense even in the time in which he lived. Many people in the Renaissance period, still more in the later seventeenth century, did not do so. Erasmus believed very little; Montaigne even less – but he had the advantage of being half-Jewish and so was outside the cocoon of traditional credulity in which most people were nurtured and enclosed. Bacon believed in a deity, but not much else; Hobbes evidently in nothing at all, except for what he thought about men: otherwise religion did not exist for him.

Earlier, in the sixteenth century, there had been Italian sceptics, who revived the classical notions of Sextus Empiricus or the relativism of Cicero on the Nature of the Gods, with his recommendation to adhere to customary rituals though the intelligent person need not believe the nonsense they inculcated for the benefit of the average fool. It is clear that Marlowe and Hariot were deists, and Ralegh too, before long incarceration and disappointment reduced him. Even so it is pathetic to watch him trying to make sense of the chronology of the Old

Testament, accepting the incredible ages of the patriarchs, the animals in the Ark, etc., in order not to offend the susceptibilities of the credulous orthodox.[1] He had his reward: his *History of the World* was taken up by the Puritans, Oliver Cromwell commending it as a most instructive work.

We observe Milton, in the book he compiled on Christian doctrine, to which he devoted years and which he regarded as his 'dearest and best possession', struggling in vain to make sense out of nonsense. It is true that what most people believe, and have believed, in all times and all places has been largely nonsense; but even in the seventeenth century Milton did not have to believe it. Neither Hobbes nor Selden did.

Milton regarded the Bible as not only 'the encyclopedia of all knowledge' but as 'the ground of all, the touchstone to try all, and the judge to determine of all truth'. This was the Protestant view, but it was simply silly. Not even the bulk of Christians – the seven-tenths or so who were Catholics – thought this: they regarded the tradition of the Church as having authority, by which the Bible itself was interpreted and authorised. For all Milton's appeal to 'reason' – i.e., his own – theirs was a more rational position: some consensus of interpretation as against the individual's very fallible judgment.

The Bible was simply a body of literature, like any other body of literature of an ancient people, Greeks or Romans, or for that matter Egyptian or Indian or Chinese. A proper world-historical perspective sees Christianity as a Mediterranean–European religion, essentially localised to that geographical area with the extensions to which Europeans have carried it with their expansion into the outer world.

In the heyday of European ascendancy in the nineteenth century it was not such nonsense as it shortly became for Newman to argue in his *Essay on the Development of Christian Doctrine* that, granted the area of Europe, and granted the last two millennia, then Catholic Christianity occupied the centre of the picture. He proceeded to conclude *Securus judicat orbis terrarum.* He was, of course, even then characteristically cooking the argument. Today the universal claim of Christianity has receded before the advance of China, India, the Middle East, Africa. It has not become parochial but remains European, with European extensions outside. Even so, within its area, Christianity is now the religion of a minority. Quite apart from the large Communist areas, like Soviet Russia and its satellites, those people are few, even within the Christian communions, who believe in its historic doctrines, or much doctrine at all. In the United States, for example, Christian subscription is largely a matter of social conformism, rather than active belief in Christian doctrine.

We confront a question that is more one of anthropology, for the community, and of psychology, for the individual, in considering the status of myth. How much of myth is believed? In what sense is a myth 'true'? It evidently does not have the truth of history, of actual events and happenings, though it may well contain, or even be based on, historical elements, e.g., the historical existence and career of Jesus, a career comparable with those of other Jewish prophets and moralists. Evidently the Jewish historical perspective is the proper one in which to see that career, rationally and without overtones, impartially and without prejudice, neither credulous nor hostile – but certainly not as subsequently overlaid by mythical beliefs and metaphysical notions, either of personal deification or ethical abstraction. The historian requires merely historical fact, the persons and events of history: these are his truths.

What was the status of myth with Milton? How and how much did he believe of it? Was the mythical factual to him? He probably believed a great deal of it to be fact, since he believed in the absolute truth and authority of Scripture. Today, we do not.

This gives us the perspective in which to view his beliefs, and may help us to discern what he regarded to be factually true.

A modern mind values myth not so much in and for itself as in so far as it provides material for art – poetry or, still more, painting. Yeats seemed to believe in a lot of spiritualist nonsense, but it provided material for his imagination to feed upon. Eliot derived a second wind of inspiration from his acceptance of Anglican beliefs. So too the chief value of Milton's *De doctrina christiana* for us is for the material it provided for *Paradise Lost* and *Paradise Regained*, though it has its importance in itself for the depiction of Milton's mind and thought.

This has only comparatively recently been realised – though the realisation hardly requires C. S. Lewis's contemptuous dismissal of aesthetic criticism of those works: rescuing 'Miltonic criticism from the drowsy praise of his "organ music" and babble about the "majesty roll of proper names" '. Lewis was no aesthete, but was more taken up with nonsense doctrines themselves. I recall a chaplain at All Souls complaining of a war-time sermon of Lewis's, when his vogue was at its height: with the perversity of an Ulsterman he insisted, you *shall* believe in the Resurrection of Christ, physical accidents, 'nails and all'. Lewis's religious preconceptions led him completely astray, to say that 'the heresies of *Paradise Lost* thus reduce themselves to something very small and rather ambiguous'.[2]

So far from this being true, the common sense of the matter is just what we should expect: the *Christian Doctrine* reveals Milton as heretical on several major points of traditional belief. He was an Arian, i.e., he did not believe in the Trinity. His 'view of the Godhead seems singularly Milton's own': it would be.[3] He disagreed further with the orthodox doctrine of the creation of the world. The Creation was not the work of Three Persons, but of the Father. Nor was the Creation the beginning of time, for the Father begot the Son before it. Nor did God create the world *ex nihilo* (out of nothing), but out of pre-existent matter. Milton was very wobbly about the Spirit, to which (or, possibly, to whom) he allotted a rather late appearance and a subordinate rôle. All this was heterodox, in which we see Milton, having accepted the ancient Scriptures as the source of knowledge and truth, struggling to make sense out of intrinsic nonsense.

The earliest of Milton's heresies, apparently, was his thnetopsychism, his belief that the human soul dies and perishes with the body – to be both renewed at the Resurrection. (But for this last superfluous piece of myth, Milton's view might accord very well with Ryle's *Concept of Mind*.) Milton had worked out for himself that man and 'soul' were just one and the same. The popular form of this conviction gave rise to a contemporary sect, the Soul-Sleepers: a position which had been strongly attacked by the odious Calvin as casting doubt on the 'truth' of eternal life. We should observe that the nonsense believed in by uneducated crackpots was hardly more nonsensical – and sometimes less so – than what was believed by the educated; for most of what people suppose themselves to think – in their very limited capacity to think at all – is strictly nonsense, i.e., does not make sense.

On the sublime issue of Predestination, which occupies such a place in seventeenth-century 'thought' and on which whole libraries of rubbish have been written, Milton was again unorthodox. We learn that he no longer agreed with the Puritan orthodoxy of Calvin on the issue after 1645. This was a significant date: it was when Milton finally turned his back on his fellow Puritans of the Assembly of Divines, after his experience at their hands over divorce. Once more we see how Milton, the most autobiographical of authors, who derived exceptional strength from his exceptional ego, was inspired by personal motivation. Calvin had urged that, as the result of Adam's transgression, man is so 'captive to the yoke of sin' that he 'can of his own nature neither aspire to good through resolve, nor struggle after it through effort'. We see not only what nonsense this was, but also how evil in its consequences. Calvinists did not fail to draw the conclusion: 'when God suffers sin to be done, he also wills it to be done'. What a conception of an all-wise, all-loving and foreknowing Deity!

Milton did not agree with it: he was a free-willer, technically an Arminian – as Archbishop Laud had been, who in this year 1645 paid the supreme penalty for his services to Church and state. In the *Christian Doctrine* Milton expounds Predestination as being 'the principal special decree of God relating to Man, whereby God in pity to mankind, though foreseeing that they would fall of their own accord, predestinated to eternal salvation, before the foundation of the world, those who should believe and continue in the faith'. These were the Elect. There went along with this the predestined damnation of the non-Elect, through no fault of their own, to all eternity.

Milton did not go along with this, any more than did many Anglicans. 'If God had decreed any to absolute reprobation, which we nowhere read in Scripture, the system of those who affirm that reprobation is an absolute decree, requires that he should have also decreed the means whereby his own decree might be fulfilled. Now these means are neither more nor less than sin. Nor will it avail to reply that God did not decree sin, but only permitted it; for there is a fatal objection to this common subterfuge, namely, that it implies more than simple permission. Further, he who permits a thing does not decree it, but leaves it free.'

Let this suffice for an example of the way in which nonsense argumentation based on nonsense assumptions can go on for ever – as whole libraries of it have done; for nonsense is (*a*) self-proliferating, and (*b*) in its nature without end. The fact is that the place of Predestination in seventeenth-century minds requires merely psychological understanding. A believer was one of the Elect himself, as Milton obviously was, simply by his genius and his gifts: God speaks in *Paradise Lost*,

> Some I have chosen of peculiar grace,
> Elect above the rest; so is my will:
> The rest shall hear me call, and oft be warned
> Their sinful state . . . etc.

But, to ordinary Puritans, what was the joy of being elect, if others were not condemned? *Schadenfreude* – it is significant that there is no word for it in English, only in German (it means, taking pleasure in the harm that befalls others) – is a constantly recurring element in human history. It was at its height with seventeenth-century Calvinists. It is to the credit of Milton that he was at odds with Calvinism on this issue.

Nor did Milton haul down his flag on the subject of divorce. He repeats his heterodox view on this subject, and again – against his declared veneration for the text of Holy Writ – tries to explain away the plain sense of Jesus' words on the subject. Once more we observe, what does not now surprise us, that Milton does not boggle at casuistry to wrest away the plain meaning of words to suit himself. (He provides a choice subject for Pareto on human thinking – the hypostatisation of one's own wishes, conscious or unconscious.) Milton had been accused of polygamy by his fellow-Puritans; in the *Christian Doctrine* he goes further, with characteristic candour and obstinacy, to approve of polygamy. How could he not, since it was practised by his Old Testament patriarchs?

The point needs no further labouring. Milton was the most individualistic of writers, the most obdurate and convinced of his own rightness. The Yale editors of the *Christian Doctrine*, pointing out how well read he was in theological controversies, comment that he found causes of dissatisfaction with everybody: with Placaeus on the Trinity, Beza on polygamy, Polanus on Christian liberty, Zanchius on hypostatic union (i.e., the union of two natures, human and divine, in Christ) and on the Mosaic Law. Earlier commentators on *Paradise Lost* did not have the *Christian Doctrine* to enlighten them – it was so heretical that it could not be published, even in Amsterdam in Latin. But Newton suspected that Milton was an Arian and did not believe in the Trinity – as Newton himself secretly was, in the next generation.

It was dangerous to express disbelief in the Trinity. In Milton's youth a couple of Arians had been burned for doing so; before the end of the century a couple more were hanged for it. So Milton had to be very careful in the expression of his heretical views in *Paradise Lost*, if his work were to be published. This is what accounts simply for the 'debatable' pages in the poem: they are to be interpreted in the light of the *Christian Doctrine*. They need no explanation in any such terms as some literary scholars have suggested, as to any growing orthodoxy of Milton's, any change of mind. The historian sees quite simply that *Paradise Lost* coheres with the *Christian Doctrine*, which provided his intellectual groundwork for the poem – he seems to have worked at them *pari passu*. And we note how wide was Milton's deviation from orthodoxy, as common sense would suggest and historical sense corroborates. C. S. Lewis was perversely anti-historical; his minimisation of the heretical in *Paradise Lost* is merely *parti pris* – contrary to common sense and to the historic fact.

*

On the issue of Justification by Faith Milton was a square Protestant. This doctrine 'often scorched the hands that touched it. Lit by Luther, it raced wildly across Western Europe setting fire to the territory on which extremists took their stand and threatening the existence of Christianity as a socially conscious *ecclesia*. Violent controversies broke out as Protestant turned on Protestant, and all against the "triple Tyrant" at their door.'[4] All very human, of course – though not in the least necessary: Erasmus did not occupy his brilliant mind with such nonsense, he had better things to do with it. His brutal opponent, Luther, was responsible for the furore, and since he was more heavily invested in nonsense he was able to defeat Erasmus' sense. Luther's final fling, 'the Holy Spirit is not a sceptic', was unanswerable: no idea, of course, that the inspiration within was simply an extrapolation of their own ego.

The nonsense went back to St Paul, himself an obvious psychological case, with his 'thorn in the flesh', and his epileptic fits, in one of which he saw a vision. It was hardly surprising that he underwent a conversion, for he had previously been a psychotic persecutor – lunging from one extreme to another. Luther was not content with Paul's statement: in his translation of the Epistle to the Romans he added the crucial word 'alone': 'a man is justified by faith *alone* without the deeds of the law'. Why this was so important to Protestants must have a psychological explanation: it went along with their view of the depravity of human nature, the predestined few who were elect, the rest damned, etc. The insistence on faith alone obviated the necessity of the priesthood of the Catholic Church, the sacramental system, the requirement of good works – which has proved itself, in accordance with the survival of the fittest, to be much better fitted to keep order in the human nursery.

St Paul's doctrine was constructed by a Jewish legalistic mind fantasying about the circumstances of the controversial life of Jesus, whom he had not known. In statements of this doctrine there remained a curious legalistic–contractual element. Professor Patrides tells us that 'Milton's interpretation in *De doctrina christiana* is couched in the forensic terminology characteristic of all Protestant expositions: "justification, in so far as we are concerned, is gratuitous; in so far as Christ is concerned, not gratuitous; inasmuch as Christ paid the ransom of our sins, which he took upon himself by imputation, and thus of his own accord, and at his own cost, effected their expiation; whereas man, paying nothing on his part, but merely believing, receives as a gift the imputed righteousness of Christ".[5] Now we know.

Without going further into these deep matters, we can at least consider to some point the Puritan conviction of the total depravity of human nature (it appears again and again in the fast-day sermons of their divines during the Civil War and Commonwealth: we need not refrain from a joke – that they had themselves to contemplate!). Their revered apostle, Calvin, was able to inform us: 'In the hidden counsel of God it was determined that Adam should fall from the unimpaired condition of his nature, and by his defection should involve all his posterity in sentence of eternal death.' Patrides adds, 'Luther was just as brutal, for he thought of man's will as manipulated in accordance with the wishes of God or Satan: "man's will is like a beast standing between two riders. If God rides, it wills and goes where God wills. . . . If Satan rides, it wills and goes where Satan wills. Nor may it choose to which rider it will run, or which it will seek; but the riders themselves fight to decide who shall have and hold it." ' This is very German: it means the abnegation of reason (by which Erasmus and civilised men hold), and following the promptings of the unconscious, thinking with the bowels – and we have seen the catastrophe to which that has led the Germans in our time.

This was Luther's view of human nature: 'whatsoever is our will is evil; whatsoever is in our understanding is error. Wherefore in spiritual matters man hath nothing but darkness, errors, ignorance, malice, and perverseness both of will and understanding.'[6] Calvin refined upon this with his view of the Fall of Man: 'Adam was not only the progenitor but also the root of man's nature, and therefore in his corruption was all mankind worthily corrupted.' Nonsense follows from nonsense premises, and we shall see the influence of this upon Milton's mind and its constructs, and how far he accorded with it.

Catholics and Anglicans did not. The sensible Jeremy Taylor, whom Laud rightly imposed upon a reluctant All Souls College, wrote: 'if by the fall of Adam we are so wholly ruined in our faculties that we cannot do any good, but must do evil – how shall any man take care of his ways? Or how can it be supposed he should strive against all vice? Or indeed how shall he strive at all? For if all actual sins are derived from the original, then no man can take care to avoid any actual sin whose cause is natural and not to be declined.' Sensible Jeremy Taylor (not all Taylors are equally sensible) was described by yet another Puritan Burgess as 'not merely Pelagian, Arminian, Papist, or Socinian, but an hotchpotch of all'. Such is the kind of thing upholders of common sense have to put up with from madmen at all times.

We can see some of the consequences in Luther's proscription of the Jews as 'wicked and ungodly' – and this after getting their religion from the Old Testament, not – alas! – from Greece. The wicked persecution of the Jews throughout European history is in itself sufficient to justify Swift's view of human beings. This does not, however, mean that man is totally depraved, merely that most of mankind are fools. Milton himself must have respected the Jews with their more reasonable monotheism. He says in the *Christian Doctrine*, abnegating a metaphysical disquisition about 'the drama of the personalities in the Godhead' (it appears in *Paradise Lost*, however): 'it is evident from numberless passages of Scripture that there is in reality but one true independent and supreme God. And as he is called one – inasmuch as human reason and the common language of mankind, and the Jews, the people of God, have always considered him as one person only, that is, one in a numerical sense – let us have recourse to the sacred writings in order to know who this one true and supreme God is.' And at once we are off again. Since Milton regarded the Jews as the people in the best position to know, and the Bible as the only source of information, it is perhaps surprising that he did not see Christianity more from a Jewish perspective – as his contemporary Spinoza did: surely the most rational and illuminating perspective in which to view it.

Milton subscribed to the lugubrious view, consequent upon his acceptance of the Fall of Man, Original Sin, etc., of death as the punishment for sin – as if it were not a perfectly natural phenomenon, common to all animals, for many a release from suffering, disease, weariness with life's troubles and trials. Milton's is the kind of nonsense construct that arises from nonsense premises. It is in total contrast to the civilised view of Bacon, not long before: 'it is as natural to die as to be born. Men fear death as children fear to go in the dark; and as that natural fear in children is increased with tales, so is the other. . . . I have often thought upon death, and I find it the least of all evils.'

Milton disclaimed metaphysical disputations, and had no hesitation in setting his own opinion 'against the whole body of theologians', where it conflicted with theirs. Yet there was plenty of theological rubbish he did subscribe to: he believed in angels, for instance; that there was such a place as Hell, a place of punishment for sin, and he cites a number of passages from Holy Writ filled with the nasty spirit of *Schadenfreude*. He believed in the general resurrection of the dead, and the Last Judgment. He seems to have expected the Second Coming of Christ shortly, as the original deluded Apostles – ignorant fishermen and such – had done. Christ's reign would occupy a millennium. 'After the expiration of the thousand years Satan will rage again, and assail the Church at the head of an immense confederacy of its enemies, but will be overthrown by fire from heaven and condemned to everlasting punishment.' He derived this fantasy from the fantastic Book of Revelation. One can object to it if he believed it to be true, while accepting it for the poetry into which it is turned in *Paradise Lost*:

> The world shall burn, and from her ashes spring
> New heaven and earth, wherein the just shall dwell,
> And after all their tribulations long
> See golden days.

One observes, as so often, the projection of himself, the imaginative compensation for actual frustration and defeat.

This is what inspired his, and others', millenarian hopes, with the onset of the Puritan Revolution: 'Thou, the eternal and shortly expected King, shall open the clouds to judge the several kingdoms of the world, and distributing national honours and rewards to religious and just commonwealths, shall put an end to all earthly tyrannies, proclaiming the universal and mild monarchy through heaven and earth. Where they undoubtedly that − by their labours, counsels and prayers − have been earnest for the common good of religion and their country [e.g., Milton], shall receive above the inferior orders of the blessed, the regal addition of principalities, legions, and thrones into their glorious titles', etc. Christopher Hill tells us that 'in 1658 Milton was still looking for the Second Coming'.[7] If so, he was as credulous as the original Apostles, though it may have had the psychological compensation of giving his morale a boost through all disillusionments.

That is, indeed, the utility and the explanation of such delusions. As a boy in Nonconformist Cornwall I had the advantage of knowing millenarian types straight out of the seventeenth century. One was a club-footed tailor named Freeman, who, in the intervals of quarrelling with his wife, spouted interminable confused brabble from the Book of Revelation. Another such was an intermittent china-clay worker, with the good Puritan name of Rogers, who varied bouts of drinking with bouts of inspired Biblical trash. His daughter, a schoolteacher who became a Christadelphian, was inspired to assure me as a somewhat apprehensive boy that the world would come to an end in 1920. When the year was safely past, I reminded her of her prophecy (or promise); without turning a hair, she assured me that the world would come to an end in 1926. Thus my education as to millenarian hopes − and human thinking − was advanced.

Enough of metaphysical moonshine! Let us come down to earth with more practical, more real, concerns throwing light on Milton the man. Since the Scriptures were the source of truth, 'every believer [what about the non-believer? likely to be more objective] has a right to interpret the Scriptures for himself, inasmuch as he has the Spirit [i.e., the wind of his own inspiration] for his guide, and the mind of Christ [i.e., non-sense] is in him'. This generous invitation to crackpots is somewhat circumscribed by the requisite qualifications to interpret. 'They consist in knowledge of languages; inspection of the originals; examination of the context; care in distinguishing between literal and figurative expressions; consideration of cause and circumstance, of antecedents and consequents; mutual comparison of texts; and regard to the analogy of faith. Attention must also be paid to the frequent anomalies of syntax. . . . Lastly, no inferences from the text are to be admitted, but such as follow necessarily and plainly from the words themselves.'

I fear that this would very much restrict the scope of utterance for the Freemans and Rogerses, the sectaries who filled the period of the Puritan Revolution with their gifts of the spirit. Moreover, it is in flat contradiction of Milton's previous assurance that the simple, even babes, could interpret Scripture. (See above, page 170.)

With so individualistic a view Milton had no use for an organised church or for ministers – once more generalising from his own self-sufficiency to ordinary simpletons who much needed such guides to keep them on the rails. To be just to Milton: he did not need these helps, from society, church or ministers. 'Ministerial labours are of no efficacy in themselves, independently of divine grace' – and of this last commodity he was sufficiently assured. He was prepared to take away from them the jobs which even Nonconformist ministers are allotted. 'With regard to the Lord's Supper the privilege of dispensing the elements is confined to no particular man, or order of men. There can be still less shadow of reason for assigning to the ministers of the church the celebration of marriages or funerals, offices which hirelings are wont to assume to themselves exclusively.' And, of course, tithes for their support should be abolished.

All this is reasonable enough in itself, and time has brought it about; but in the seventeenth century it was utterly unpractical, or practicable only within a specialised small sect like the Quakers, with whom Milton had some affinity, though less sympathy. No organised church could exist on his basis; and he thought set forms of worship superfluous.

The inferiority of women to men is enforced in the *Christian Doctrine* as throughout his work: man is the superior sex and it is for him to rule. What a contrast this offers with the fully masculine Shakespeare's sympathy and love for women! But Milton's was the Puritan view, and Shakespeare the opposite of a Puritan. This had the curious consequence that Milton attached more importance to chastity in men than in women. 'If unchastity in a woman, whom St Paul terms the glory of man, be such a scandal and dishonour, then certainly in a man, who is both the image and glory of God, it must, though commonly not so thought, be much more deflowering and dishonouring. In that he sins both against his own body, which is the perfecter sex, and his own glory, which is in the woman – and that which is worst, against the image and glory of God which is in himself'!

This is a perfect example of Milton's doctrinairism and of the way in which adherence to doctrine led him up against clear common sense. No wonder his view was 'commonly not so thought': for obvious biological reasons chastity in women – until the age of birth-control – was vastly more important than chastity in men: for the sake of the family, children and the succession. Not only in royal families and aristocracies, where this was the acknowledged rule, but right down through society, women needed to take more care; men have had much more freedom since they do not produce the children. With better birth-control the rule in societies has become more relaxed – reasonably so, with less need for it.

Milton had no illusions about equality or democratic rule: 'for unto the wisest man nature gives command over men less wise, not unto the wicked man over good men, a fool over wise men; and consequently they that take the government out of such men's hands, act quite contrary to the law of nature'. This is carried over, like so much else, into *Paradise Lost*:

> Unjustly thou deprav'st it with the name
> Of *Servitude* to serve whom God ordains,

Or Nature. God and Nature bid the same,
When he who rules is worthiest, and excels
Them whom he governs.

The rule of the elect – i.e., Milton – is what is put forward. In dispensing charity and almsgiving, 'we are to be guided by geometrical rather than arithmetical proportion, regulating our bounty according to the rank and dignity, the education and previous condition of each individual – lest we fall into the absurdity of equalising those whom nature never intended for an equality'.

This, we see, is contrary to the whole assumption of a socialist society. Milton was no egalitarian, but a middle-class man with middle-class perspectives. He was opposed to the voluntary poverty of monks and friars, and considered their vows 'superstitious'. The scrivener-usurer's son approved of usury, with the usual limitations that facilitated commercial contracts: 'that usury is in itself equally justifiable with any other kind of civil contract is evident from the following considerations', and there follow a number of citations from Scripture. No luxury or ostentatious wealth, however, the accent is all on abstinence and temperance: we see the perfect picture of the Nonconformist *bourgeois*, his beliefs and doctrines simply projections of his inner urges and his place in society.

There is not much emphasis on love, the central and abiding virtue of Catholic Christianity – any more than there is ever a good word for his Catholic fellow-Christians – seven-tenths or so of Christianity. I am reminded of a Cornish bishop who remained always a Nonconformist in his outlook, and should never have ceased to be one. Reminded of the parable of the Good Samaritan, he said, 'I wouldn't have gone to his help – not if he was a Roman Catholic.' This was Milton's spirit, not much love, charity, or compassion, but plenty of self-righteousness and cantankerousness, along with genuine rectitude. 'Love is a general virtue, infused into believers by God the Father in Christ through the Spirit, and comprehending the whole duty of love which each individual owes to himself and his neighbour.' It is a very cool conception of

love; many an unbeliever has had a warmer and more effica-
cious conception. Perhaps we may condone this in one whose
life had not much love in it.

'The opposite of this is uncharitableness; which renders all
our other qualities and actions, however excellent in appearance, of no account.' We observe here the gap – a gap Pareto
would have been aware of – between precept and practice.
There was not much charitableness in Milton's mind, much
more censoriousness – in this a good prototype of later Dissent.
'Charity towards our neighbour', he tells us, 'consists in loving
him as ourselves' – there seems an element of humbug in this,
when himself was so unself-aware.

Compassion? 'The third modification of absolute love is
compassion. . . . The opposite of this is, first, unmercifulness.'
No compassion, but a harsh unmercifulness, was to be seen in
Milton's attitude towards King Charles I in his sufferings.
Perhaps he would have excused himself by the consideration
that 'hatred is in some cases a religious duty – as when we hate
the enemies of God or the Church'. I recall a New England
virago, of Puritan persuasion, grinding her dentures, with 'I
don't want to hate people, but I must uphold virtue.' I regis-
tered that perhaps she didn't try hard enough – she was more
Puritan than Christian.

'Placability consists in a readiness to forgive those by whom
we have been injured.' In the case of Milton's first wife he considered himself injured (he would, anyway); we do not know her
side of the story. But Milton was placable enough in taking her
back, and putting up with her family into the bargain. On the
other hand, when at the end of his life he came to write his will,
he wrote: 'the portion due to me from Mr Powell, my former
wife's father, I leave to the unkind children I had by her, having
received no part of it; but my meaning is, they shall have no
other benefit of my estate than the said portion, and what I
have besides done for them, they having been very undutiful to
me'.

He himself had been brought up to be a gentleman; he
brought his daughters up as servants, to go out into the world
and earn their living. Doctrine or no, here we have the man.

Shakespeare, who began with little and had a hard apprentice-ship, was able to leave his granddaughter an estate and thereby to make a titled lady of her.

It is only recently that critics have come to realise the impor-tance of Milton's *Christian Doctrine* for the making as well as the interpretation of *Paradise Lost* and *Paradise Regained*. Milton seems to have begun work on *Paradise Lost* about 1655, prob-ably with some suspension when he was so agitatedly pamphleteering from Cromwell's death to Charles II's Restoration. He began the *Christian Doctrine* about the same time and pursued it until he had a fair copy by 1660. He kept it by him, amending and altering to the end, for it could not be published.

We now realise that the two works 'express in two different forms the same body of religious beliefs'.[8] Thus debatable pas-sages in *Paradise Lost* are interpretable by reference to the *Christian Doctrine*. They do *not* represent any change of view, any greater orthodoxy; they represent all that it was possible for Milton to say and be published. Verse is sometimes a form of covering-up: one can say anything in verse, and most people will not recognise what one is saying. Milton sailed as close to the wind of heresy as was possible.

The book grew out of his collection of texts from the Bible under headings. He had other compendia, notably those of Ames and Wolleby, to aid him. Above all he had an extraordi-nary knowledge of the Bible, an extremely retentive memory and intellectual command – as one sees from the long verse-paragraphs this blind man could memorise and dictate. On top of this Milton was well enough read in theological controversies and Biblical criticism. He was well aware of textual corruptions exposed by Erasmus and Beza. He was, in general, conserva-tive about the text of the Bible, since God had imparted divine truth to its authors, who then wrote it down. This did not pre-vent Milton from a certain amount of textual criticism on his own, good scholar as he was, on grammatical points, ob-scurities of language, etc. When it came to the opinions of theologians he had no compunction at all about correcting them, finding causes of dissatisfaction with everybody. A main motive with him was to establish what *he* thought as against the errors and dishonesties of the theologians. Very few of them had been so candid as the rugose St Jerome: 'the true profession of the mystery of the Trinity is to own that we do not comprehend it'.

The Book of Revelation became a major source for the earlier books of *Paradise Lost*, in particular for the three-day battle in Heaven. A recent critic tells us that the incidents of *Paradise Lost* were 'as profoundly true as the Book of Revelation itself'. In what sense *true* – historical or mythical? In proclaiming the dogma of the Assumption of the Virgin Mary into Heaven, not long ago, Pope Pius XII asserted that it was 'not a terrestrial truth, but a celestial truth', i.e., not true at all. Myth can be accepted as material for poetry, but not as true, or as doctrine.

Christopher Hill tells us that in the free-ranging discussions of the 1640s and 1650s the Book of Revelation was especially to the fore, and inspired the lunacies of Fifth Monarchy men, Baptists, Diggers, Ranters, Quakers, Muggletonians, and that in all this discussion Milton's radical friends participated. 'At the time of writing the *De doctrina* (and therefore of writing *Paradise Lost*) Milton certainly still expected that Christ and his Saints would ultimately reign on earth.' This may have helped to keep him going. But we must be careful not to go too far and say that he 'consciously and consistently' shared the heresies (and lunacies) of 'some of his very radical contemporaries'. I think this underestimates Milton's essential solitariness: much too individualistic, and too arrogant intellectually, to share anybody's views, he was determined to think out everything for himself alone.

In the dedication of his book to 'All the Churches of Christ' (!) Milton emphasises this. 'I resolved not to repose on the faith or judgment of others in matters relating to God. . . . I was concerned to discover in many instances adverse reasonings either evaded by wretched shifts, or attempted to be refuted, rather speciously than with solidity, by an affected display of formal sophisms, or by a constant recourse to the quibbles of the grammarians.' And so on: pure Milton, here is the man himself speaking. 'According to my judgment, therefore, neither my creed nor my hope of salvation could be safely trusted to such guides.' He addressed himself to the learned. 'For my own part, I adhere to the Holy Scriptures alone – I follow no other heresy or sect.' He was himself, alone.

Ironically enough, it was Daniel Skinner – the rather discreditable son of Samuel Pepys's housekeeper (if that was her function) – who tried, after Milton's death, to publish the *De doctrina christiana* in the more liberal Netherlands. Skinner, a promising Westminster and Trinity (Cambridge) man, had been in a position to 'cull out' Milton's manuscripts after his death; Professor Parker informs us that 'the elderly Milton was much drawn to bright young men'. The English government was standing no more trouble from that quarter, and prevented the publication of the book – in the revealing phrase of respectable Secretary of State Williamson – of 'that late Villain Milton'.

Such was the estimation in which the defender of regicide was contemporaneously held.

CHAPTER TEN

Paradise Lost

THE Restoration was the best thing that could have happened to Milton. It *forced* him to drop dealing with the ephemera of politics, back upon his own true genius, the life of the imagination and its expression in poetry. The extraordinary thing is that, with his sense of dedication, his early determination to write an epic, he should have taken such risks of never getting round to writing it. The *Christian Doctrine* was necessary preparation; it provided the groundwork and the scaffolding by which he was to erect his glorious building. But the monument, by so narrow a shave, might never have come into existence at all: Clarendon had only to suggest his name to the Commons, and he would have been hanged according to his deserts. Even the carcases of those he had defended – Cromwell, Bradshaw, Ireton – were taken up from their graves and hanged in chains.

Everything about Milton was strange and different from other people – such a contrast to Shakespeare! Milton's waiting so long before embarking on the work is the more odd because of his long-announced intention 'to leave something so written to aftertimes as they should not willingly let it die'. It showed sublime assurance to announce it beforehand: any normal person would not have dared, or would have been more dubious about the chances of accomplishing

Things unattempted yet in prose or rhyme.

By a pleasant irony *Paradise Lost* received its *imprimatur* from Laud's successor on the throne of Canterbury, Archbishop Sheldon, through his chaplain as licenser, one Tompkins, *Ecclesiae Anglicanae contra Schismaticos assertor eximius* ('Admir-

215

able protagonist of the Anglican Church against the Schismatics'). However, the Anglican censorship was exercised with a notable degree of toleration – far more so than any Presbyterian censorship would have been. Milton had reason to be grateful. Moreover, contrary to popular belief, the poem had considerable success. Published in 1667, it sold out its first edition of 1300 copies by 1674, when it went into a second in the year of Milton's death.

Then it gathered momentum. In 1678 came a third, and in the year of the Revolution which turned out James II came a fourth, with a roll-call of distinguished names as subscribers. Among them were the Poet Laureate, Dryden – a Catholic, be it noted; eminent Anglicans like Dean Aldrich and Dean Atterbury – all more tolerant than Milton; the poet Waller, the dramatist Sir Robert Howard; peers like Lord Dorset and the great lawyer, Somers, to become a peer; Milton's old Tory antagonist, Sir Roger L'Estrange. Four years later there followed a fifth edition, a fine folio; three years later a sixth, and then there poured from the press no less than nine more editions before the great scholar Bentley's extraordinary edition, embellished by portraits engraved by Vertue and emendations as if the text were Virgil or Homer, in 1732. Meanwhile translations were appearing abroad.

The fact was that *Paradise Lost* soon began to be appreciated for the wonderful work it is. A historian observes that the Revolution of 1688, which effectively inaugurated a Parliamentary monarchy, gave a strong impulse to Milton's renown. He entered Whig temples of Fame as a defender of liberty, with busts of him venerated as such. To the Dissenters, immensely strengthened by the 'glorious' Revolution, he became patriarch and prophet, *Paradise Lost* along with *The Pilgrim's Progress* promoted to the status of secondary bibles. In the end Milton had fortune on his side.

Persons of taste appreciated the greatness of the work from the first, led by Dryden. He based an opera on Milton's work, *The State of Innocence, or the Fall of Man*, acknowledging that 'this poem has received its entire foundation, part of the design, and many of the ornaments, from him'. He apologised for the inadequacy of his own work, 'the original being undoubtedly one of the greatest, most noble, and most sublime poems which either this age or nation has produced'. How generous a tribute this was, and every word of it rings sincere! According to Aubrey, Dryden, 'who very much admired him [Milton], went to him to have leave to put his *Paradise Lost* into a drama in rhyme. Mr Milton received him civilly, and told him he would give him leave to tag his verses.' (Tags were points, sometimes of metal or silver, which decorated the ends of laces or ribbons on dress.)

In a prefatory note on 'The Verse' Milton had disclaimed rhyme – as usual with him, too vehemently – as 'being no necessary adjunct or true ornament of poem or good verse, in longer works especially, but the invention of a barbarous age, to set off wretched matter and lame metre'. This is unnecessarily dismissive, especially when one thinks of his favourite Spenser. He allows that rhyme had been 'graced indeed since by the use of some famous modern poets, carried away by custom, but much to their own vexation, hindrance, and constraint to express many things otherwise, and for the most part worse, than else they would have expressed them'. There is cogency in this second point: it left him free to express things in the best way possible.

In fact, a practising poet notices that there is a great deal of rhyme in *Paradise Lost,* less in *Paradise Regained*, yet still more in *Samson Agonistes*. This is in accordance with aesthetic decorum, partly deliberate, partly instinctive. To a born poet, rhyme comes naturally (one can hardly tell why; it is such a subtle matter psychologically). *Paradise Lost* is so gorgeously carried out as to be, in a sense, a baroque poem. Many rhymes occur at the ends of lines; still more occur between the end of a line and the next half-line, or vice versa. Here are opposite examples, from opposite pages:

> We should be quite abolished and exp*ire*.
> What fear we then? what doubt we to incense
> His utmost *ire*?

> Scorning surp*rise*. Or, could we break our way

> By force, and at our heels all Hell should *rise*. . . .

Milton had such intellectual command as to carry whole verse-paragraphs in his head; so it is not surprising to find the clang of rhyme often occurring at intervals of several lines:

> His glory to augm*ent*. The bold design
> Pleased highly those Infernal States, and joy
> Sparkled in all their eyes: with full ass*ent*. . . .

In addition to this there is the frequent clang of half-rhyme or consonantal rhyme. Take such a passage as this:

> With shuddering horror pale, and eyes agh*ast*,
> Viewed first their lamentable lot, and found
> No *rest*. Through many a dark and dreary vale
> They p*assed*. . . .

Sometimes there are passages where rhymes, half-rhymes or consonantal alternate. All this is partly conscious artistry, partly instinctive. The effect in *Paradise Lost* is greatly to enrich the verse and strengthen it, to band it together and impress it on the mind, make it sparkle and far more interesting. For a double reason *Paradise Regained* is barer, though rhyme and half-rhyme do recur in it – partly by reason of aesthetic decorum, and partly because the poet is less inspired, not gripped emotionally to the same extent. In *Samson Agonistes* he is even more emotionally gripped, more autobiographically involved than before, and there is more rhyme than ever.

To the second edition of *Paradise Lost*, having won its acclaim, Marvell prefaced a tribute:

> When I beheld the Poet blind, yet bold,
> In slender book his vast design unfold. . . .
>
> Thou sing'st with so much gravity and ease,
> And above human flight dost soar aloft
> With plume so strong, so equal and so soft. . . .

He concludes by taking up Milton's point about rhyme:

I too, transported by the mode, offend
And, while I meant to praise thee, must commend;
Thy verse, created, like thy theme sublime,
In number, weight, and measure, needs not rhyme.

My aim, however, is not to repeat the commonplaces of literary criticism. In this appalling egalitarian age, without sense of quality or distinction, without taste or savour, in which so much writing is characterless chaff, there is an inflationary Milton industry as there is a Shakespeare industry, neither of which illuminates the writer, but buries him under a mountain of commentary without significance. I prefer to concentrate on portraying his mind and the character of his thought.

We are struck at once with how much of these poems is continuous with his prose work, not only the *Christian Doctrine* but also the political tracts. So much of *Paradise Lost* is political, as one should expect from the cast of his thought, his feverish interest in politics; it shows the unity of his mind, the consistency of all his work. The historian particularly notices how much the poem reflects, as always with a real writer, his own experience: of Civil War and Commonwealth, the Restoration, his sense of strain and suffering, his anger and grief at heart. Saintsbury, one of the best of Milton critics, noticed the upheaval of emotions reflected in the inequalities and differing levels of the work.

The subject is the Biblical one of the Fall of Man, but leading themes are rebellion, defeat, revenge; one recognises Civil War, Commonwealth, Restoration, all living and contemporary, filled with emotions: anger, envy, exasperation, jealousy, admiration, pride, arrogance – the whole gamut of Milton's temperament. This is why the poem is so much alive and vibrant with feeling, unlike other deliberate and self-consciously heroic poems – his opposite number Davenant's *Gondibert*, or some of Dryden's. And, of course, Satan is the hero – Lucifer proud and arrogant, of ambition illimitable, rebellious, defeated but unrepentant, unyielding, never giving in. This was what would have Milton's sympathy; this was his own spirit. A practising poet would also notice that the inner sympathy is expressed in the inspired poetry Satan commands – far finer than that in which God expresses himself (occasionally like a club bore orotundly, like the Almighty when his antiquated cosmology is exposed by a scientific Father of the Church at the beginning of *Penguin Island*).

Here is Satan:

> What though the field be lost?
> All is not lost – the unconquerable will,
> And study of revenge, immortal hate,
> And courage never to submit or yield;
> And what is else not to be overcome?
> That glory never shall his wrath or might
> Extort from me. To bow and sue for grace
> With suppliant knee, and deify his power
> Who, from the terror of this arm, so late
> Doubted his empire – that were low indeed:
> That were an ignominy and shame beneath
> This downfall. . . .[1]

This comes at the beginning of the poem and would have been written not long after the Restoration, Milton's own situation with regard to which it closely recapitulates. It is Satan speaking; it is also Milton.

Satan carries on: after defeat

> the mind and spirit remains
> Invincible, and vigour soon returns

– as was indeed the case with Milton –

> Though all our glory extinct, and happy state
> Here swallowed up in endless misery.
> But what if he our Conqueror – whom I now
> Of force believe almighty, since no less
> Than such could have o'erpowered such force as
>   ours. . . .

This was true enough even in 1660; there was something surprising in the way the Restoration came about. Such was the
strength of the Cromwellian armies, the prestige of Cromwell's
rule, that it took the breakdown into faction-fighting and, even
then, twenty months before Charles II came back.

Faction had opened the way. Milton had urged unity against
the enemy in all his tracts and pamphlets in 1659–60, as Satan
does in the poem:

> with this advantage, then,
> To union, and firm faith, and firm accord.

Instead of that, they had taken to faction:

> men only disagree
> Of creatures rational, though under hope
> Of heavenly grace and, God proclaiming peace,
> Yet live in hatred, enmity, and strife
> Among themselves. . . .

One recognises a type he was familiar with, in the 'bad men'
who

> should boast
> Their specious deeds on earth, which glory excites,
> Or close ambition varnished o'er with zeal.

Zeal had been the special quality, almost the vocational disease, of Puritans. Yet many who had been brave in the field
faltered when it came to the political course to follow:

> I laugh when those who at the spear are bold
> And venturous, if that fail them, shrink, and fear
> What yet they know must follow – to endure
> Exile, or ignominy, or bonds, or pain,
> The sentence of their conqueror. This is now
> Our doom – which, if we can sustain and bear. . . .

To bear it, Satan's motto was Milton's:

> to be weak is miserable,
> Doing or suffering.

Never give up:

> for who would lose,
> Though full of pain, this intellectual being,
> Those thoughts that wander through eternity,
> To perish rather, swallowed up and lost
> In the wide womb of uncreated Night?

This was Milton's consolation, the real paradise; the splendour of the poetry at this point reveals what inspired him.

The first two Books of *Paradise Lost* are full of reminders of late events. We need hardly cite the lengthy description of war. We remember how the City saved the situation after Edgehill, when the Royalists got their nearest to London at Brentford, and the City marched out its trained bands, 20,000 strong, to turn the tide of war at Turnham Green:

> the gates wide open stood,
> That with extended wings a bannered host,
> Under spread ensigns marching, might pass through
> With horse and chariots ranked in loose array.

These early Books are filled with councils, consultations, debates, speeches, such as Milton had witnessed and, as a civil servant, listened to during the Commonwealth. After Moloch speaks in council, up rises Belial:

> A fairer person lost not Heaven; he seemed
> For dignity composed, and high exploit.
> But all was false and hollow; though his tongue
> Dropped manna, and could make the worse appear
> The better reason, to perplex and dash
> Maturest counsels. . . .

A plausible Parliamentary orator evidently; one cannot but think Milton had some particular person in mind, the type was familiar:

                              for his thoughts were low –
To vice industrious, but to nobler deeds
Timorous and slothful. Yet he pleased the ear,
And with persuasive accent thus began:
'I should be much for open war, O Peers,
As not behind in hate, if what was urged
Main reason to persuade immediate war
Did not dissuade me most and seem to cast
Ominous conjecture on the whole success. . . .'

We spare the reader this sarcastic reconstruction of a Parliamentary debate. It was noted of Milton in later life that, instead of humour, his turn was for sarcasm. Belial was a Parliamentary type all right. Milton was a good hater, and these early Books breathe hate.

The upshot of defeat was the Restoration of the King – rendered recognisably.

                    Suppose he should relent,
And publish grace to all, on promise made
Of new subjection; with what eyes could we
Stand in his presence humble, and receive
Strict laws imposed, to celebrate his throne
With warbled hymns, and to his Godhead sing
Forced Halleluiahs, while he lordly sits
Our envied sovereign, and his altar breathes
Ambrosial odours and ambrosial flowers,
Our servile offerings?

The imagination boggles at the thought of Milton warbling hymns at the Court of Charles II; yet the Court is recognisable. Adam's primitive state, in all its magnificent nudity, was

                    More solemn than the tedious pomp that waits
On princes, when their rich retinue long
Of horses led and grooms besmeared with gold
Dazzles the crowd and sets them all agape

– just what Milton had enforced in his last tract, the *Ready and Easy Way to establish a Free Commonwealth*. Were they now

> to consult how we may best,
> With what may be devised of honours new,
> Receive him coming to receive from us
> Knee-tribute yet unpaid, prostration vile!
> Too much to one! but double how endured –
> To one and to his image now proclaimed?

Satan encourages his followers to conspiracy:

> But what if better counsels might erect
> Our minds, and teach us to cast off this yoke?

– as the reviving spirits of the Republicans were to do, thus
encouraged, throughout Charles II's reign.

> Will ye submit your necks, and choose to bend
> The supple knee?

They would not, if Satan knew them aright:

> if not equal all, yet free,
> Equally free; for orders and degrees
> Jar not with liberty, but well consist.

This is a fascinating statement, for in two lines it sums up the
whole Whig position: they were protagonists of liberty, but –
aristocrats as they were – they firmly believed in the hierarchi-
cal order of society, with its orders and degrees. No wonder the
Republican Milton became their prophet. (The monarchy was
more popular, in the precise meaning of the term.)

How could they have lost the game, and been defeated in
1660?

> For who can yet believe, though after loss,
> That all these puissant legions, whose exile
> Hath emptied Heaven, shall fail to re-ascend,
> Self-raised, and re-possess their native seat?
> For me, be witness all the host of Heaven,
> If counsels different, or dangers shunned
> By me, have lost our hopes.

They were to live, to fight another day:

> But he who reigns
> Monarch in Heaven till then as one secure

— as Charles I had done —

> Sat on his throne, upheld by old repute,
> Consent or custom, and his regal state
> Put forth at full, but still his strength concealed. . . .

In 1640, no one had suspected the latent strength of the monarchy:

> Which tempted our attempt, and wrought our fall.

Now, after 1660:

> our better part remains
> To work in close design, by fraud or guile,
> What force effected not. . . .

They had only to wait till 1688, fourteen years after Milton's death, when the Revolution would accomplish their hopes – or some of them.

Meanwhile, there was much to endure. Belial is depicted as a Parliamentary hypocrite:

> than whom a Spirit more lewd
> Fell not from Heaven, or more gross to love
> Vice for itself. To him no temple stood
> Or altar smoked; yet who more oft than he
> In temples and at altars, when the priest
> Turns atheist, as did Eli's sons, who filled
> With lust and violence the house of God?

How much one would like to know whom Milton had in mind for his portrait of Belial! *Paradise Lost* is not a satire, like Dryden's *Absalom and Achitophel*, with its specific identification of Achitophel as Shaftesbury. All the same, that plausible orator

who had served Cromwell and fallen from grace to serve
Charles II was generally held to be both atheist and
whoremaster. The depiction is, with Milton, generalised:

> In courts and palaces he also reigns,
> And in luxurious cities, where the noise
> Of riot ascends above their loftiest towers,
> And injury and outrage; and when night
> Darkens the streets, then wander forth the sons
> Of Belial, flown with insolence and wine.

This was all too exact. The streets were unsafe with the young
rakes of courtiers running riot – Rochester and Sedley were
actually streakers, well before today's exhibitions; there were
constant duels, nose-slitting of opponents, and Monmouth, the
King's handsome young bastard, killed a poor parish-beadle
who tried to interfere with one of his assaults.

Milton must have felt more than ever justified by the course
the Restoration took: the licence and frivolity of Charles II's
Court (unlike Charles I's – was it for this that Parliament had
destroyed a virtuous king?); defeat at sea, the Dutch in the
Medway (people began to wish for Old Noll again); the Great
Plague of 1665 and the Fire of London in 1666. Heaven did not
seem to be rewarding the Restoration. Milton's poem came out
in 1667.

He never gave in. By the time we come to Book VI, it is:

> 'Servant of God, well done! Well hast thou fought
> The better fight, who single hast maintained
> Against revolted multitudes the cause
> Of truth, in word mightier than they in arms –
> And for the testimony of truth hast borne
> Universal reproach, far worse to bear
> Than violence; for this was all thy care:
> To stand approved in God, though worlds
> Judged thee perverse.'

Whom does this describe but Milton himself? He always identified 'truth' and 'right reason' with himself; and there is a note
of reproach, as well as a reminder of his *Defences*, in the words,

> nor is it aught but just
> That he who in debate of truth hath won
> Should win in arms, in both disputes alike
> Victor.

He was indeed not only intransigent, but exorbitant:

> there be who faith
> Prefer, and piety to God, though then
> To thee not visible when I alone
> Seemed in the world erroneous to dissent
> From all: my Sect thou seest; now learn too late
> How few sometimes may know when thousands err.

Utterly unyielding, he cared nothing for what anybody else thought, alone in the world, and blind.

Book III begins with the marvellous hymn, 'Hail, holy Light', for which one would forgive him anything:

> but thou
> Revisit'st not these eyes, that roll in vain
> To find thy piercing ray, and find no dawn. . . .
> Thus with the year
> Seasons return; but not to me returns
> Day, or the sweet approach of even or morn,
> Or sight of vernal bloom, or summer's rose,
> Or flocks, or herds, or human face divine;
> But cloud instead and ever-during dark
> Surrounds me, from the cheerful ways of men
> Cut off. . . .

We learn from this long prelude to the Book how much the poem owed to Milton's active dream-life, and the memories he drew on of the early country life at Horton, which inspired 'L'Allegro' and 'Il Penseroso', before the excitement of the Civil War deflected him from poetry. There remained the never-quenched ambition for greatness to inspire him – and surely to console, now that he was fulfilling that for which he was born: recalling

> Those other two equalled with me in fate,
> So were I equalled with them in renown,
> Blind Thamyris and blind Maeonides,
> And Tiresias and Phineus, prophets old.

His ardent wish was to be fulfilled.

Milton put the whole of his life's experience – except, perhaps significantly, the ardour of his feelings for Diodati – into his great poem. Delicious pastoral descriptions recall the landscapes of the earlier poems; there are two references to remind us of his meeting with Galileo, and the famous lines about the Val d'Arno and the autumnal leaves in Vallombrosa. Equally there are passages to recall what he had seen in Italy, the disapprobation of the trappings of Catholicism that had made him, so hospitably entertained – so good-looking when young – unpopular for his outspoken views:

> Embryos and idiots, eremites and friars,
> White, black and grey, with all their trumpery . . .
> And they who, to be sure of Paradise,
> Dying put on the weeds of Dominic,
> Or in Franciscan think to pass disguised. . . .
>   Then might ye see
> Cowls, hoods, and habits, with their wearers tossed
> And fluttered into rags; then relics, beads,
> Indulgences, dispenses, pardons, bulls,
> The sport of winds: all these, upwhirled aloft,
> Fly o'er the backside of the World far off
> Into a Limbo large and broad, since called
> The Paradise of Fools. . . .[2]

The Church's hirelings reappear, not only from the prose tracts but all the way from 'Lycidas':

> So clomb this first grand Thief into God's fold:
> So since into his Church lewd hirelings climb.

His consistent view of the futility of metaphysical disputation is summed up in a few famous lines, to which we may well subscribe:

Others apart sat on a hill retired,
In thoughts more elevate, and reasoned high
Of Providence, Foreknowledge, Will, and Fate –
Fixed fate, free will, foreknowledge absolute –
And found no end, in wandering mazes lost.

He reaffirms his un-Calvinist view of Predestination. Adam and Eve had been granted reason by God, and 'Reason is Choice'. In Book V the Angel Raphael warns the happy couple:

to persevere
He left it in thy power – ordained thy will
By nature free, not over-ruled by fate
Inextricable, or strict necessity.

God, in a somewhat casuistical argument, exonerates himself from responsibility for their Fall: they

'So were created, nor can justly accuse
Their Maker, or their making, or their fate,
As if predestination overruled
Their will, disposed by absolute decree
Of high foreknowledge. They themselves decreed
Their own revolt, not I. If I foreknew. . . .'

In these circumstances Mr Empson, not unreasonably, thinks their treatment rather unkind of God.[3]

We come to what, in modern secular terms, may be regarded as a central issue of the poem: the relation between the sexes. Man (Adam) was created first, as lord of creation; then Woman (Eve) was created out of a rib of his, to be his solace and recreation. As a child I believed this charming fable and that males, in consequence, were minus a rib. (Sad experience enlightened me, on both counts.)

In their looks
The image of their glorious Maker shone

> Truth, wisdom, sanctitude severe and pure –
> Severe, but in true filial freedom placed,
> Whence true authority in men: though both
> Not equal, as their sex not equal seemed;
> For contemplation he and valour formed,
> For softness she and sweet attractive grace;
> He for God only, she for God in him.

To a modern ear the last line sounds ludicrous; *nous avons changé tout cela*: the case is almost completely reversed.

We have had reason to see that Milton had virtually no sense of humour, and in the relations of Adam and Eve this is made abundantly clear – as when she addresses her partner:

> 'O thou for whom
> And from whom I was formed flesh of thy flesh,
> And without whom am to no end, my guide
> And head! what thou hast said is just and right. . . .
>   I chiefly, who enjoy
> So far the happier lot, enjoying thee
> Pre-eminent by so much odds, while thou
> Like consort to thyself canst nowhere find.'

We may well wonder whether these were the terms exchanged between Mary Powell, the Cavalier's daughter, and her Puritan husband. Cavaliers were apt, *per contra*, to make rather a cult of women.

With Milton, beauty is regarded as feminine only – again a Puritan view, when one thinks of the Renaissance cult of male beauty, in portraits and sculpture, or in the delighted renderings of handsome young men at Charles I's Court by Van Dyck; but here

> How beauty is excelled by manly grace
> And wisdom, which alone is truly fair.

The subjection of women is submissively accepted by Eve, who thus accosts Adam:

> 'My author and disposer, what thou bidd'st

Unargued I obey. So God ordains:
God is thy law, thou mine: to know no more
Is woman's happiest knowledge, and her praise.'

Adam receives this with fatuous complacency, and

in delight
Both of her beauty and submissive charms,
Smiled with superior love. . . .

Anyone with a little more knowledge of women than Milton had – walled up in his egoism – might have surmised a piece of feminine flattery and dissimulation; in any case one could expect matrimonial trouble ahead.

The hymn, 'Hail, wedded Love', in Book IV puts forward a fatally idealistic view of marriage, all from the man's point of view and with the constant refrain of the inferiority of women:

Hail, wedded Love, mysterious law, true source
Of human offspring, sole propriety
In Paradise of all things common else!
By thee adulterous lust was driven from men . . . etc.

Anthropology informs us how restricted a conception this is, and that most of the propagation of the species goes on outside marriage. Milton has his Puritan tilt against 'illicit' pleasures and another kick at Courts: love is not to be found or, at least, sought

in Court amours,
Mixed dance, or wanton mask, or midnight ball,
Or serenate, which the starved lover sings
To his proud fair, best quitted with disdain.

This shows a rather nasty spirit, along with the incorrigible Puritan habit of laying down the law about other people's pleasures. We have already noticed in a prose tract his contemptuous dismissal of the enchanting love-poetry of the Caroline poets. Some of them were as sincere in the love that inspired

them as ever Milton was, if not more so, though the faint eroti-
cism of Adam and Eve's relations would indicate that Milton
was not altogether averse to the pleasures of the bed – within
the strict bond of matrimony, of course. Chaste Charles I had
been too uxorious, if anything; the hypocritical rule of the
Saints produced a shocking reaction with Charles II's Court:
but for them society would hardly have gone so flagrantly to the
other extreme.

What is the common sense underlying the mythical nonsense
of the Fall of Man, Original Sin, etc., which carries no conviction to a modern mind? If we strip away the familiar trappings
of the Biblical fable – rapidly becoming less familiar in an
uneducated, egalitarian society – we are still left with the relation of the sexes as a central theme in the poem; naturally
enough, for it sprang out of the crucial experience of Milton's
personal life, the problem posed for him by marriage. (He
would have done better not to marry.) At one point, in
describing the idealised relations of Adam and Eve, a personal
cri de cœur rises from Milton's lips:

> Oh, when meet now
> Such pairs, in love and mutual honour joined?

This occurs after Eve's exclusion from the instruction Adam
receives from the Angel Raphael about the cosmos, since knowledge is not the sphere of woman. She goes off to tend to her
flowers and fruits in the nursery – as it has been expressed in
a more brutal clime, her province is the *Kinder, Küche* and
Kirche. Milton divides the rôles with a somewhat fatuous smug-
ness:

> Her husband the relater she preferred
> Before the Angel . . .
>   he, she knew would intermix
> Grateful digressions, and solve high dispute
> With conjugal caresses.

In discourse with the Angel, as between two men, Adam con-
fides that too much was subducted from his side in creating
woman:

> 'at least on her bestowed
> Too much of ornament, in outward show
> Elaborate, of inward less exact.
> For well I understand in the prime end
> Of Nature her the inferior, in the mind
> And inward faculties, which most excel;
> In outward also her resembling less
> His image who made both.'

Man, we see, is God-like. After this, we are not surprised by Milton's candid recommendation of self-esteem:

> 'Ofttimes nothing profits more
> Than self-esteen, grounded on just and right
> Well managed. Of that skill the more thou know'st,
> The more she will acknowledge thee her head,
> And to realities yield all her shows.'

It hardly seems a recipe for a happy marriage.

The concept of love is no less cool:

> 'What higher in her society thou find'st
> Attractive, human, rational, love still:
> In loving thou dost well; in passion not,
> Wherein true Love consists not. Love refines
> The thoughts, and heart enlarges – hath his seat
> In Reason, and is judicious. . . .'

Once more we have this over-emphasis on reason; love itself is virtually (or virtuously) reduced to reason. One can well see that the masculine condescension in the whole depiction would drive a modern woman frantic. And Milton seems not to have realised that, unconsciously, this overbearing attitude opened the way to the subtler seductions of the Serpent: Eve was not wholly satisfied with her subjection.

Very revealingly, when she yields to temptation, and eats of the Tree of Knowledge, she considers whether not to

> 'keep the odds of knowledge in my power
> Without co-partner? so to add what wants
> In female sex, the more to draw his love.'

This is not merely feminine dissimulation but the desire to

> 'render me more equal, and perhaps –
> A thing not undesirable – sometime
> Superior; for, inferior, who is free?'

One can but sympathise with the sinner, after her inferiority has been so constantly, so tediously, rubbed in. Even when Adam falls, his male superiority is saved, for he does it deliberately, well knowing what *he* is doing:

> He scrupled not to eat,
> Against his better knowledge, not deceived,
> But fondly overcome with female charm.

One draws the moral that one should not be fondly overcome with female charm.

Immediately follow the reproaches of marital life; one recognises the familiar answering-back:

> 'What words have passed thy lips, Adam severe?
> Imput'st thou that to my default, or will
> Of wandering, as thou call'st it, which who knows
> But might as ill have happened thou being by,
> Or to thyself perhaps?'

It is the wearisome note of self-justification, and the too-frequent retort:

> 'Is this the love, is this the recompense
> Of mine to thee, ingrateful Eve, expressed
> Immutable when *thou* wert lost, not I . . .', etc.

The moral is driven home:

> 'Thus it shall befall
> Him who, to worth in women overtrusting,

> Lets her will rule: restraint she will not brook;
> And, left to herself, if evil thence ensue,
> She first his weak indulgence will accuse.'

God himself condemns Adam for giving way to woman:

> 'was she made thy guide,
> Superior, or but equal, that to her
> Thou didst resign thy manhood, and the place
> Wherein God set thee above her, made of thee
> And for thee, whose perfection far excelled
> Hers in all real dignity?'

We are given the gramophone record again, at higher strength
from such a source:

> 'her gifts
> Were such as under government well seemed –
> Unseemly to bear rule; which was thy part.'

(But what about Elizabeth I, or Catherine the Great?)
   Milton never lets up on woman. God's sentence is handed
down through the Archangel Michael:

> 'From Man's effeminate slackness it begins,'
> Said the Angel, 'who should better hold his place
> By wisdom, and superior gifts received.'

In the course of the bitter marital recriminations exchanged
between man and wife, a good many home-truths are uttered.
The better part is allotted to Adam, and that he speaks
for Milton is clear from the urgency, the conviction, of the
verse:

> 'Oh, why did God,
> Creator wise, that peopled highest Heaven
> With spirits masculine, create at last
> This novelty on earth, this fair defect
> Of Nature, and not fill the world at once
> With men as angels, without feminine?'

(Many male homosexuals have had the same thought.)

> 'This mischief had not then befallen,
> And more that shall befall – innumerable
> Disturbances on Earth through female snares,
> And straight conjunction with this sex. For either
> He never shall find out fit mate, but such
> As some misfortune brings him, or mistake;
> Or whom he wishes most shall seldom gain,
> Through her perverseness, but shall see her gained
> By a far worse or, if she love, withheld
> By parents; or his happiest choice too late
> Shall meet, already linked and wedlock-bound
> To a fell adversary, his hate or shame:
> Which infinite calamity shall cause
> To human life, and household peace confound.'

It is, at last, a realistic summing-up of the chances and dangers of marriage in actual fact. Here is again the Milton of the divorce tracts. Adam and Eve were reduced to making the best of a bad job, as Milton and Mary Powell had done.

The poem is indeed alive – as all true works of art are – with personal references, direct and indirect. At the beginning of Book VII – more than half-way through his gigantic task – Milton apostrophises himself:

> More safe I sing with mortal voice, unchanged
> To hoarse or mute, though fallen on evil days,
> On evil days though fallen, and evil tongues,
> In darkness, and with dangers compassed round,
> And solitude. . . .

He then repeats to us the touching information that the Muse visited him in the watches of the night, and often in dreams. At the opening of Book IX he again recognises the aid

> Of my celestial Patroness, who deigns
> Her nightly visitation unimplored,
> And dictates to me slumbering, or inspires
> Easy my unpremeditated verse,

Since first this subject for heroic song
Pleased me, long choosing and beginning late.

This corroborates the importance of his subconscious inspiration and brings home to us that we must never neglect that
factor in the inspiration of his work or our understanding of it.
No less characteristically he at once goes on to dismiss other
epics, such as Tasso's or Spenser's,

Heroic deemed, chief mastery to dissect
With long and tedious havoc fabled knights
In battles feigned. . . .

And so on. He had once admired these; now no longer, dedicated to the Biblical mythology of Puritanism.

Justice compels us to admit that he had a far more significant
subject, even apart from the myth he and so many others have
believed. He had set out to justify the ways of God to men.
Before the end he was obliged to conclude that they were
inexplicable. This reminds us of one or two places in the
Christian Doctrine where even he was unable to untie nonsense
knots, the kind of insoluble dilemma that arises from subscription to nonsense premises. Like that of the Problem of Pain,
which gave C. S. Lewis such excruciating difficulty: how an
omnipotent and omniscient Creator, an all-wise and all-loving
God, could inflict such suffering on his creatures. Well, people
who believe nonsense must expect awkward consequences.

The more real problem, also the theme of *Paradise Lost* – still
alive with us, though the force of the fable has fallen – is the
human dilemma with regard to knowledge. So colossal is the
mystery of the universe that no mere human faculties can comprehend it – much less localised religions, Christian or any
other, explain it. Here the Angel Raphael is still relevant, in his
promise to answer man's desire

'Of knowledge within bounds; beyond abstain
To ask, nor let thine own inventions hope
Things not revealed, which the invisible King,
Only omniscient, hath suppressed in night,

To none communicable in Earth or Heaven.'

It was to be expected that Milton, with his background and prejudices, would have no sympathy with the scientific views of the Royal Society, for all the prominence of its activities just at the time that he was writing *Paradise Lost* – it was patronised by Charles II and leading members of it were Royalists like Wren and Evelyn, Tories like Pepys. Milton preferred to operate on the basis of the antiquated Ptolemaic view of the universe, though he was acquainted with the Copernican. (We see how absurd was Christopher Hill's pre-judged conclusion: 'Royalists were Ptolemaics, Puritans Copernicans.' Almost, though not precisely quite, the opposite was true.)

With Milton's dominant interest being religion, *his* religion, he settled for an indifferent view:

> This to attain, whether Heaven move or Earth
> Imports not, if thou reckon right; the rest
> From man or angel the great Architect
> Did wisely to conceal, and not divulge
> His secrets, to be scanned by them who ought
> Rather admire.

This reminds one of Newman's subterfuge, when confronted with the contradiction between the Bible and science on the point: 'whether the sun moves round the earth, or the earth moves round the sun, we shall never know until we know what motion is'. (He also believed in the liquefaction of the blood of St Januarius at Naples.)

Milton went on to an uncharacteristic touch: perhaps the Almighty had left the question open

> to move
> His laughter at their quaint opinions wide
> Hereafter, when they come to model Heaven,
> And calculate the stars. . . .

We need only comment that it was by the scientific outlook and methods of the Royal Society, inspired by Bacon, that the stars have been calculated, that man has landed on the moon and is in a way to explore space.

Milton was interested in geography, and *Paradise Lost* exemplifies remarkable knowledge of the subject, especially for a blind man. We find him, rather pathetically, ordering in these years the best new available atlas – his amanuenses would have to read it for him. The information went in detail into Book XI, and into *Paradise Regained*. Everything he knew and had experienced, everything he believed in, went into these last works. He felt justified indeed, as he contemplated the world into which he had survived: he is describing Noah, but it is himself he has in mind:

> So all shall turn degenerate, all depraved,
> Justice and temperance, truth and faith, forgot;
> One man except, the only son of light
> In a dark age, against example good,
> Against allurement, custom, and a world
> Offended. Fearless of reproach and scorn. . . .

He would denounce the wrath to come on their impenitence. We have already observed that the wrath was not long in coming in those two years before the publication of the book – the fearful visitation of the Plague of 1665, from which Milton took refuge in the country at Chalfont St Giles, then the Great Fire. He had proved a true prophet.

Moving towards his conclusion with Book XII, he reinforces the lesson, what he had always thought:

> Since thy original lapse, true liberty
> Is lost, which always with right reason dwells
> Twinned, and from her hath no dividual being.
> Reason in man obscured, or not obeyed,
> Immediately inordinate desires
> And upstart passions catch the government
> From Reason, and to servitude reduce
> Man, till then free.

The poem ends with a vision of the future, which enables Milton to recapitulate the past, with his old fixations. This is a

bore. The clergy are described now as 'wolves' – we remember
the Roman wolf of 'Lycidas': now all are condemned.

> Wolves shall succeed for teachers, grievous wolves,
> Who all the sacred mysteries of Heaven
> To their own vile advantages shall turn
> Of lucre and ambition, and the truth
> With superstitions and traditions taint,
> Left only in those written records pure,
> Though not but by the Spirit understood.

He had become practically one with the Quakers, though he
would hardly have welcomed the thought: he was himself
alone.

On top of all this, *Paradise Lost* would be remembered for ever in
our language for its style alone: there is nothing else in literature like it. Much has been said of its classicism and the turn it
gave the language in the eighteenth century. But, really, it is a
baroque poem, gorgeous in its magnificence when it chooses to
be – as with the description of the progress of the Serpent
towards Eve:

> not with indented wave,
> Prone on the ground, as since, but on his rear,
> Circular base of rising folds, that towered
> Fold upon fold, a surging maze; his head
> Crested aloft, and carbuncle his eyes;
> With burnished neck of verdant gold, erect
> Amidst his circling spires, that on the grass
> Floated redundant.

There then follows a roll-call of reverberating names, a regular
feature contributing crystal and chalcedony and chrysoprase to
the poetry. (If one may have such baroque splendour in verse,
why not in church? But Milton was visually defective here,
inhibited by his Puritanism.)

The magnificence of the verse is sometimes varied by
charming pastoral passages, remembered scenes: one sees him

As one who, long in populous city pent,
Where houses thick and sewers annoy the air,
Forth issuing on a summer's morn, to breathe
Among the pleasant villages and farms
Adjoined, from each thing met conceives delight –
The smell of grain, or tedded grass, or kine,
Or dairy, each rural sight, each rural sound.

Such passages of pastoral simplicity are not frequent; more so are lines of quasi-romantic evocation, especially in Book IV, to remind one that the magic of *Comus* and the earlier poems had not been lost. It is appropriately overlaid and transcended by grandeur, the grandeur proper to the heroic and the epic.

The poem is not without its barer and more monotonous sections, much of Book VI, for example, and especially the speeches of the Almighty:

'Effulgence of my glory, Son beloved,
Son in whose face invisible is beheld
Visibly, what by Deity I am,
And in whose hand what by decree I do.
Second Omnipotence! two days have passed . . .', etc.

Milton could not command a simple style: one reason why his translation of the Psalms into common measure does not appeal. It looks, psychologically, as if he could not afford to let his hair down, and be simple and natural.

It is a curious thing psychologically that with Milton everything had to be bigger and grander, more vehement if not more pompous. Was it the case of a small man, acutely conscious of physical inferiority, engaged in filling himself out, asserting his masculinity, 'compensating' as the psychologists say? He certainly over-compensated himself.

George Saintsbury, our best critic of Milton's style, a prime authority on prosody, sums up: 'the peculiar stateliness which redeems even conceit from frivolity or frigidity; the unique combination of mass and weight with easy flow; the largeness of conception, imagery, scene; above all, perhaps, the inimitable stamp of phrase and style – attained, chiefly, by cunning selection and collocation of epithet – give the true Milton'.[4] (To 'cunning' I should prefer the word 'discriminating', instinctively discriminating.) Saintsbury goes on: 'It is only on the rarest occasions – when he attempts humour, or when he becomes simply didactic – that the style is other than consummate in its own way. . . . In his poetry, he particularly affects proper names of resonance and colour, scattering them over the verse-paragraphs with an effect that is almost pyrotechnical.'

Saintsbury considers that Milton derived the inspiration for his verse-paragraphs particularly from the soliloquies of Shakespeare. He says, fairly enough, that for all the splendour and grandeur 'he never, perhaps, attains to the absolute zenith of expression – as does Shakespeare often, and Dante sometimes'. I think this is because there is something wanting to the heart in Milton. Some lines in Shakespeare are, as I have said, the *ne plus ultra* of the language[5] – such lines as

> The odds is gone, and there is nothing left
> Remarkable beneath the visiting moon.

> Burn the great sphere thou mov'st in, darkling stand
> The varying shore of the world.

But Milton achieved and sustained, over a vast poem of twelve Books, the grand manner proper to epic. In his own time, the poet second only to him in genius perceived that: Dryden paid tribute to the old Puritan's loftiness of mind and majesty of expression. Saintsbury underlines this: 'in loftiness – sublimity – of thought and majesty of expression, both sustained at almost superhuman pitch, he has no superior, and no rival except Dante'. Perhaps, after all, it was an advantage to be not so very human. 'The magnificence of his poetical command of the language in which he writes has only to be perceived in order to carry all before it.' And we may say of its grandest expression, *Paradise Lost*, what Hazlitt said of *King Lear*: 'all that we can say must fall far short of the subject, or even what we ourselves conceive of it.'

CHAPTER ELEVEN

Milton, Christ and Samson

MILTON wrote easily and fast – as did Shakespeare; and *Paradise Regained*, the sequel to *Paradise Lost*, was written speedily. His nephew tells us: 'in a wonderful short space considering the sublimeness of it. However, it is generally censured [estimated] to be much inferior to the other, though he could not hear with patience any such thing when related to him.'[1] How like Milton that would be! He would know only too well how incapable of critical judgment ordinary people are, and how tedious it is for an original writer to hear their opinions expressed. Phillips, himself a writer, goes on reasonably: 'possibly the subject may not afford such variety of invention. But it is thought by the most judicious to be little or nothing inferior to the other for style and decorum.' That seems to me to put the case exactly, and to be right in both terms: naturally there is less variety in the shorter poem and from the nature of the subject. The subject itself dictates the decorum of a somewhat barer style; but as a work of art it is hardly at all inferior. though it appeals less to the reader.

Thomas Ellwood, the Quaker, liked to think that he had suggested the subject, and Masson considered that there is nothing against this. Ellwood was another of Milton's young men, to whom he had lent the manuscript of *Paradise Lost*. The young Quaker brought it back to the poet when visiting him at Chalfont during the Plague. Milton asked him how he had liked it and what he thought of it; after some talk, Ellwood chaffed him with: 'Thou hast said much here of Paradise Lost, but what hast thou to say of Paradise Found?' 'He made me no answer, but sat some time in a muse.'[2] (We know that Milton liked to sit back in an easy chair when dictating, with one leg over an arm.)

243

They broke off talk on that subject, and turned to another. Some time later, when Ellwood was visiting him in London, Milton showed him a manuscript of *Paradise Regained*, with: 'This is owing to you; for you put it into my head by the question you put to me at Chalfont, which before I had not thought of.'

Quakers are truth-telling people, and evidently Ellwood believed it. Actually, the subject is an obvious sequel to *Paradise Lost*, anticipated in that poem – though anticipatory lines could well have been incorporated in the manuscript, since it was not published for another two years. If Milton were merely being polite, as he was in personal conversation – as opposed to his writings, where his convictions blinded him to everything else – it shows once more his pleasant ways with young men, whom he had a way of attaching to him. Evidently the attraction was mutual.

Masson considers that there is no evidence of long premeditation with this poem as with the other, though it was not published till 1671. Once more we are not out to discuss the fable – Christ's Temptation by Satan in the Wilderness – but to descry and delineate the mind of the man behind it. We recognise the author, and his inspiration, from the first lines: the invocation to the Holy Spirit, to

inspire,
As thou art wont, my prompted song, else mute

– he can only write of these high subjects now –

> And bear through height or depth of Nature's bounds,
> With prosperous wing full summed, to tell of deeds
> Above heroic, though in secret done,
> And unrecorded left through many an age:
> Worthy to have not remained so long unsung.

There we have our author – of insuperable self-esteem, the unbending spirit, the unyielding claim – as against Shakespeare's gracious and bending naturalness and courtesy. And yet again the exorbitant claim is justified, apparently there had been no other poem on the theme.

We have several times observed the self-identification of sentiment and circumstance frequent with this so self-absorbed a writer. Others have noticed the frequent identifications with Christ's situation or Job's in this poem; and it is not difficult to recognise Milton in this description of Christ's child-hood:

> When I was yet a child, no childish play
> To me was pleasing; all my mind was set
> Serious to learn and know, and thence to do
> What might be public good; myself I thought
> Born to that end, born to promote all truth,
> All righteous things.

Truth, as always, is with Milton.

> Therefore, above my years,
> The Law of God I read, and found it sweet.

This is enforced again towards the end:

> The childhood shows the man,
> As morning shows the day. Be famous, then,
> By wisdom; as thy empire must extend,
> So let extend thy mind o'er all the world
> In knowledge; all things in it comprehend.[3]

Our minds go back to those years at Horton, when Milton had taken all knowledge for his province and built up the vast reading which served him well for his life's work, in prose as well as verse.

A charming reminiscence of Italy occurs with the simile:

> Or as a swarm of flies in vintage-time,
> About the wine-press where sweet must is poured,
> Beat off, returns as oft with humming sound.

Again we recognise the contemporary situation in

> For God hath justly given the nations up
> To thy delusions; justly, since they fell
> Idolatrous. . . .

and we hear once more the gramophone record against the clergy:

> Thy Father, who is holy, wise, and pure
> Suffers the hypocrite or atheous priest
> To tread his sacred courts, and minister
> About his altar, handling holy things. . . .

Satan finds Christ a much harder nut to crack than Eve had been; he consults with Belial, who appears again, as to what will best tempt him. Evidently not women, any more than with Milton, for

> What woman will you find,
> Though of this age the wonder and the fame

– Milton probably had Queen Christina of Sweden in mind, to whom he had written Latin letters for the Council of State –

> On whom his leisure will vouchsafe an eye
> Of fond desire? Or should she, confident,
> As sitting queen adored on Beauty's throne,
> Descend with all her winning charms begirt
> To enamour . . .

as Christina had since descended from her throne to enjoy the charms of private life. Christ, like Milton, was impervious to feminine allure:

> For Beauty stands
> In the admiration only of weak minds
> Led captive; cease to admire and all her plumes
> Fall flat, and shrink into a trivial toy.

Christ (Milton) was of more exalted mind than the susceptible, if wise, Solomon:

> Made and set wholly on the accomplishment
> Of greatest things. . . .
> Therefore with manlier objects we must try
> His constancy – with such as have more show
> Of worth, of honour, glory, and popular praise
> (Rocks whereon greatest men have oftest wrecked).

(Had he Cromwell in mind? We have seen that, though he had continued to serve the Protector, he had been recruited under the Commonwealth, and cannot have wholly approved of the Protectorate.)

Nor are riches a temptation to such as Jesus or Milton. Jesus replies for both:

> And what in me seems wanting but that I
> May also in this poverty as soon
> Accomplish what they did, perhaps, and more?

'They' were the heathen heroes of old, of Republican Rome. As for Milton, he was by no means so well off as he had been, since his financial losses with the Restoration and that of his pension from the state. Nevertheless, he was still independent – and he had not brought up his daughters to be fine ladies, but household servants.

> Extol not riches, then, the toil of fools,
> The wise man's cumbrance, if not snare; more apt
> To slacken virtue and abate her edge
> Than prompt her to do aught may merit praise.

Here is the Miltonic ideal, expressed by Christ –

> Yet he who reigns within himself, and rules
> Passions, desires, and fears, is more a king –
> Which every wise and virtuous man attains.

The aim should be not to rule 'headstrong multitudes',

> But to guide nations in the way of truth
> By saving doctrine, and from error lead
> To know and, knowing, worship God aright.

'Truth', 'right', 'right reason' are Miltonic signature-tunes.

These are the values of the elect – not glory, awarded by the mob. And our Saviour, speaking for Milton, is quite as hard on the people as the latter: no nonsense about democracy falls from his lips.

> For what is glory but the blaze of fame,
> The people's praise, if always praise unmixed?
> And what the people but a herd confused,
> A miscellaneous rabble, who extol
> Things vulgar and, well-weighed, scarce worth the
>   praise?
> They praise and they admire they know not what,
> And know not whom, but as one leads the other.

This had been Oliver Cromwell's view, we have seen, quite as much as Charles I's. What was praise from them worth?

> And what delight to be by such extolled,
> To live upon their tongues and be their talk?
> Of whom to be dispraised were no small praise –
> His lot who dares be singularly good.

One cannot mistake Milton's personal accent in this – the reproach that the lot of the singularly good is to receive small praise. He had always the consolation that

> The intelligent among them and the wise
> Are few, and glory scarce of few is raised.

One cannot avoid the suspicion that arises from the note of reproach that Milton would have liked glory. Who wouldn't prefer it to the obloquy he incurred, even though he had richly earned it? By a familiar psychological turn – sour grapes, no less – he denigrates worldly renown:

> Where glory is false glory, attributed
> To things not glorious, men not worthy of fame.
> They err who count it glorious to subdue
> By conquest far and wide, to overrun
> Large countries, and in field great battles win,
> Great cities by assault.

He had not objected to the victories of the *Civil* war – Marston Moor and Naseby, the assaults on Bristol, Gloucester,

Leicester, Chester – nor to Cromwell, Ireton, Fairfax, Lambert and their kind. Now, with years and disillusionment,

> What do these worthies
> But rob and spoil, burn, slaughter and enslave
> Peaceable nations, neighbouring or remote,
> Made captive, yet deserving freedom more
> Than those their conquerors, who leave behind
> Nothing but ruin whereso'er they rove,
> And all the flourishing works of peace destroy. . . ?

One cannot but welcome this new scale of values on the part of this combative Puritan, so bellicose in his vehement prose, who had challenged the issue in the 1640s. Now he was on his way to the pacifism of the Quakers or – a more unexpected approximation – to Chillingworth, who, Clarendon tells us, 'did really think all war unlawful'. Milton's heroes now were not Fairfax and Cromwell, but Job and Socrates:

> Who names not now with honour patient Job?
> Poor Socrates – who next more memorable?

Milton identified himself with Job in his trials: there are no less than five references to him in *Paradise Regained*. However, if there was no hope left there was at least no fear – though the thought is given to Satan:

> For where no hope is left is left no fear.

When Satan spreads the lure of power, Milton writes in irony:

> The world thou hast not seen, much less her glory,
> Empires, and monarchs, and their radiant Courts –
> Best school of best experience, quickest in sight
> In all things that to greatest actions lead.

These greatest actions were, of course, war; and there follows one of the many roll-calls of exotic names, which give glitter like mail to the verse – we cite the following for an example of what appealed to Milton:

> From Arachosia, from Candaor east,
> And Margiana, to the Hyrcanian cliffs
> Of Caucasus, and dark Iberian dales:

> From Atropatia, and the neighbouring plains
> Of Adiabene, Media, and the south
> Of Susiana, to Balsara's haven.

Evidently the latest new atlas had not been read to him in vain. This trick of reciting grand names he got from Shakespeare, who got it from Marlowe, initiator of so much – a spirit closer to Milton, for all his 'atheism'.

Milton's own experience of politics and diplomacy, as Secretary in the Foreign Tongues, is reflected in Satan's putting forward schemes, described by 'our Saviour':

> Long in preparing, soon to nothing brought,
> Before mine eyes thou hast set, and in my ear
> Vented much policy, and projects deep
> Of enemies, of aids, battles, and leagues,
> Plausible to the world, to me worth naught.

In other words, the ephemera of politics; in spite of his dismissal of them, Milton's fingers itched to be in them. He still could not keep his mind off them; this is why they appear in the transparent disguise of *Paradise Lost* and *Paradise Regained*. In spite of total defeat and a narrow escape from the gallows in 1660, then a dozen years of an unbroken front presented by the Restoration, the moment a crack in it appeared in 1672 with Charles II's Declaration of Indulgence Milton was ready to launch yet another prose tract: *Of True Religion, Heresy, Schism, Toleration, and what best means may be used against the growth of Popery* (1673). This was issued in the last year of his life – his last message to the world, not the great poems.

In *Paradise Regained* he continues with the sentiments based on his governmental experience:

> Then embassies thou show'st
> From nations far and nigh! What honour that
> But tedious waste of time, to sit and hear
> So many compliments and lies,
> Outlandish flatteries?

He means by 'outlandish' simply foreign – in spite of his earlier Italian culture, there was something insular about Milton, owing again to his Puritanism. This partly accounts for the defective appreciation of Milton abroad (a German, who knew no English, once described him to me as 'a kind of Klopstock'!). Here is yet another contrast to Shakespeare, who was fairly certainly never abroad and had no such depth of foreign culture, classical or Italian, and yet succeeds in being universal, because supremely human.

Milton goes on – the Son of God is speaking:

> Then proceed'st to talk
> Of the Emperor, how easily subdued,
> How gloriously.

This takes us straight back to that time in office, when he proposed to take a day off with young Cyriack Skinner, intermission from

> . . . what the Swede intend, and what the French.

In the poem Christ rejects the temptation of political power, as in the Bible, though there would seem to have been some ambivalence, some confusion in his aims, in historic fact, which brought about his death. There is, then, an ironic propriety in Milton's unconscious ambivalence: of course he longed for political power, as all Puritans did, to impose their Puritanism on an unregenerate people. One can descry this, in the moment of Milton's disclaiming it: Christ was not sent to free

> That people, victor once, now vile and base,
> Deservedly made vassal – who, once just,
> Frugal and mild, and temperate, conquered well . . .

as under Cromwell! we may add.

It would seem that Christ spoke for Milton in his aims from early years:

> Victorious deeds
> Flamed in my heart, heroic acts – one while
> To rescue Israel from the Roman yoke

– there is double-talk here, the further suggestion in 'the Roman yoke'.

> Then to subdue and quell, o'er all the earth,
> Brute violence and proud tyrannic power,
> Till truth were freed, and equity restored.

We must remember how tyrannous the power of the conquering Counter-Reformation seemed at its summit in the Thirty Years' War, especially to one who had seen the superb aggressive Rome of Sixtus V and Bernini, resplendent and new. Christ, speaking for Milton,

> Yet held it more humane, more heavenly, first
> By winning words to conquer willing hearts,
> And make persuasion do the work of fear;
> At least to try, and teach the erring soul,
> Not wilfully misdoing, but unware
> Misled; the stubborn only to subdue.

Milton has little idea how unpersuasive his prose tracts were, but there is no mistaking the objective – either about teaching the erring soul, or subduing the stubborn.

Christ's rejection of Greek philosophy expresses once more Milton's long-held objection to metaphysical speculation. We have noticed a nasty obscurantism as an element in Puritanism, along with its philistinism. It is sad to find the most learned of our poets in the end giving vent to it; it is also perverse – there is so much in Milton that was perverse, from what psychological source?

> However, many books,
> Wise men have said, are wearisome; who reads
> Incessantly, and to his reading brings not
> A spirit and judgment equal or superior
> (And what he brings what needs he elsewhere seek?)

– how very like Milton! –

> Uncertain and unsettled still remains,
> Deep-versed in books and shallow in himself,
> Crude or intoxicate, collecting toys
> And trifles for choice matters, worth a sponge,
> As children gathering pebbles on the shore.

Supercilious as ever, we may comment; and, yet again, justified.

Since these last works sum up the experience, the findings
and prejudices of a life-time, we are not surprised to find Milton's dismissal of philosophic speculations once more:

> But these are false, or little else but dreams,
> Conjectures, fancies, built on nothing firm.
> The first and wisest of them all professed
> To know this only, that he nothing knew.

Thus is Socrates dismissed; then Plato and the Sceptics:

> The next to fabling fell and smooth conceits;
> A third sort doubted all things, though plain sense.

Lastly, Milton dismissed the Stoic philosophy, though he himself – perverse and unself-critical as always – exemplified Stoic,
rather than Christian, virtues. Nor can we allow his perverse
denigration of classical literature, to which he owed so much, in
the interests of his Puritan cult of the Bible. The mulish Luther
had held that the finest Greek tragedies were nothing compared
with the Psalms of David – little would he know, though prepared to lay down the law (like laying down the law about
Milton without knowing the language – and such a marvellous
master of it!).

Now at the end of his career Milton perversely says that
Greece had rather derived her arts from the Hebrews!

> Ill imitated while they loudest sing
> The vices of their deities, and their own,
> In fable, hymn, or song, so personating
> Their gods ridiculous, and themselves past shame.

To such absurd lengths can doctrine drive one! He goes on to
say, ludicrously, that the classics of ancient Greece,

> Thin-sown with aught of profit or delight,
> Will far be found unworthy to compare
> With Sion's songs, to all true tastes excelling,
> Where God is praised aright and godlike men,
> The holiest of Holies and his Saints.

And then – ugh! – he adds the Puritan moralist's qualification:

> Unless where moral virtue is expressed
> By light of Nature, not in all quite lost.

He even goes so far as to regard the Bible as a better school of government, savage old Hebrew Prophets – Isaiah, Jeremiah, Amos and the rest – superior to Thucydides, Plato, Aristotle, Isocrates! (One is reminded of the eighteenth-century French lady on first reading the Prophets: 'Mais quel ton! Quel mauvais ton!')

> But herein to our Prophets far beneath,
> As men divinely taught, and better teaching
> The solid rules of civil government,
> In their majestic, unaffected style,
> Than all the oratory of Greece and Rome.
> In them is plainest taught, and easiest learnt,
> What makes a nation happy, and keeps it so,
> What ruins kingdoms, and lays cities flat.

One can only say that the turbulent, factious history of the ancient Jews, with its ulcerated conflicts and constant upheavals, was no recommendation for the Prophets, who, much as their people may have needed their advice, were singularly ineffective in impressing it on them. Nor was such a pattern a good one for anyone else to follow – rather the majestic peace imposed upon the nations by Imperial Rome.

This, with its overtones, and its sequel in Papal Rome, which Christianised the barbarians and imposed its own creative universality upon Europe, would not be sympathetic to a Puritan. However, the Puritan épopée, changeable and factious as it was after its Biblical model, was of short duration. And it is thought that, in Christ's rejection of temporal power, Milton took leave at last of any Fifth Monarchy delusions he had once entertained. A Marxist would say it was to be 'pie in the sky' after all.

Hanford perceives well 'the final flare-up of creative energy in *Samson Agonistes*, whether it came immediately on the completion of *Paradise Regained* or after an interval of one or more years'.[4] All persons of insight into literature and the ways of writers are agreed that *Samson Agonistes* is the most autobiographical work of this most autobiographical of writers. Hanford notices Milton's revealing additions to the Bible story: in particular, that 'he has carried over into the interpretation of the simple Israelite his own messianic conviction, making him generalise – as Christ himself had generalised – on the fate of corrupt nations fallen and the ingratitude of the common herd toward those who toil to free them from their common bonds'.[5]

> But what more oft, in nations grown corrupt,
> And by their vices brought to servitude,
> Than to love bondage more than liberty –
> Bondage with ease than strenuous liberty –
> And to despise, or envy, or suspect,
> Whom God hath of his special favour raised
> As their deliverer? If he aught begin,
> How frequent to desert him, and at last
> To heap ingratitude on worthiest deeds!

The Restoration situation is easily recognisable, with Milton's all too familiar reaction to it, his bitter reproach at its corruption and vices. His contempt for the people who have readily sold themselves to its easy bondage instead of striving for strenuous liberty, his personal sense of desertion – for many earlier fellow-travellers had gone over to it.

It is absurd to suppose that *Samson Agonistes* could ever have been written before the Restoration. The traditional view is usually right and has common sense with it. The massive sense, and authority, of Masson make no bones about it: 'we have no information as to the date of the composition, except what is conveyed in the poem itself. That certifies it beyond all doubt as a post-Restoration poem; and the most probable date is between 1666 and 1670.'[6] The flecks of historical reference within the poem corroborate this. W. P. Ker, whose judgment one must always respect for its combination of historical with common sense, says: 'Milton was driven by the strength of his own genius to write the tragedy of *Samson*. Till that was done he had not uttered himself to the full.'[7] The earliest testimonies also confirm this view. The early biographer, almost certainly

Cyriack Skinner, says: 'It was now that he began that laborious
work of amassing out of all the classic authors, both in prose
and verse, a Latin *Thesaurus* . . . also the composing *Paradise
Lost*, and the framing a body of divinity out of the Bible. All
which, notwithstanding the several calamities befalling him in
his fortunes, he finished after the Restoration. Also the British
History down to the Conquest, *Paradise Regained, Samson
Agonistes*, a tragedy, Logic and Accidence commenced
Grammar, and had begun a Greek Thesaurus, having scarce
left any part of learning unimproved by him.'[8] Jonathan
Richardson made careful inquiries from which we learn vivid
details, such as that Millington the bookseller used to lead
Milton by the hand when he went abroad. After his official
work came to an end, 'his time was now employed in writing
and publishing, particularly *Paradise Lost*; and, after that,
Paradise Regained and *Samson Agonistes*.'[9] To reverse the traditional order shows neither historical nor much literary sense –
as in the more notorious case of Shakespeare's Sonnets.[10]

So, too, with the autobiographical inspiration of *Samson*,
quite as much as with the Sonnets. Earlier, Milton had jotted
down Samson along with other possible subjects, Masson says,
'little knowing how much of his own future life was to corres-
pond with the fate of that particular hero of the Hebrews. The
experience had come, coincidence after coincidence, shock
after shock, till there was not one of all the Hebrew heroes so
constantly in his imagination as the blind Samson captive
among the Philistines. . . . A tragedy on Samson would be in
effect a metaphor of the tragedy of his own life. That, therefore,
by destiny as much as by choice, was Milton's dramatic subject
after the Restoration.'[11] And, as Saintsbury puts it succinctly,
'the other common saying [besides the one that Satan is the
hero of *Paradise Lost*] that "Samson is Milton" contains the
general truth again'.[12] I think we may see not only a final burst
of creative energy in *Samson Agonistes* but a final summing-up of
Milton's experience of life and his reflection on it.

Milton's prefatory note on 'That Sort of Dramatic Poem
called Tragedy' is again very personal, learned, incisive and, as
always, controversial. Masson sees that, with the Civil War

and Milton's intense involvement, his Puritan views hardened with regard to the drama as with everything else – sadly for the delicate author of *Comus*. Now, with his personal relegation and withdrawal, Milton defends tragedy after the ancient models, if no more. 'This is mentioned to vindicate tragedy from the small esteem, or rather infamy, which in the account of many it undergoes at this day, with other common interludes; happening through the poet's error of intermixing comic stuff with tragic sadness and gravity, or introducing trivial and vulgar persons: which, by all judicious, hath been counted absurd, and brought in without discretion, corruptly to gratify the people.' This is a palpable hit against Shakespeare, whom he had once loved. Milton continues: 'of the style and uniformity, and that commonly called the plot . . . they only will best judge who are not unacquainted with Aeschylus, Sophocles, and Euripides, the three tragic poets unequalled yet by any, and the best rule to all who endeavour to write tragedy'. Once more, superior as ever – and completely justified: his implicit claim places him beside Aeschylus, Sophocles and Euripides.

The very first line introduces us to blind Samson being led forward by a guiding hand, while thoughts crowd in upon him of

> Times past, what once I was, and what am now.

Immediately the Miltonic theme announces itself:

> Why was my breeding ordered and prescribed
> As of a person separate to God,
> Designed for great exploits, if I must die
> Betrayed, captived, and both my eyes put out,
> Made of my enemies the scorn and gaze?

Milton's enemies had not hesitated to taunt him with his blindness, and to say that he deserved it, a just punishment for his crime against the King. Samson's 'heaven-gifted strength', his glorious gift, had been a pledge:

> promise was that I
> Should Israel from Philistian yoke deliver!

The personal reference is unmistakable in the pathetic force of
the address that immediately follows:

> O dark, dark, dark, amid the blaze of noon,
> Irrecoverably dark, total eclipse
> Without all hope of day! . . .
> O first-created beam, and thou great Word –
> 'Let there be light, and light was over all',
> Why am I thus bereaved thy prime decree?

Thus the famous apostrophe carries on to its conclusion – not
only blindness to bear but, worse, the obloquy of enemies:

> But made hereby obnoxious more
> To all the miseries of life,
> Life in captivity
> Among inhuman foes.

As we have seen, Milton was lucky to have got off so lightly –
the Restoration had not been inhuman in its treatment of him.
However, no word of gratitude escaped this implacable man:
he was more acutely conscious of his enemies. And, indeed, he
was a target for attack by many scribblers of the time – we will
not burden the reader with their journalist names – and by
some who were more than mere scribblers. Masson notes how
Milton's paranoiac concern with his enemies – though he had
provoked them himself – goes straight into *Samson*, transmuted
into art, as so much of his experience had safely gone into the
fable of *Paradise Lost*.

Here is Masson's discerning judgment of *Samson Agonistes*.
'The marvel is that this purely artistic drama, this strictly
objective poetic creation, should have been all the while so profoundly and intensely subjective.'[13] But this is how great works
of art are made – as with comparable titanic figures,
Michelangelo or Beethoven – out of the experience of the whole
man, conscious and unconscious, not just fabricated by the
intellect. 'Nothing put forth by Milton in verse in his whole life
is so vehement an exhibition of his personality, such a
proclamation of his own thoughts about himself and about the
world around him, as his *Samson Agonistes*.' This is, of course,
why it throbs and thrills with life still. 'But, indeed, there is no

marvel in the matter. The Hebrew Samson among the Philistines and the English Milton among the Londoners of the reign
of Charles II were, to all poetic intents, one and the same
person. They were one and the same not only by the similarity
of their final circumstances, but also by the reminiscences of
their previous lives. That was, no doubt, the great recommendation to Milton in his last years of the subject he had
thought of only casually, amid so many others, a quarter of a
century before. By choosing that subject he had taken means to
be thoroughly himself once more in addressing his countrymen,
to be able to say what he would as tremendously as he could,
and yet defy the censorship.'

This is obvious enough: in the drama he could speak out
indirectly; in his last prose tract, *Of True Religion*, he spoke out
directly. These are the two last expressions of his exorbitant
autobiographical inspiration. Samson's situation is paralleled,
even in detail, in points we have already noticed in the prose
works.

> Am I not sung and proverbed for a fool
> In every street?

– as Milton. What adds to the bitterness of the irony is that he
had been a fool, judged by practical worldly considerations, of
expediency, etc.

> Do they not say, 'How well
> Are come upon him his deserts'?

This is exactly what his enemies did say. As for friends,

> How counterfeit a coin they are who 'friends'
> Bear in their superscription (of the most
> I would be understood).

Once more, this is exact: Milton's closest friends stood by him,
but they were few. The majority of his acquaintance, former
Puritans – even the egregious Prynne – had come to terms with
Charles II's régime, scandalous as it was. (This was what these
virtuous fanatics had won by their war.) Milton remained
upright, unreconciled, unbending, though blind. As for former
acquaintance,

> In prosperous days
> They swarm, but in adverse withdraw their head,
> Not to be found, though sought.

Samson has been blinded by his enemies:

> Blind among enemies! O worse than chains,
> Dungeon or beggary, or decrepit age!

For Milton, age and illness were creeping on; he was

> exposed
> To daily fraud, contempt, abuse, and wrong.
> Within doors or without, still as a fool,
> In power of others, never in my own.

What fate worse for a man so proud? Hanford points out that in this we come close to Milton's own household situation in these years: 'we recollect that his daughters attempted to cheat him in his marketings and that he did not in his dying hour forgive them'.[14] Though it is Samson who is speaking, we need hardly doubt that he speaks for Milton himself:

> That these dark orbs no more shall treat with light,
> Nor the other light of life continue long,
> But yield to double darkness near at hand;
> So much I feel my genial spirits droop,
> My hopes all flat . . .
> My race of glory run, and race of shame,
> And I shall shortly be with them that rest.

In Samson's services to his country we see repeated what Milton had claimed, again and again, of his own.

> In seeking just occasion to provoke
> The Philistine, thy country's enemy,
> Thou never wast remiss. . . .

Samson's acts 'God had done singly by me',

> Acknowledged not, or not at all considered,
> Deliverance offered. I, on the other side,
> Used no ambition to commend my deeds.

We have seen Milton say precisely that about his own service rendered in writing the *Defences*, and that such reward as he received he had made no interest for or pushed himself forward.

We may comment here that his reward had been not inconsiderable, as a secretary to the Council of State; but that – such was his self-esteem – membership of the Council itself would not have been above his ambition. Hanford has seen with perception that what the little man had wanted was power: 'the drama becomes then, in its central incident, a last imaginative gratification of the poet's will to power'.[15]

Samson's fate flowed from his disastrous marriage, and Milton puts it down to his weakness: he had married out of his own people, among the enemy, undermined by female charm. Milton had come to think weakness the worst of evils, from which the rest arose: the delicate nature, of feminine sensibility in youth, had become hardened. Masson sees the crucial importance of the disaster of Milton's first marriage – as it would be to a man of his exceptional egoism, poised on such an edge psychologically. 'The chief blunder in his life, that which had gone nearest to wreck it, and had left the most marring consequences and the most painful reflections, was the very blunder of which Samson had to accuse himself. Like Samson, he had married a Philistine woman – one not of his own tribe, and having no thoughts or interests in common with his own; and, like Samson, he had suffered indignities from this wife and her relations. The effects of Milton's unhappy first marriage on his temper and opinions are discernible in his biography far beyond their apparent end in the publication of his Divorce Pamphlets. . . .'[16] The experience had been a searing one, never healed by the apparently happy but brief interlude of the second marriage; while the third, to a woman below him in station, provided him with but a comfortable housekeeper. Fruits of his first marriage were with him to the end of his life in his unsatisfactory daughters – one mentally defective – and in his works. After all, this was the central experience of his personal life: what went into the reproaches (and self-reproaches), the marital recriminations of Adam and Eve, is given even more forceful and final expression in those of Samson and Dalila.

> Nay, what good thing
> Prayed for, but often proves our woe, our bane?

Milton's protected youth, brought up as a young Benjamin
with highest expectations (and the psychological consequences
to be expected), had prolonged his innocence and made him,
specially chosen, specially vulnerable:

> I was his nursling once and choice delight,
> His destined from the womb,
> Promised by heavenly message twice descending.
> Under his special eye
> Abstemious I grew up and thrived amain . . .
> But now hath cast me off as never known,
> And to those cruel enemies,
> Whom I by his appointment had provoked.

Milton was always convinced that he was doing God's work in
provoking and confronting his enemies – to be now cast off, and
at their mercy, blind.

The personal inspiration is unmistakable in the famous
hymn that immediately follows, questioning God's justice, or at
least finding it inexplicable (as it is on his religious assumptions):

> God of our fathers, what is man!
> That thou towards him with hand so various,
> Or might I say contrarious,
> Temper'st thy providence through his short course
> Not evenly, as thou rul'st
> The angelic orders and inferior creatures mute,
> Irrational, and brute.

Well might he wonder – not as regards inferior folk whose existence was of no importance and unmemorable, but even with
God's own elect. Uncharitable and un-Christian as this is, this
was what Milton really, and consistently, thought:

> Nor do I name of men the common rout,
> That wandering loose about
> Grow up and perish, as the summer fly,
> Heads without name no more remembered. . . .

Matthew Arnold had these lines in mind two centuries later

with his hardly less famous dismissal of the common herd of men. What was so inexplicable was God's treatment of those specially called to do his holy work:

> But such as thou hast solemnly elected,
> With gifts and graces eminently adorned
> To some great work, thy glory,
> And people's safety, which in part they effect.

'Which in part they effect' is a nice qualification: Milton would never have admitted that his work had been of no effect altogether.

> Yet towards these thus dignified, thou oft
> Amidst their height of noon,
> Changest thy countenance, and thy hand with no
>   regard
> Of highest favours past
> From thee on them, or them to thee of service.

What a reproach to the Almighty, and how Miltonic! to have received special favours, and rendered special service – to be treated thus!

> Nor only dost degrade them, or remit
> To life obscured, which were a fair dismission,
> But throw'st them lower than thou didst exalt them
>   high . . .

exactly what had happened to Milton, lower in status and circumstances now than those with which he had begun, let alone his elevation as a servant of the Commonwealth. Not only that, but exposed to opprobrium, scorn and persecution:

> Oft leav'st them to the hostile sword
> Of heathen and profane, their carcases
> To dogs and fowls a prey, or else captived . . .

as Cromwell's, Bradshaw's, Ireton's carcases had been dug up, others hanged, and yet more imprisoned, sentenced for life:

> Or to the unjust tribunals, under change of times,
> And condemnation of the ingrateful multitude.

We have had that precise phrase before: the people at large are always condemned of ingratitude for what the Puritan Revolution had done for them. Milton describes himself here:

> If these they scape, perhaps in poverty
> With sickness and disease thou bow'st them down,
> Painful diseases and deformed. . . .

Milton was now suffering from gout, the pains from which he found harder to bear than blindness, his hands deformed by chalkstones. The sufferings of the elect were 'causeless', not

> The punishment of dissolute days: in fine,
> Just or unjust alike seem miserable,
> For oft alike, both come to evil end.

Such was Milton's reflection on divine justice in the end – unanswerable, and inexplicable on his premises, as with C. S. Lewis and his Problem of Pain.

Hanford makes the penetrating observation – important psychologically, for the keynote of Milton's character was pride – 'the self-reproaches which Milton never allows himself to utter in his own person find free expression through the dramatic personality':[17]

> Whom have I to complain of but myself,
> Who this high gift of strength committed to me . . .
> But weakly to a woman must reveal it,
> O'ercome with importunity and tears?

Yet again he blames his fatal mistake as weakness:

> Of what now I suffer
> She was not the prime cause, but I myself,
> Who, vanquished with a peal of words, (O weakness!)
> Gave up my fort of silence to a woman.

The continual harping on this makes one suspect that Milton was afraid of weakness in himself, and that would be in keeping with our psychological interpretation of him: the youthful femininity, the fear of being taken for feminine, the over-emphasis on masculinity, the assertiveness, and consequent strain.

Enter Dalila, the wife: Woman, like Eve, making a plausible case for the fate she has brought on her husband. Whom Samson receives with:

> these are thy wonted arts,
> And arts of every woman false like thee,
> To break all faith, all vows, deceive, betray,
> Then as repentant to submit, beseech,
> And reconcilement move with feigned remorse,
> Confess, and promise wonders in her change.

Why had he not taken a wife among his own people? His father had not approved,

> but thou did'st plead
> Divine impulsion prompting how thou might'st
> Find some occasion to infest our foes.

We have noticed before Milton's propensity to impute his mistakes to the Almighty; but why give way to a wife's blandishments after the mistake of marrying her,

> when mustering all her wiles,
> With blandished parleys, feminine assaults,
> Tongue-batteries, she surceased not day nor night
> To storm me over-watched and wearied out.
> At times when men seek most repose and rest,
> I yielded. . . .

We do not know whether this lets us into the secrets of the Miltons' domestic interior; all we know is that Milton yielded and received his incompatible Cavalier wife back.

After that, the secrecy of marriage, in those days and in a Puritan household, closes round them – though there are the evidences of continuing disputes with the wife's family, and the angry reference of Milton's last words in his will. The exchanges between Dalila and Samson remind one of those between Eve and Adam. Here is womankind: Dalila says,

> In argument with men a woman ever
> Goes by the worse, whatever be her cause.

Samson refuses to take her back,

> To bring my feet again into the snare
> Where once I have been caught; I know thy trains
> Though dearly to my cost, thy gins, and toils,

> Thy fair enchanted cup, and warbling hymns
> No more on me have power.

Yet, when Samson has dismissed her, the Chorus comments:

> Yet beauty, though injurious, hath strange power,
> After offence returning, to regain
> Love once possessed, nor can be easily
> Repulsed, without much inward passion felt
> And secret sting of amorous remorse.

For what we may take it to be, this is the only indication we have of a more kindly emotional reaction.

Even so, Samson responds:

> Love-quarrels oft in pleasing concord end,
> Not wedlock-treachery endangering life.

The Chorus proceeds to ask what *is* it that women want?

> It is not virtue, wisdom, valour, wit,
> Strength, comeliness of shape, or amplest merit

– all of which, we may assume, Milton regarded himself as possessing –

> That woman's love can win or long inherit;
> But what it is, hard is to say,
> Harder to hit. . . .

There follows a disillusioned comment. Once the woman has got her man:

> Whate'er it be, to wisest men and best
> Seeming at first all heavenly under virgin veil,
> Soft, modest, meek, demure,
> Once joined, the contrary she proves, a thorn
> Intestine, far within defensive arms
> A cleaving mischief, in his way to virtue
> Adverse and turbulent. . . .

No one would assert this view of marriage as general, but that it was Milton's we may gather from its frequent repetition: what a writer constantly enforces is an index to his inner nature. That this was Milton's is clear from the signature-tune that immediately follows:

> Therefore God's universal law
> Gave to the man despotic power
> Over his female in due awe,
> Nor from that right to part an hour,
> Smile she or lour:
> So shall he least confusion draw
> On his whole life, not swayed
> By female usurpation, nor dismayed.

He does not seem to have reflected that his life would have incurred less confusion if he had not married at all, and had remained celibate. But that was not a Puritan solution of the problem. Thus was Samson frustrated in his aim:

> I was no private but a person raised
> With strength sufficient and command from heaven
> To free my country; if their servile minds
> Me, their deliverer sent, would not receive. . . .

For the purpose of his revenge, Samson beguiles the officer sent by the Philistines to bring him to them with:

> And for a life who will not change his purpose?

It is very obvious that Samson-Milton would not. Then follows the dismissive reflection:

> So mutable are all the ways of men.

Samson's father, seeking his son's liberty from the Philistine lords,

> Some much averse I found and wondrous harsh,
> Contemptuous, proud, set on revenge and spite –
> That part most reverenced Dagon and his priests

– as it might be the High Cavaliers and their Anglican clergy, from one of whom, Samuel Parker, an offensive attack on Milton came.

> Others more moderate seeming, but their aim
> Private reward, for which both god and state
> They easily would set to sale

– such were the moderates and those who had come to terms, in Milton's view –

> a third
> More generous far and civil, who confessed
> They had enough revenged, having reduced
> Their foe to misery beneath their fears,
> The rest was magnanimity to remit. . . .

Such was Clarendon – who, in the very year of *Paradise Lost*'s appearance, was sent into exile, for all the services he had rendered to the Stuarts.

Clarendon had no idea of revenge in him; he merely wrote a book to justify himself. The last section of *Samson* is dominated by the theme of revenge, the vindictive wish-fulfilment that runs all through the Old Testament. Samson's chance has come on one of the holy days of the people,

> Impetuous, insolent, unquenchable.

A great noise is heard – the shattering and rending of their temple. Who knows whether

> He now be dealing dole among his foes,
> And over heaps of slaughtered walk his way?

Manoa comments, in good Old Testament spirit:

> That were a joy presumptuous to be thought.

The Chorus approves:

> Yet God hath wrought things as incredible
> For his people of old; what hinders now?

(It was only fourteen years after Milton's death that the Stuarts received their dismissal with the Revolution of 1688.)

Then the story of Samson's pulling down the temple upon the heads of his enemies –

> The vulgar only scaped, who stood without

– the Chorus celebrates his victory in death:

> O dearly bought revenge, yet glorious!
> Living or dying thou hast fulfilled

The work for which thou wast foretold. . . .

The wish-fulfilment theme of revenge receives expression in the famous lines:

> O, how comely it is and how reviving
> To the spirits of just men long oppressed,
> When God into the hands of their deliverer
> Puts invincible might,
> To quell the mighty of the earth, the oppressor . . .
> Tyrannic power, but raging to pursue
> The righteous, and all such as honour truth!

Milton had always identified truth and righteousness with himself. He goes on, as if describing his own situation:

> But he, though blind of sight,
> Despised, and though extinguished quite,
> With inward eyes illuminated,
> His fiery virtue roused
> From under ashes into sudden flame. . . .

We might apply that, not inappropriately, to the writing of *Samson Agonistes* itself, with the moral:

> So Virtue, given for lost,
> Depressed and overthrown . . .
> Revives, reflourishes, then vigorous most
> When most unactive deemed.

The general moral is enforced, that people bring their own destruction upon themselves:

> So fond are mortal men,
> Fallen into wrath divine,
> As their own ruin on themselves to invite . . .

as indeed 1660 had been followed by the disasters of 1665 and 1666, Plague and Fire.

Samson's father pronounces the famous panegyric:

> Nothing is here for tears, nothing to wail
> Or knock the breast; no weakness, no contempt,
> Dispraise, or blame; nothing but well and fair,
> And what may quiet us in a death so noble.

In the final words Milton answers the question he had posed as
to God's inscrutable justice:

> All is best, though we oft doubt,
> What the unsearchable dispose
> Of Highest Wisdom brings about,
> And ever best found in the close.
> Oft he seems to hide his face,
> But unexpectedly returns. . . .

This is the proper conclusion of a tragedy, and it is, no doubt,
what Milton's religion told him he ought to think. There was,
however, an extreme tension between Milton's temperament,
far from Christian, and his intellectual convictions: out of the
conflict came the intensity of his genius. Hanford sees that
'neither the spirit nor the reception of the act is Christian. . . .
It is in vain that he repudiates stoicism as a futile refuge and a
false philosophy; he is betrayed by the vehemence of his
declarations against it, and he instinctively adopts its
weapons.'[18] We may go further to recognise that Milton was a
better Stoic than he was Christian; we doubt whether the whole
man really thought that all was for the best.

In these last years Milton was rounding up his life's work by
sending to the press various prose pieces that remained on his
hands, along with the products of his poetic genius. Since 1640
he had been a prolific provider of material for the printing
press; publishers were in want of matter, and it is probable that
in his last years Milton was glad of what money it brought in.

In 1658, before Cromwell's death, Milton published a
manuscript of Sir Walter Ralegh that had come into his possession: *The Cabinet-Council, containing the Chief Arts of Empire, and
Mysteries of State*. Ralegh had become something of a hero with
the Puritans – rather paradoxically, since he certainly had not
liked *them*. But he was a victim of the Stuarts, and that was
enough; these notes and aphorisms of his, with his reflections
on James I, made him something of a Parliament man.

More in his spirit was congenial to Milton: both were

extremely arrogant men, inspired by pride, and there was a certain integrity in Ralegh's later stance, as always in Milton's. Ralegh was a Machiavellian, and there was a Machiavellian strain in Milton's political thinking, as we have seen. Even in the *Christian Doctrine* there is a surprising admission that lying was upon occasion justifiable – especially for a holy cause, of course. It is not surprising that Milton should have found something congenial in Ralegh's political thinking, and have published him: 'I thought it a kind of injury to withhold longer the work of so eminent an author from the public.'

Now in 1669 Milton published his *Accidence Commenced Grammar*, and next year his *History of Britain*. *Paradise Regained* and *Samson Agonistes* came out together, though with separate title-pages, in 1671. In 1672 there followed his (Latin) *Art of Logic*. Next year, 1673, was signalised by his republication of his earlier poems. As Masson says, this was a judicious move, to remind the world that he had been a poet among those of happier earlier days. Perhaps it is significant that, in republishing, Milton reprinted the foreign tributes to himself and his verse, while omitting the English.

In this same year he returned to the political fray with his tract *Of True Religion, Heresy, Schism, Toleration; And what best means may be used against the growth of Popery*. Politics must have been the stuff of life to him for, the moment it was at all possible, he returned to his old vomit. Even Masson asks, 'what shall we say to Milton's re-appearance once more in his old and hazardous character of political pamphleteer? Nothing can show more strongly the inveteracy of his interest in public affairs, his passion for inserting his hand into any current controversy. . . . Were not Poetry, Latin Grammar, British History and Logic sufficient to occupy the blind old political offender, that he must venture once more on ground so perilous to him heretofore?'[19] That his last writing, his last public bid for attention, should have been political is a most significant pointer to the nature of the man.

The political situation had drastically changed and, now that he was free to speak out on it, he pounced. For twelve years the Cavalier and Anglican ascendancy had held firm; it was

Charles II who broke it, or tried to. Indifferent to religion, he was not indifferent to power; he did not wish to be dependent on Parliament, which kept him on a tight-rope financially, even when Parliament was Anglican and Royalist. The clue to Charles II's moves and calculations was that he was out to form a King's party, and end both the Anglican monopoly and his own dependence by building up a coalition of dissident Anglicans, Dissenters and Roman Catholics. Meanwhile, he sought to free himself from Parliamentary dependence by accepting subsidies from his cousin, Louis XIV, in return for collaboration with French foreign aims – e.g., the conquest of the Netherlands – and the promise (impossible of fulfilment) to bring Britain over to Catholicism. In 1672 Charles made the secret Treaty of Dover with Louis to this effect. It was an utterly unpatriotic deal, contrary to the interests of Britain, and contributed handsomely to French ascendancy in Europe, which it took all William III's (and Marlborough's) life's work to contain.

To recruit support among Dissenters, Charles II issued a Declaration of Indulgence, giving them freedom to worship in their conventicles; hundreds emerged from the holes and corners to which they had been relegated by the Anglican reaction. The danger was that they might fall for the King's policy, unaware of its true import, which was to advance Catholicism in accordance with his secret understanding with Louis XIV. The Dissenters were in danger of being divided and to fall into the trap; the Quakers did, for example – William Penn played into James II's hands, who had nothing else in mind but Catholic supremacy.

It was to this danger, division among Protestants, that Milton addressed his tract; in this last political writing, for the first time, he became really statesmanlike. At last he had learned the lesson of a life-time, and urged the necessity of a union among Protestants, *along with the Anglican Church*. This was, in fact, the formation that defeated the Stuarts, and sent them flying, with the Revolution of 1688. The inwardness of that decisive event was that the governing class was not going to make the mistake again, which they made in 1642 and then opened the way to civil war by getting themselves divided. Milton in 1673, the last year of his life, was at last taking up a majority position, which won through to triumph fifteen years later, in 1688.

Literary people rarely understand politics; Milton who, for a period, was on the fringe of politics, had nothing of the political comprehension of a Cromwell or a Clarendon. But at last he saw clear. Even the sympathetic Masson, a literary man and a professor, failed to see the significance of Milton's plea. Masson describes the tract as 'a plain and simple, not to say feeble, performance'.[20] It was not feeble, it was mild and comprehensive; that was the whole point of it, to appeal to as wide a front as possible, a union of all Protestants against Charles II's suspected treachery and the declared Catholicism of his heir to the throne. Catholicism was on the march: soon would come Louis XIV's revocation of the Edict of Nantes, the *dragonnades* and forced conversions, the drives against the Huguenots, their dispersal as exiles over Europe; and, in England, the accession of a Catholic king.

Milton's argument is all for unity against the common enemy, and a new note is heard, of comprehension, and sinking of doctrinal differences that held the Protestant communions apart. 'The Lutheran holds consubstantiation: an error indeed, but not mortal. The Calvinist is taxed with predestination, and to make God the author of sin: not with any dishonourable thought of God, but – it may be – overzealously asserting his absolute power, not without plea of Scripture. ['It may be' is something new to hear from Milton!] The Anabaptist is accused of denying infants their right to baptism: again, they deny nothing but what the Scripture denies them. The Arian and Socinian are charged to dispute against the Trinity: they affirm to believe the Father, Son, and Holy Ghost, according to Scripture and the Apostolic Creed. .... Their other opinions are of less moment. The Arminian lastly [here Milton was in agreement with Laud] is condemned for setting up free will against free grace; but that imputation he disclaims in all his writings, and grounds himself largely upon Scripture only. It cannot be denied that the authors or late revivers of all these sects or opinions were learned, worthy, zealous and religious men, as appears by their lives written. . . .'

All this is a welcome, new and kindly note in Milton, coming at the very end of his life, his last message. It is also the most sensible thing he ever wrote, perceiving at last that, if the advance of Catholicism was to be stayed, it needed the Anglican Church, along with other Protestants. For the first time in his life he makes a friendly reference to the national Church. 'All Protestant churches with one consent, and particularly the Church of England in her Thirty-Nine Articles (Articles VI, XIX, XX, XXI, and elsewhere), maintain these two points as the main principles of true religion: that the rule of true religion is the Word of God only; and that their faith ought not to be an implicit faith – that is to believe, though as the Church believes, against or without express authority of Scripture.'

This last was the position of the Catholic Church; he regarded it as heresy, which he defined as being 'in the will and choice professedly against Scripture'. Such was the basis of Milton's intellectual position against Catholicism. It has no authority with us today, and Protestantism has weakened with the collapse of the authority of Scripture. The real conflict, as always in history – Hobbes would agree – was one of power. Milton puts forward the argument on this front too. We need not go into it in detail: Catholic claims were universal, totalitarian and exclusive; there was no hope of toleration for anybody else if they were allowed to get on top. Declarations of indulgence were chiefly means to that end.

Milton was anxious lest the Dissenters should be taken in. In the event the majority refused to be seduced by the offers of Charles II or James II. They stood with the Church of England in resisting the advance of Popery, and got their reward after the victory of 1688. This was, in part, a victory for Milton too; this minority-minded man ended up with the majority at last.

He continued to be attacked, and one of these attacks called forth a notable defence of him by Andrew Marvell. This happened in the course of a controversy between Marvell and Samuel Parker, but it was not often that any of Milton's friends came to his defence – perhaps they considered him all too capable of defending himself. Milton was thin-skinned and easily provoked, but what aggravated the offence was that Parker was a former Puritan, bred up as one by his father – the lawyer who had sentenced the Duke of Hamilton, the Earl of Holland and Lord Capel to death, immediately after Charles I's; moreover, Milton had been kind to the young man. It is a not unfamiliar pattern, and Milton apparently took strips off the offender in something he wrote in reply.

Marvell, perhaps wisely, prevented the publication and dealt with Parker with more dignity, and more effectively. Had Milton 'took you in hand, you would have had cause to repent the occasion, and not escaped so easily. . . . J.M. was, and is, a man of great learning and sharpness of wit as any man. It was his misfortune, living in a tumultuous time, to be tossed on the wrong side, and he writ, *flagrante bello*, certain dangerous treatises. . . . At his Majesty's happy return J.M. did partake, even as you yourself did for all your huffing, of his regal clemency, and has ever since expiated himself in a retired silence. It was after that, I well remember it, that, being one day at his house, I there first met you, and accidentally. . . . Then it was when you wandered up and down Moorfields, astrologising upon the duration of his Majesty's government, that you frequented J.M. incessantly, and haunted his house day by day. What discourse you there used he is too generous to remember. But, he never having in the least provoked you, for you to insult thus over his old age, to traduce him by your scarramuccios as a schoolmaster, who was born and hath lived much more ingenuously and liberally than yourself . . . it is inhumanly and inhospitably done. . . .'[21]

The affair corroborates our picture of Milton: we note again his touchiness and extremism – not even Marvell wholly approved the side he was 'thrown' on (i.e., chose) – and his kindness and generosity towards young men. Perhaps also it shows his bad judgment, for Parker did not turn out well from Milton's point of view. A priggish young Puritan at Oxford, addicted to fasts and prayer-meetings, when he went over to the Church he 'wrought himself dexterously by short graces and sermons, and a mimical way of drolling upon the Puritans' – to which they lent themselves by their ridiculous mannerisms, caricatured by Samuel Butler and Swift. To become a bishop Parker advocated the absolute power of the Crown, for which James II made him Bishop of Oxford as well as President of Magdalen; as such Parker lent himself to all James's Romanising projects. It seems, however, that he was a genuine upholder of toleration, only – unlike Milton – he extended it to Catholics.

All his life Milton had been such a hard worker that, in addition to his many publications, he left a mass of material, to be published posthumously. A keen publisher, Brabazon Aylmer, wrote before Milton's death, 'I had reason for some time to hope that I might be permitted the printing of both the Public and the Familiar Letters of our author in one volume.' Evidently Milton wished, and had discussed, publishing both. In the event, only the latter were permitted; the official Letters of State he had written on behalf of Commonwealth and Protectorate had to attend a more propitious time. The *Christian Doctrine*, 'my dearest and best possession', had to wait still longer, arrested among State Papers, until the early nineteenth century.

We may regard Milton's work as rounded and complete, with an almost providential propriety, in his last poetic work, *Samson Agonistes*, with its moving personal overtones, and his last prose tract, *Of True Religion*, opening new vistas of comprehension. He was nearly sixty-six when he died on Sunday, 8 November 1674, 'with so little pain that the time of his expiring was not perceived by those in the room'. His life's work, so full and prolific, was well complete.

The Man

WE BEGAN this portrait with the striking contrast between the two out-topping poles in our literature, Shakespeare and Milton; and the contrast continues, with much more that might be said. We know more about Milton because he lived a couple of generations later, when more information about people was generally available; and also because he was so autobiographical a writer that he has given us a great deal of information in his work. All things considered, it is remarkable that we should know as much about Shakespeare as we do, especially now that the crucial questions in his personal relationships have been cleared up.

Various people who knew Milton or people close to him have given us descriptions of the man. It is well to begin with the earliest, John Aubrey, who also gave us our first biographical notice of Shakespeare. Aubrey is always revealing – he had such a quirk for observation, such insatiable curiosity and penetration into character; he was also conscientious in collecting information, inquiring from Milton's widow, brother and nephew. 'He was scarce so tall as I am. He had light brown hair, his complexion very fair; oval face, his eye a dark grey.... The pictures before his books are not *at all* like him. His harmonical and ingenious soul did lodge in a beautiful and well-proportioned body. He had a very good memory, but I believe that his excellent method of thinking and disposing did much to help his memory. Of a very cheerful humour, he was very healthy and free from all diseases, and only towards his latter end he was visited with the gout, spring and fall. He would be cheerful even in his gout-fits, and sing.

'He was an early riser, yea, after he lost his sight. He had a man read to him: the first thing he read was the Hebrew Bible, and that was at 4 a.m.; then he contemplated. At 7 his man came to him again, and then read to him and wrote till dinner. His daughter Deborah could read to him Latin, Italian and French and Greek. The other sister is Mary, more like her mother. After dinner he used to walk three or four hours; he always had a garden where he lived; went to bed about 9. Temperate man, rarely drank between meals. Extreme pleasant in his conversation, and at dinner, supper, etc.; but satirical. He pronounced the letter R very hard – a certain sign of a satirical wit: from John Dryden.'[1]

Jonathan Richardson, who was industrious in gleaning details later from those who knew Milton, adds a convincing gloss to that. 'Milton had a servant, who was a very honest, silly fellow, and a zealous and constant follower of those teachers [Nonconformist preachers]. When he came from the meeting, his master would frequently ask him what he had heard, and divert himself with ridiculing their fooleries or, it may be, the poor man's understanding: both one and t'other probably. However, this was so grievous to the good creature that he left his service upon it.'[2] How characteristic and convincing an episode! Everybody deplores it, even the good Masson, and sympathises with the poor fellow. My sympathies are with Milton: average persons have no idea what it is to listen to their fatuities in matters of thought, let alone of those below average. Milton was for taking it out of them – so like him.

Then again Aubrey gives us a recognisable trait: 'he was much visited by learned: more than he did desire'. For a man with such inexhaustible inner resources as he had he would not wish to be bored by those with markedly fewer. 'He had a delicate tunable voice and had good skill; his father instructed him. He had an organ in his house; he played on that most. . . . His widow assures me that Mr Hobbes was not one of his acquaintance, that her husband did not like him at all; but he would acknowledge him to be a man of great parts, a learned man. Their interests and tenets were diametrically opposite; v. Mr Hobbes's *Behemoth*.'

This is, of course, exact: the one an idealist to the point of fanaticism, the other a realist to the point of cynicism. Hobbes had no illusions to begin with, Milton finished with few.

We are interested only in the early information about the great man. The next biography in point of time is fairly certainly by Cyriack Skinner, who adds some convincing observations. He tells us, what we might have guessed, that Milton could not bear wasting time, and that he married in a hurry, courting, marrying Mary Powell and bringing her home to London all in a month. His discipline with his pupils was strict: young Lord Barrymore, 'sent by his aunt, the Lady Ranelagh, Sir Thomas Gardiner of Essex, and others were under his tuition. But whether it were that the tempers of our gentry would not bear the strictness of his discipline, or for what other reason he continued that course but a while.'[3]

From this source too we learn that, during his time in office, Milton was able to procure relief for Spenser's grandson, 'a Papist suffering in his concerns in Ireland', and also for Sir William Davenant when taken prisoner; these among others. 'By the great Fire in 1666 he had a house in Bread Street burnt, which was all the real estate he had.' The rest, with most of his capital, he had lost. Methodically he used to allot different portions of the day to different studies and work. 'Of these the time friendly to the Muse fell to his poetry; and he, waking early, had commonly a good stock of verses ready against his amanuensis came: which, if it happened to be later than ordinary, he would complain, saying "he wanted to be milked". [Isn't there something unconsciously feminine about that?] The evenings he likewise spent in reading some choice poets, by way of refreshment after the day's toil, and to store his fancy against morning.'

It is a tribute to Milton that the elder nephew, Edward Phillips, whom he brought up so strictly, should write so enthusiastic a eulogy of him. 'Take him in all respects, for acumen of wit [i.e., intellect], quickness of apprehension, sagacity of judgment [we may qualify here – literary, not political], depth of argument and elegancy of style, as well in Latin as English, as well in verse as prose, he is scarce to be paralleled by any the best of writers our nation hath in any age brought forth.'[4] An interesting detail is that he derived the weakness of his eyes from his mother, who was of Welsh stock by origin. This suggests that Milton may have turned after that side: he certainly bore the stigmata of the Celtic temperament, the intellectual passion and doctrinairism, the vehemence and touchiness, the extremism, the personal egoism. It is all in strong contrast to William Shakespeare, in whose glass the English nature and temperament are mirrored at their best.

The fullest of the early biographies is that of John Toland, of a brilliant and unconventional intelligence best capable of appreciating the subject. Bred up a Catholic, he lost his faith without acquiring much of another; seeing through both sides of the controversy between Catholic and Protestant, his book *Christianity Not Mysterious* initiated the Deist dispute of the eighteenth century. A Deist, he believed even less than he dared say, and had the freedom from convention to appreciate the originality (and abnormality) of Milton's mind.

Toland collected what information was available, but was the first to base himself upon a study of all Milton's work, correlating and quoting what he told of himself. He told a great deal. Toland's eye for what was significant picked up things that were important – for example, how much Milton owed to his conversations with Manso about Tasso in influencing his mind towards epic. So it would be Tasso that Milton had rather ungratefully in mind in disclaiming for *his* epic:

> Not sedulous by nature to indite
> Wars, hitherto the only argument
> Heroic deemed, chief mastery to dissect
> With long and tedious havoc fabled knights
> In battles feigned . . .
>   or to describe races and games,
> Or tilting furniture, emblazoned shields,
> Impresses quaint, caparisons and steeds,
> Bases and tinsel trappings, gorgeous knights
> At joust and tournament. . . .

So much for Tasso and Spenser; undoubtedly the years had hardened Milton since those days when he had charmed Italy. With his epic he intended higher things:

> Me, of these
> Nor skilled nor studious, higher argument
> Remains, sufficient of itself to raise
> That name, unless an age too late, or cold
> Climate, or years, damp my intended wing
> Depressed. . . .

Once more we must admit that his arrogant claim was totally justified: his was the grander, more universal, theme.

Toland perceptively quoted Milton's Latin verses declaring both his ambition and a self-esteem to equal it. (It is possible that this abnormal self-stimulation was psychologically necessary to him to steel himself to such a task.) Toland quotes several such passages from the works to build up his picture. He had the advantage of sharing most of Milton's heterodox views, even to his dislike of Presbyterians. Writing in 1698, Toland said, apropos of Milton's exposure of their intolerance: 'on this occasion I must remark that, by reason of the Presbyterians warmly joining with others the last Parliament to pronounce penal laws against the Socinians [i.e., Rationalists], I find few people will believe that those in England differ from their brethren in Scotland about persecution, nor that their own sufferings of late have made 'em more tender to the consciences of others'.[5] This refers to the recent Stuart campaigns against the fanatical Covenanters. The one deleterious consequence of the Revolution of 1688 was that it shackled dreary Presbyterianism upon the neck of the Scottish nation, with the usual consequence of blasting creativeness in culture and the arts.

Toland emphasises a point that is insufficiently appreciated, and rather unexpected – that *Paradise Lost* was written quickly: 'this piece was composed in half the time he was thought to be about it'. Milton confirms this –

> Easy my unpremeditated verse

– and Toland tells us how it came to him. 'He was by reason of his blindness obliged to write, by whatsoever hand came next, ten or twenty or thirty verses at a time.' We have already remarked on the extraordinary memory that could hold all these in his mind at once, and the intellectual control that could maintain the structure of whole verse-paragraphs. Shakespeare could do this too, but he had the advantage of his actor's training and could *see* what he was writing.

As for critics and criticism, Toland – who, being a highly original mind, had had much to put up with himself – dismissed them with a bull's-eye: 'to incur the displeasure of certain ignorant and supercilious critics argues free thinking, accurate writing, and a generous profession of truth. . . . As to the regularity of the poem, I never knew it questioned by any but such as would build themselves a reputation on the flaws and mistakes they discover in other men's labours. But the unparalleled sublimity and force of the expression, with the delicacy of his thoughts and the copiousness of his invention are unanimously owned by all ranks of *writers*. He has incontestably exceeded the fecundity of Homer, whose two Poems he could almost repeat without book. Nor did he come much short of the correctness of Virgil: which is affirmed by one whose judgment in this province will be acknowledged by every man that is not willing to expose the defect of his own. I mean the famous John Dryden, the best English poet alive.'[6] We need go no further.

Sir Robert Howard, the dramatist and aristocratic brother-in-law of Dryden – he had been imprisoned in Windsor Castle under the Commonwealth – was 'a great admirer of Milton to his dying day. And, being his particular acquaintance, would tell many pleasant stories of him. He himself, having once demanded of him what made him side with the Republicans, Milton answered, among other reasons, because theirs was the most frugal government; for that the trappings of a monarchy might set up an ordinary commonwealth.'[7] There we have the old Nonconformist, with his limited, or inhibited, aesthetic response. Another aristocratic friend was the Earl of Anglesey, upon whom Milton bestowed some of his papers: he, 'as well as several of the nobility and gentry, was his constant visitor. Nor was he less frequented by foreigners to the last.' Toland much regretted that Milton did not find leisure to 'bring down his History to his own times'. It would certainly have given scope for his gifts of denigration and invective.

As to his religion, Toland notices Milton's crab-like progress away from previous associations: from the general Puritan position towards the Independents and sectarians, until in the end there was nobody he could agree with. 'In the latter part of his life he was not a professed member of any particular sect among Christians; he frequented none of their assemblies, nor made use of their particular rites in his family.' He was alone, John Milton.

Then, to conclude, Toland says the most remarkable thing, which no one has noticed: '*I never met with any of his acquaintance who could be positive in assigning the true reasons of his conduct.*'[8]

We cannot hope to be more positive, though modern psychology certainly has had some success in penetrating the recesses of the subconscious, uncovering the springs of unconscious motivation. The chief intellectual revolution of our time has been in the sphere of psychology; there is an abyss between modern self-awareness and the pre-modern era when people – however aware they were of conscious motivation (as Clarendon, Hobbes, Laud, Halifax all were) – were yet unaware of the unconscious predispositions, fixations, neuroses.

William Shakespeare was divinely normal – that is not the least wonderful thing about him, for most men of genius are far from normal. He was happily heterosexual, grafted into family life, accepting its usual obligations, while widely responsive to beauty of every kind, in nature as well as in human beings; free and easy with women, not tormented by religious belief, conventional about all that, sociable and neighbourly; a merry, sportive disposition, as we know, an out-of-doors man; above all, an *accepting* nature: and this was wisdom, in all the chances and ills of life, doubled then.

John Milton was in complete contrast to all this. He could accept nothing on trust: he had to go into everything for himself, satisfy himself intellectually on every point – hence his construction of a whole system of divinity, settling precisely what he did believe, before he could accomplish his epic. Why was this? Where William Shakespeare trusted to his instinct – and in consequence his unconscious worked for him day and night, as one can tell from his imagery – John Milton could not trust himself to his instinct, obviously felt that he could not afford to: where would it have led him? (We know where it led Christopher Marlowe.) Hence Milton's unconscious was at war with his Puritan intellectual convictions; Hanford has seen that the creativeness, in his case, arose from tension.

In the region of motives one cannot be certain; Milton himself was probably unaware of them – certainly much less so than Shakespeare would have been, the most aware of men. The keynote of Milton's character was pride – no wonder the other name for his hero was Lucifer – probably inflamed and set on edge by a sense of physical inferiority, smallness, femininity, which he was determined to suppress, and certainly overcompensated. He always over-reacted, a psychologist would say; and a perceptive American scholar has wondered whether Milton was *emotionally* honest with himself. His line of conduct and his actions, which baffled his acquaintance, followed from the position he early took up, which became a fixation – as observant and sophisticated people in Italy noticed with the pretty Englishman. He became fixed, hardened and obdurate – nothing of the adorable fluency and flexibility of Shakespeare's nature.

Yet we must never forget – when so much in Milton's intellectual make-up was utterly charmless – that Milton had personal charm. Here is the paradox; here is the conflict. His intellectual position was intolerable, even hateful; yet he was a poet of very great genius, the second in our language.

My purpose is not literary criticism, and I do not propose to go into what constitutes the genius, or how it expresses itself in his work. I would, however, point out that *pride* is in the very nature of his language: he could not be, or in general did not choose to be, simple. This is why his versification of the Psalms – which he admired above all other works – is unsatisfactory: he could not manage simple measures very well. He had to be more complex – in a curious way, more evasive – like his nature. I believe that this was at the root of Eliot's distaste for his classic language and usage, though he did not put his finger on precisely why.

The point can be illustrated – though hardly defined, it is so subtle – by the contrast between Shakespeare's grand language and Milton's. Both can be grandiloquent, yet they are curiously different. Shakespeare regularly uses the grandest words, in the lordliest way, and yet somehow they are natural. I think this is because they rise up from his subconscious, answering to his limitless imagination. Milton uses grand words, classic constructions, reversed word-order, all the tricks, but consciously and deliberately. It is all imposed by his overriding, controlling intellect. All is under control; but the control is imposed. That is the difference.

The style expresses the nature of the genius: Milton's so deeply concerned with ethics, with righteousness, 'right reason', and truth, with the sublime problems of divinity and man's fate; a spirit naturally lofty and solitary, not much related to other men or like them; learned and bookish; his one relaxation, music, a self-regarding one. Naturally he has not the endless variety of Shakespeare, instinctively versed in the knowledge of the ways of men. Both, however, have universality – Milton's that of his probing depiction of our universal fate, which holds good for humanity even if the terms of its depiction are outmoded in belief and more than ever mythical.

Hence the propriety of the first great critic of Milton, Dryden, in singling out the keynotes of his style: loftiness of mind, majesty, sublimity. Saintsbury accords with this, while adding: 'great variety he has not; in his longer and later poems certainly not; while the contrast of earlier and later only supplies it to a limited extent'.[9] However, he concludes, 'his influence is omnipresent in almost all later English poetry, and in not a little of later prose English literature. At first, at second, at third, hand he has permeated almost all his successors. Without Milton, you cannot understand, in the real sense of understanding, writers so different as Landor and Tennyson, as Thomson and Wordsworth.' And then concludes our leading authority on English prosody, 'so far as Milton's historical position is concerned, he is almost the central figure in the whole history of our verse'.

As for the man, Saintsbury diagnoses his 'tendency to "ray

out" nonconformity in almost all directions and on almost all subjects'. He was at issue with all sects and all parties: anti-Catholic, anti-Anglican, anti-Presbyterian, anti-Independent; anti-Trinitarian, anti-Predestinarian; against the monarchy, not really in agreement with the Protectorate, and no more a Fifth Monarchy man or millenarian. By the end he was in a party of one.

An admirable critic in our time considers that Ezra Pound was false to his genius as a lyric poet, 'led astray by a compulsive need to teach and preach economic theories, goaded by political ambition'. If we may compare a lesser spirit with an altogether grander, there certainly was something of this in Milton's extraordinary case.

A fine French phrase has it that 'une grande âme doit contenir plus de douleurs qu'une petite'. We must allow, in the end, that Milton was a great soul, not a small one; what Oliver Cromwell was in the world of action, that John Milton was in the realm of poetry: a heroic figure.

Notes

Chapter 1. Milton's Early Years

1. Cf. in more detail my *William Shakespeare: A Biography* (1963).
2. Cf. my essay 'The Milton Country' in my *Times, Persons, Places* (1965).
3. J. H. Hanford, *John Milton, Englishman* (1949), p. 21.
4. Ibid. p. 27.
5. Ibid. p. 36.
6. Cf. D. C. Dorian, *The English Diodatis* (1950).
7. An authoritative article in the *Encyclopedia Britannica* (11th ed.) informs us that the Arminians 'reacted against both the supra-lapsarian and the infralapsarian developments of the doctrine of Predestination and combated the irresistibility of grace; they held that Christ died for all men and not only for the Elect, and were not sure that the Elect might not fall from grace'. We see once more what a large part in history is occupied by disputes about non-sense. The decisions of the Synod were 'unconditional election, limited atonement [i.e., Christ did not die for all men], irresistibility of grace, final perseverance of the saints'. On this enlightened basis persecution was let loose.

Chapter 2. Milton and the Church

1. *The Life of Edward, Earl of Clarendon*, 3 vols (1827), vol. 1, pp. 65–6.
2. G. Burnet, *Memoirs . . . of the Dukes of Hamilton* (1677), p. 28.
3. Samuel Butler, *Characters*, ed. A. R. Waller (1908), p. 18.
4. Edward Hyde, Earl of Clarendon, *History of the Rebellion*, 6 vols (1888), vol. 1, pp. 124–5.
5. Quoted in B. Manning, *The English People and the English Revolution* (1976), p. 1.
6. Ibid.
7. John Aubrey, *Brief Lives*, ed. A. Clark, 2 vols (1898), vol. 1, p. 408.
8. E. H. Emerson, in *The Prose of John Milton*, ed. J. Max Patrick (1968), p. 97.
9. John Selden, *Table Talk*, Temple Classics, pp. 111 ff.
10. Ibid. p. 62.
11. Ibid. p. 150.
12. Ibid. p. 95.
13. Ibid. p. 50.

Chapter 3. Milton, Marriage and Women

1. John Selden, *Table Talk*, Temple Classics, p. 79.

2. Helen Darbishire, *The Early Lives of Milton* (1932), p. 24.

Chapter 4. Milton on Education and Free Thought

1. J. H. Hanford, *John Milton, Englishman* (1949), p. 124.
2. Ibid. p. 123.
3. Quoted by T. R. Hartmann, in *The Prose of John Milton*, ed. J. Max

Patrick (1968), p. 222.
4. Ibid. p. 220.
5. Ibid. p. 249.
6. Ibid. p. 258.

Chapter 5. Milton as Historian

1. Sir Charles Firth, *Essays Historical and Literary* (1938), p. 61.
2. Ibid. p. 74.

3. Not 'patrician' as Christopher Hill describes him, with some confusion of class.

Chapter 7. Milton on Monarchy and Himself

1. W. R. Parker, *Milton, A Biography*, 2 vols (1968), vol. 1, p. 455.
2. *The Prose of John Milton*, ed. J. Max

Patrick (1968), pp. 433–4.
3. Quoted in Parker, *Milton*, vol. 1, p. 463.

Chapter 8. The Puritan Collapse

1. Abraham Cowley, *Essays, Plays and Sundry Verses*, ed. A. R. Waller (1906), pp. 342 ff.
2. *The English Works of Thomas Hobbes*, ed. Sir William Molesworth, 11 vols (1839–45), vol. 6, pp. 165 ff.
3. Quoted in J. H. Elson, *John Hales of Eton* (1948), pp. 32 ff.
4. Quoted in B. H. G. Wormald, *Clarendon* (1951), pp. 170 ff.

5. Godfrey Davies, *The Early Stuarts, 1603–1660* (1937), pp. 241 ff.
6. John Aubrey, *Brief Lives*, ed. A. Clark, 2 vols (1898), vol. 1, pp. 288–90.
7. Davies, *Early Stuarts*, pp. 252, 253.
8. G. N. Clark, *The Later Stuarts, 1660–1714* (1934), p. 1.
9. Helen Darbishire, *The Early Lives of John Milton* (1932), p. 74.

Chapter 9. Milton's Christianity

1. Cf. my *The Elizabethan Renaissance: The Cultural Achievement* (1972), pp. 292 ff.
2. C. S. Lewis, *A Preface to 'Paradise Lost'* (1942), pp. 89, 91.
3. John Milton, *Complete Prose Works*, Yale edition, vol. 6, introduction.
4. C. A. Patrides, *Milton and the Christian Tradition* (1966), p. 188.
5. Ibid. pp. 187, 192 ff.
6. Quoted in ibid. pp. 101–2.
7. Cf. *English*, Spring 1976, pp. 38 ff.
8. Milton, *Complete Prose Works*, Yale edition, vol. 6, introduction.

Chapter 10. *Paradise Lost*

1. This passage well illustrates what I have said above about rhyme. Notice the end-rhymes 'hate' and 'late', with the half-rhyme 'might'; the internal rhyme 'me' with 'knee' in the next line. Also the repetition of the word 'lost' in 11. 1 and 2 – another regular usage to reinforce verbal strength and effect.
2. Note here again the verbal echoes of 'Parad*ise*', 'disgu*ised*'; '*tossed*', 'al*oft*', '*off*'.
3. Cf. William Empson's amusing book, *Milton's God* (1965).
4. *Cambridge History of English Literature*, vol. 7 (1934), pp. 110 ff.
5. Cf. my *William Shakespeare: A Biography* (1963), pp. 386–7.

Chapter 11. Milton, Christ and Samson

1. Helen Darbishire, *The Early Lives of Milton* (1932), pp. 75–6.
2. David Masson, *The Life of John Milton*, 6 vols (1859–80), vol. 6, pp. 652, 654.
3. This short passage offers another example of the not infrequent rhymes in *Paradise Regained*: 'ext*end*' and 'compreh*end*', the half-rhyme of '*man*' and '*then*', the repetition of 'ext*end*'; there is even a clang of '*mind*' with 'ext*end*'.
4. J. H. Hanford, *John Milton, Englishman* (1949), p. 229.
5. Ibid. p. 217.
6. Masson, *Milton*, vol. 6, p. 662.
7. W. P. Ker, *The Art of Poetry* (1923), p. 59.
8. Darbishire, *Early Lives*, p. 29.
9. Ibid. p. 275.
10. This is the marked defect of Professor J. Carey's edition of *Samson Agonistes* in the recent Longman *Milton*, ludicrously placing the tragedy in the middle of his work and dating it '1647–53?'. In those years Milton was fully occupied with his prose tracts and his work for the Council of State. Fancy basing this on such a doubtful consideration as that there is more rhyme in *Samson* than in

Paradise Lost! As we have seen, there is a great deal of rhyme in the latter: Milton's disclaimer means simply that *Paradise Lost* was not to be a poem in regular rhyme, like Spenser's *Faerie Queene* and others. Professor Carey confesses an inability to perceive the obvious autobiographical element in *Samson Agonistes* everybody else has seen – in itself a disqualification for an editor of the work. We are given a long note on 'various sources for the Dalila/ship simile', and another to the effect that 'no source has been found for Milton's representation of Fame as male, double-mouthed', etc. Milton might have thought of these things for himself. Such pedantry, com-

bined with such impercipience, qualify for my strictures above, Preface and p. 219.

11. Masson, *Milton*, vol. 6, p. 664.
12. *Cambridge History of English Literature*, vol. 7 (1934), p. 136.
13. Masson, *Milton*, vol. 6, p. 670.
14. Hanford, *John Milton, Englishman*, p. 215.
15. Ibid. p. 222.
16. *The Poetical Works of John Milton*, ed. David Masson, 3 vols (1874), vol. 2, p. 580.
17. Hanford, *John Milton, Englishman*, p. 214.
18. Ibid. pp. 224–5.
19. Masson, *Milton*, vol. 6, p. 690.
20. Ibid. vol. 6, p. 693.
21. Andrew Marvell, *The Rehearsal Transprosed*, ed. D. I. B. Smith (1971), pp. 312–13.

Epilogue: The Man

1. Quoted in Helen Darbishire, *The Early Lives of Milton* (1932), pp. 3 ff.
2. Quoted in David Masson, *The Life of John Milton*, vol. 6, pp. 683–4.
3. Darbishire, *Early Lives*, pp. 22 ff.
4. Ibid. p. 50.
5. Ibid. pp. 139 ff.
6. Ibid. p. 169.
7. Ibid. p. 186.
8. Ibid. p. 195.
9. *Cambridge History of English Literature*, vol. 7 (1934), pp. 135 ff.

Index